# Just Hold Her

## A FOSTER MOTHER'S MEMOIR OF MEDICINE, CAREGIVING, AND THE LONG NIGHTS TOGETHER

JUDY WRIGHT

# Contents

Published by Held Close Books
United States of America
www.heldclosebooks.com

First Edition: April 2026
ISBN 979-8-9952251-1-9


A portion of the proceeds from this book supports the John and Judy Wright Scholarship in partnership with the Ennis Center for Children.

**A Note on Memory and Medical Witness**
This memoir reflects the author's recollections of experiences over time. Some names and identifying details have been changed to protect the privacy of individuals, including foster children and medical personnel. The author has made every effort to ensure the accuracy of medical observations recorded in contemporaneous journals. This work is intended as a personal narrative and should not be considered medical advice.

Author: Judy Wright
Editor: Andrew Wright
Copyeditor: Conor Gallogly
Proofreader: Stacie Doughtie and Stephanie Sun
Afterword: Callie Nelson

**For John** —
*who held me.*

# Author's Note

Every detail is true.
Every bottle. Every injection.
Every number written in the margins of
a spiral notebook that stayed with me.

Some names have been changed. Others remain.
Not to soften what happened, but to protect the
people who lived it.

The notebook held the hours.
The glucose readings. The weights.
The small adjustments that meant the difference
between staying and slipping.

The notebook kept the record.
This is what it couldn't hold.

She was here.
She was held.
And for a time, that was everything.

# June 12, 2009 — Friday

That morning with John was the last time things made sense.

John was home Friday, relaxing in his plaid lounge pants and a Pink Floyd T-shirt. It was a welcome break from the starched white shirt and epaulets he wore as a corporate pilot, flying executives worldwide. Dudley, our cockapoo, slept across his lap while John leaned forward, eyes fixed on the TV as Captain Sullenberger answered questions about the Hudson River landing. His tuna sandwich sat untouched.

I was in the kitchen, working on a floral arrangement for the dining room table. Red and purple flowers, eucalyptus for filler, arranged in a brass planter I was sure I could make work with a bit of finesse. Just a small touch to make the house feel less empty. I wasn't especially crafty, just too frugal to buy one already made.

The phone rang. Caller ID read Ennis Center for Children.

Beth's voice made me sit up. Our foster care caseworker didn't usually sound careful. But that morning her tone was soft and measured. My body braced. I gripped the phone and steadied my breath.

"Mrs. Wright," she said gently, "would you consider taking care of a baby girl born two months early with serious complications, and not expected to survive?"

The room went still.

We were used to hard calls. We'd taken them before. But this little girl hadn't even left the NICU. The world felt like it was grieving.

I was scared. As the fear tightened, a voice rose within me.

*This is why you are here.*

Beth continued, her composure thinning.

"There is nothing optimistic in the reports. This infant has survived a horrific first eight weeks of life. The hospital staff believes NICU-level care is no longer helping her."

She paused, her voice shaky.

"Would you, please... just hold her until she dies?"

I heard her exhale, as if she'd been holding it all morning.

Then silence.

I gave her the same rote answer I'd given so many times before.

"I need to speak with my husband. I'll call you back."

I held the last red rose of the floral arrangement when the hollow dial tone snapped me back.

My stomach flipped.

I set down the phone, loud enough to cut through the TV's drone.

John looked up. I had his full attention.

My whole body shook when I told him.

"A baby girl. Born two months early. They don't think she'll make it."

The words kept going, spilling into the air before I could catch them.

He listened, then leaned back and let out a slow breath.

"How are we supposed to let go of that?" he asked.

He named the ache we knew too well. Letting go.

Some children go home. Some move on. It never gets easier.

This baby wouldn't be going anywhere. She would die in our care.

I settled into my recliner beside John. Dudley curled on my lap, ears perked as if he understood every word.

We talked about our four grown children, doing well on their own. We agreed that if this baby didn't survive, her loss wouldn't impact their day-to-day lives the same way it would affect ours.

This would be our grief to carry.

We sat in silence.

Then John reached across the table, placed his hand over mine, and looked into my eyes.

"Call her back."

That simple touch, warm and grounding, reminded me of the weight we shared. Helping children wasn't about convenience. It was about compassion.

We could give this baby what she needed most: to be held. To be loved.

When I called Beth back, she explained that the state had already filed a petition to terminate parental rights. The next step was to place the baby in a licensed foster home.

On our application, we checked nearly every box: age range, siblings, special needs, medical fragility, ethnicity.

We kept our arms open wide. This baby fit our criteria. More than that, she fit our purpose.

To meet her, Ennis Center needed permission from the Department of Human Services (DHS), which was overseeing her case. Because we were licensed through a private agency, DHS would need to accompany us on the initial visit.

So we waited.

Four long days passed as Beth processed the paperwork.

This wait was different. We weren't just organizing the bin of "Girl 0–3 months, summer" that sat in our basement. We were bracing ourselves.

<hr>

WHEN THE DAY FINALLY CAME, we set out for the hospital with hot coffee in John's hand and a full gas tank. It was a forty-five-minute drive to a stone building perched high on a hill.

I was glad John could be with me on this first visit. His job took him away often, and I learned to run our fostering life in the gaps between his flights. I handled the logistics, the calls, and the day-to-day care. I learned not to wait to feel ready.

But John was never a visitor in our home. When he was here he stepped in like this mattered as much to him as it did to me. Because it did. He loved the children we took in. He loved me.

That day, his presence reminded me that I was not stepping into this alone.

<hr>

FROM THE ATTACHED PARKING GARAGE, we stepped onto the polished tile just inside the hospital entrance. A white-haired volunteer pointed us to the elevators. "NICU's on three." She smiled, as if this was good news.

We rode up in silence.

We'd arrived early, knowing that entering the NICU meant following a strict protocol. Walking in was like stepping into another world: bright, sterile, and humming with quiet urgency. Every beep and rustle had meaning. I didn't speak the language. Not yet. But I could feel its weight.

We scrubbed in at the deep basins just outside the unit, between the sliding glass entrance and the locked metal doors, lathering up to our elbows with harsh, ammonia-scented disinfectant. The laminated signs above each sink reminded us what was at stake.

I dried my hands with coarse, sterile towels as John leaned into the intercom, pressing the buzzer with his elbow.

We waited.

He squeezed my hand. His fingers trembled.

I glanced at his face. His eyes had softened, filling with tears he hadn't expected. He tried to hold himself upright, but I could see it. The weight was already on his shoulders. I whispered a prayer for strength just as the door buzzed.

Inside, the unit was hushed and fluorescent, filled with glowing machines and delicate lives. Rows of incubators lined the halls like lanterns, each one cradling a frail, flickering hope. Nurses moved in practiced silence, their gloved hands adjusting wires and soothing limbs the size of fingers.

We had been in NICUs before. Met fragile babies. Held their hands.

But this felt different.

Sunlight poured in through the windows, casting a warm June glow across the floor. Yet, I shivered.

I reached for John again.

His palm was damp, but he gripped back.

We stood there, side by side.

But neither of us felt steady.

---

THE DOOR CLICKED SHUT behind us.

Before we could take another breath, the caseworker from DHS appeared. No smile. No introduction. Her boxy gray suit looked like armor. She spotted us by the nurses' station and walked over briskly, clipboard in hand, wasting no time on pleasantries.

She launched into the baby's case. The facts. The forecasts. The kind of list they thought a foster parent needed to hear before saying yes.

Moments later, Nurse Carolyn joined us. Her hair was pulled tightly into a bun, and her cheerful Disney scrubs clashed with the heaviness in her eyes. She stepped in where the caseworker faltered, filling in the clinical details with calm precision.

The more she spoke, the smaller I began to feel.

I didn't need a speech. I needed to see her.

To hold her.

I've always trusted my gut. I knew if I could just cradle her, even for a moment... I would know whether I could do this.

But Nurse Carolyn wasn't rushing. She wanted us to

understand what we were stepping into. She knew this baby well.

"Born April 17. Two months early. Three pounds fifteen ounces."

*So tiny.* I gripped the rail behind me.

"She was exposed to cocaine, alcohol, and nicotine. Likely dependent on all three."

My chest tightened.

"She was born with no skin on her hands or feet."

I flinched. My body reacted before my mind could.

*No skin.*

I couldn't picture it.

"She failed both hearing screenings. Her eyes are covered in a yellow film. No retinal response."

Probable deafness. Probable blindness.

Nurse Carolyn's voice dropped to a whisper.

"She was born with congenital syphilis. The doctors blamed it for much of what they were seeing: her insulin dependence, her blindness, her deafness, her fragile body."

I pressed deeper into John's side. He stood with freckled forearms folded tightly across his chest, pinning down the sleeves of his plaid button-down. His stance was wide. Grounded. Bracing for impact.

I, on the other hand, needed something solid to lean on. My knees wobbled. My breathing was shallow.

We listened as Nurse Carolyn continued to read from the chart and the DHS worker scribbled notes into her folder. They were giving us everything we needed to make an informed decision. But I couldn't absorb it. It was all so clinical. The room tilted.

Everything slowed.

Nurse Carolyn paused.

"It's a lot."

The chart in her hand stayed open, but her face softened.

Not with pity. With truth.

I stared at the floor, trying to breathe.

———

THE BABY'S mother had disappeared from the hospital just hours after giving birth, leaving her daughter behind before she had even learned to cry.

No calls. No visits. No one left to ask questions or fight for better options.

With her mother's milk not available, she was started on formula, fed through tiny, measured bottles. Her sterile incubator was her only constant. She couldn't regulate her own body temperature, so the machine did it for her. Day after day, week after week, she lay beneath the dome, cocooned in synthetic comfort.

Doctors and nurses came and went... poking, prodding, charting.

The incubator became her gurney, wheeled to imaging suites and diagnostic labs: MRIs, CT scans, blood draws.

Everything about her care was monitored. Precise. Every move, a calculation. Even her feedings felt mechanical. Her little head lifted, tilted. The formula dropped in, milliliter by milliliter. Enough to prove she was still here.

The staff did their jobs. The machines did theirs. But for all the wires and charts and protocols, something essential was missing.

"Failure to thrive." The phrase stamped her file like a forecast. Not a diagnosis, but a warning. A sign the world had given up.

What was a cannula?

What did sub-Q mean?

We had fostered medically fragile babies before. I had learned to read charts, decipher acronyms, track every dose and decimal.

This case felt different. Heavier. The learning curve just to keep her comfortable was steep. The stakes were high.

Still, beneath the swirl of questions, something steadier stirred.

We didn't have the answers. Not yet. But we already knew.

We were going to say yes.

*This is why you are here.*

We needed to steady our fears. We needed to see her. Because the more we learned about this baby's start, the more miraculous it seemed that she survived at all.

After an hour of briefings, Nurse Carolyn closed the chart and looked up.

"Are you ready to meet her?"

I nodded, my throat still too tight to speak.

The lights blurred as we walked. We passed rows of incubators, each one decorated with pink or blue teddy bears, cheerful mobiles, and hand-lettered name signs. Proof of parents who visited often.

Nurse Carolyn walked to the very end of the hall. Then stepped aside.

Alone in the shadows, the last incubator sat quiet.

No stuffed animals. No name. No signs of anticipation or joy.

The area surrounding her incubator overflowed with medical supplies. Bins stacked high, items tilting off shelves. The air buzzed with the hum of machines.

And there, deep in the dim enclosure, was a tiny, swaddled bundle beneath a tangle of wires and faint light. She lay curled on her right side with her impossibly small hands tucked beneath her chin. Oxygen tubing looped under her nose. Wires spilled out from beneath the familiar blue-and-pink striped blanket, each one tethered to a machine keeping watch. Someone had placed a small green bow on the crown of her head, the color vivid against her soft black curls.

Sleeping. Still fighting.

And somehow... mine to hold.

Only then did I look at John. His jaw trembled as tears welled in his eyes. A lump rose in my throat. Neither of us could speak.

She was beautiful in a way that hurt.

We hadn't held her yet, but she was already holding us.

I understood, in that silent moment, why they insisted on telling us the worst first. Why the placement manager had chosen her words so carefully.

That was our out.

Our chance to walk away before her face made it impossible.

But now we had seen her.

And we weren't going anywhere.

———

Two hours after we arrived, Nurse Carolyn finally opened the incubator.

I lifted the four-pound newborn into my arms, careful not to disturb a single wire or tube.

*Just hold her.*

The words echoed. My heart swelled.

Tears slipped down my cheeks as my arms folded around her.

Nurse Carolyn guided me to a wooden rocker beside the incubator. Its low arms and lumpy cushion offered little comfort. But then she placed a two-ounce bottle into my hand, the kind with the red rubber nipple I'd seen in every nursery I'd ever known. That small familiarity grounded me.

I had done this before. I could do it again.

Nurse Carolyn reminded me that the feeding had to be completed within thirty minutes. For her, sucking alone burned calories nearly as fast as she could take them in. Every minute at the bottle was a battle not to lose more than she gained.

I cradled her close, watching her chest rise and fall with quiet determination. Around us, nurses gathered, sharing pieces of her story. How she fought for her very first breath, and every one since. Defying the odds.

"There must be a reason she's alive," one shy nurse murmured.

And at that moment, I saw it too.

A presence. Fierce and fragile.

Every breath a defiance. Every heartbeat a reason.

What this baby needed most wasn't medicine or machines.

She needed a place to belong.

And that's what we would give her.

Not a cure.

A place in this world.

A place in our home.

# June 17, 2009 — Wednesday

She met the discharge weight: four pounds six ounces. The agency paperwork was in place. The hospital would send her home once we proved we could manage her care. So we would learn her body, her rhythms, how to keep her comfortable. Lancet. Meter. Insulin. Formula. A new language for keeping her alive.

We tried to eat a proper breakfast, pretending it was an ordinary day. Dudley kept circling my legs as I got him outside, acting like he knew something was coming. John filled Dudley's food and water bowls to last the day. We had no idea how long we'd be at the hospital.

I dressed for long hours in the rocker. Soft cotton, nothing that might scratch her skin. John grabbed a blue spiral notebook and blue pen, his trusted tools.

With Dudley settled, we locked the house and took our usual seats in the car. John had his stainless-steel coffee mug secured in the center console, the warm scent of French vanilla creamer filling the cabin. I had my iced tea with lemon.

The drive was quiet. Not morning quiet, something

heavier. The silence of two people bracing for what came next, carrying our own questions and fears, trying to steady ourselves for the third-floor NICU.

One thought kept circling louder than the rest.

Could I hold her through her last breath?

I knew death. I had cared for John's father in his final months: feeding, bathing, medications, every small need. When Pap passed, I was left hollow. Overwhelmed. A strange stillness after weeks of constant vigilance.

But Pap was seventy-four. Cancer gave us time to prepare. This was different. She weighed less than five pounds.

Was I ready to lose her?

Doubt hollowed me, but my hands stayed open.

I would have to hold her. Love her. And let her go.

---

JOHN and I stood silently as Nurse Carolyn read more from the baby's chart.

This fragile baby girl had endured daily blood draws in addition to frequent CT scans, MRIs, and other lab work. Many tests had to be repeated. Gas in her tummy blurred the results. IV lines often failed because her veins collapsed.

Her nurses worked to stabilize her. They followed a strict insulin and feeding schedule, trying different formulas to help her gain weight. The goal was narrow: hold her until her body learned to grow.

In those first few weeks, she did not grow. She shrank. Her weight dropped to two pounds eight ounces. Life-threatening. When the doctors said sepsis, hope thinned.

Tears filled my eyes as I listened. The more I fought them, the more they came.

Twenty-seven diagnoses in her chart: sepsis, brain bleed, syphilis, insulin dependence, no vision, no hearing. Her hands and feet were raw. My throat tightened as Nurse Carolyn named each one.

She had made it this far in the NICU, under the care of professionals who knew every alarm by heart. After a few days of watching and practicing, her care would be in my hands. I was afraid of the impact on her as I learned the alarms, the numbers, and the signs from her frail body. Still, something in me was drawn to her.

I kept my focus on this fragile child. All I wanted was to ease her suffering. She needed someone. I would be the one to stay.

When I held her against my chest, I prayed our home would be a safe, loving place for this newborn to be at peace when she passed. I wanted to believe her life, no matter how short, had purpose. That our love might be enough to hold her until the end. I didn't let myself imagine survival. I didn't ask how long. I had one thing to do.

*Just hold her.*

I'd always told myself I could manage anything for a little while. That's what I was prepared to do. But what if she stayed longer than a little while?

Would she live long enough that I would need to find ways to communicate with her, even without hearing or vision? Sometimes I imagined learning to sign, but all I could see was letters traced into a palm. Her hands were so small, her skin still healing. How could I ever know if she understood me?

No. Not now. I looked down at her sleeping face. I had to stay here. Rocking her, feeding her, loving her, following routines, giving her everything I had, moment by moment.

The routines were no longer something I watched from the edge of the room. They were being placed into my hands, one at a time.

Nurse Carolyn showed me how to start each feeding with a glucometer reading and insulin injection. "Aim for 100–225 mg/dL," she said, warning that her numbers fluctuated wildly, dropping as low as 30 and spiking to 480. Either extreme could be life-threatening.

"That's it," Nurse Carolyn said. I nodded. My hands hovered, not yet trustworthy.

"Next time," she said, "you can try."

Next time, I pressed the razor-shaped lancet to her heel and drew blood. My heart ached knowing that I'd be the one causing pain to this struggling four-pound baby. Soon, I would measure her insulin and slide the needle into her thigh. Long-acting insulin in the morning and evening, shorter-acting before each feeding. For now, I watched.

I couldn't hold back my tears as Nurse Carolyn swabbed her thigh. A small lift of skin. The needle touched, then slipped in. A thumb on the plunger. Slow pressure. I held my breath.

She flinched, then stilled. A dot of red. A square of gauze.

Nurse Carolyn warned that she might resist her feedings and showed me how to hold her and support the baby's head so she could conserve energy. She propped the baby in a sitting position in her incubator, with the baby's head leaned back so that gravity eased some of her need to suck. Nurse Carolyn kept coming back to the same thing: weight gain.

"Go ahead, try it." Nurse Carolyn eased the baby into

my hands, mentioning she'd gained an ounce. It felt like a hundred. I supported her head as Nurse Carolyn had shown, tested different bottle angles, and watched every movement she made.

I did the hands-on training while John took notes. Pages of them. Not in his usual scribble. He wrote slowly, deliberately, as if precision could keep her safe. When the doctors spoke, his hands paused over the page. He met every nurse's eyes and thanked them by name, as if they'd given us more than knowledge.

We took turns holding her. Every chance he got, he cradled her against his chest and promised the same thing. "You are safe. You are loved," he'd repeat, each word a gentle hymn.

"You're the luckiest little girl in the world," he would whisper. "You're coming home with us."

---

After five hours of training, we drove home. Our bodies were slow; our minds raced.

We met the team. The pediatrician walked us through her weight chart, careful arrows marking each rise and fall. "Slow, but gaining," he said softly, as if speaking to the baby more than us.

The infectious disease doctor did not mince words. Congenital syphilis. Insulin dependence. A body under strain. He believed there was a chance her body might heal as it matured. "Weight gain would change everything," he said, "if she could manage it."

The dermatologist showed us photos from her first days. Her hands and feet were raw, the skin stripped and weeping. I could not unsee it. Now her hands and feet were covered in medicated dressings, protecting skin that had not fully formed at birth. Only her heels remained uncovered, scarred and raw from repeated lancet sticks.

"Manageable," he said. "If her body can grow."

An intern asked if the photos could be used in his dissertation. I told him he'd need permission from DHS. This was not our story to share.

John's pen moved slowly across the page as each doctor spoke. I rocked our baby, patting her bottom, humming under my breath.

The endocrinologist studied her glucometer readings with Nurse Elizabeth, adjusting insulin doses by fractions. "It's a work in progress," he said. He admitted he had never treated a newborn like her. He thought the insulin might be temporary, if her pancreas recovered. He apologized for the adult-sized lancet; there was nothing smaller available. He examined her scabbed heels and shook his head.

Amor, his nurse, lingered. She touched my shoulder before leaving, promising to check on us every day.

The dietitian was brisk and clinical, focused only on calories and ounces. By then, John's notebook was full and my head was louder than the monitors.

Each specialist held a piece of her. Each one seemed surprised she was still alive. And yet she was.

As foster parents, protocol was simple: names stayed private. In public, we relied on terms of endearment. The boys were all "Buster." The girls were "Deedle," borrowed from our youngest's refrain, "She's just a Deedle girl."

John stopped at the grocery store for milk, lemons, and a chance to share. Before he set the basket down, the cashier asked, "How's the baby?" A bagger drifted over. The manager leaned on the endcap.

John told them about our Deedle in the NICU. Today's small win: an ounce gained. "Keep her in your prayers," he said.

We ate deli food and kept talking through our plan as Dudley slept in John's lap.

One day wasn't enough. We needed more time.

---

LATER THAT EVENING, sitting in the matching brown rocker-recliners I had recently convinced John to buy, we mapped a new layout for the room. Then we moved furniture until it fit. We made room for the feedings. The oxygen tank. The monitor and its leads.

We didn't talk about how long she might stay.

We just made room.

John promised to plan ahead. Each time he traveled, he would make sure the fridge was stocked, meals were ready, and supplies were set out. When he was home, he'd handle bottle duty, laundry, and groceries. John made it clear: my only job was to care for this baby. And of course, give Dudley some attention, too.

As I listened, I felt blessed, strangely steadied. By the end of the conversation, we had a plan. Not perfect. Manageable. For now.

---

FOR THIS BABY, I wanted to give her a name that could be hers alone. A name with strength, one she could grow into if she survived. She already had an extraordinary story. She deserved something unique, not often heard.

That night, long after the world slept, her name came to me.

We would call her Jayden.

It meant *"God has heard."*

It held her fight. The calm in her face.

If she lived, she could grow into it.

If she didn't, we would hold her name and speak it for her.

# June 19, 2009 —
# Friday

John was in Germany. He hated to leave me. Maybe he missed time with Jayden even more. The solo drive to the hospital showed me what life might be when he was away.

My first NICU visit without him. None of our experience helped. I kept reaching for his hand. I was grateful for the sunshine. Its warmth helped to settle the nervous shivers I couldn't quite control. My white sneakers tapped the tile and echoed through the quiet room as I made my way to the back corner where Jayden lay. Alone.

I set down my bag and moved the rocking chair closer to her, careful not to disturb the delicate web of tubes and wires connecting her to the machines. I unbuttoned the top buttons of my soft cotton shirt and gently lifted her from the incubator, supporting her delicate head in my hands.

I settled into the rocker and opened her blankets, drawing her against my chest. I had to see her. To speak her name for the first time.

"Jayden, my sweet girl. I am going to love you forever."

She didn't stir. She couldn't hear me. But something about the moment felt right. Her name fit.

I wrapped her blankets tightly around her and drew her close to my heart. Her body melted into mine. For the first time that day, I was calm.

As I held her, beautiful and delicate, already mine to love... the nurses moved quickly from one incubator to the next, tending to the dozens of babies in the NICU. None of them had time to sit and cradle a baby. Their attention was stretched thin as they charted vitals, managed tests, prepared medications, and kept a rigid feeding schedule, repeated across so many fragile lives.

Most days, parents provided that connection. Mothers and fathers weaving in and out during visiting hours, offering tender moments of touch, the quiet comfort of being held.

But Jayden didn't have that. Two months old. Failure to thrive. She didn't know the warmth of arms that lingered. She hadn't been cradled simply because she was loved.

I looked down at the little dumpling in my arms and whispered a vow.

"I will be the person in your life who loves you forever."

NURSE ELIZABETH LIFTED Jayden from my arms to check her blood sugar, then administered insulin before the feeding. I watched as the adult-sized lancet pierced Jayden's tiny heel, drawing blood but no tears. Afterward, Nurse Elizabeth wrapped her and handed her back with a two-ounce bottle, the familiar kind with the red rubber nipple. Ordinary. Trembling.

I cradled Jayden in my arms and offered her the bottle. At first, Jayden took it quickly, working on the newly introduced high-calorie formula like she'd been waiting for it. But she wouldn't settle in my arms. Her chin lifted. Her head pulled back. Her back arched. Her whole body tensed, resisting rest. The longer she drank, the harder it became. Gagging. Choking. The apnea alarm blared. Nurses rushed in. The only way to silence the alarm was to pull the bottle away, press Jayden to my chest and rub and tap her back.

Maybe feeding was so difficult that she needed the repetition of being held up and the familiarity of the incubator. Perhaps the closeness of being held felt like too much when she was already struggling to drink. I didn't know. So for now, I decided to follow her lead, to meet her where she was. In time, we could try something gentler.

As Nurse Elizabeth fed the red-haired boy in the incubator beside us, she reminded me to pull the bottle from Jayden's lips. She'd reached her thirty-minute limit. I looked down. Jayden had swallowed only one ounce. Half the formula she needed, despite how hard she worked. I was so focused on helping her finish, I'd lost track of time. I worried the short feed would look like a failure. I needed Nurse Elizabeth to believe in us. Would she think I wasn't capable of caring for such a fragile child?

The lesson Nurse Elizabeth had for me today was learning to inject the insulin. I did not want to do this. But it was absolutely necessary. Jayden's need for insulin became apparent within the first hours of her life. If she had any chance at all of survival, it would be up to me to continue with the injections.

Nurse Elizabeth stood at her station, handing me the

supplies. First, a swab of alcohol to sterilize the injection site. Next, the syringe, drawing the exact dose based on her glucometer reading. Then Nurse Elizabeth explained the Sub-Q process: lift the skin, insert the needle above the muscle while slowly pushing the plunger to release the insulin into her thigh. Pull the syringe away from Jayden's thigh and gently massage the injection site to help with absorption.

Nurse Elizabeth talked me through each step, speaking softly but with authority. As the tears fell on my cheeks, my vision blurred. My stomach ached and my hands shook. My heart raced. How could I do this to such a delicate person? But I proceeded. Nurse Elizabeth's hand on my shoulder felt like her confidence in me was all I needed.

When I completed the task, I cried. I cried more than the baby did. Jayden had very little reaction to the injection. She seemed to already accept the pain of everything that nurses, doctors, and her own body put her through. My heart continued to ache as I realized she expected nothing more. Pain. Always. Pain.

After her feeding, I noted the amount of formula and her glucose reading in my spiral notebook. I unwrapped Jayden and held her against my bare chest, as exposed as I could and still be decent. I eased her head beneath my chin, hoping she could feel the vibration of my voice. Then I draped a soft cotton blanket over us both, tucking the edges beneath my arms. I slid one hand beneath the blanket and rubbed her back. The skin felt dry. Brittle. Her preemie-sized diaper was the only thing separating her from me.

I rocked her in the old rickety chair. I sang softly.

The same lullaby, over and over.

This became my daily rhythm. Six to eight hours a day in the NICU.

Holding her.

Learning.

Sometimes I turned the rocker toward the window. Other times, toward the work area. Either way, I opened my shirt and held Jayden skin to skin. She couldn't see or hear me. But she could feel my warmth. My heartbeat.

It was the only way I knew to say:

"I am here. I love you. You are safe."

---

EVEN FROM GERMANY, John called me every night, his voice carrying the calm I leaned on, no matter how many miles between us. Our conversations no longer centered on the stories from his travels. Now, all he wanted to hear about was his Deedle.

"How's Deedle doing?" he'd ask, cautiously.

Some days brought encouraging news. She'd gained an ounce or two. Other days, a drop in weight. Her blood sugar levels wouldn't stabilize. The numbers spiked and plummeted without pattern or warning. Her prognosis remained unchanged.

"She knows you love her. You're doing great." His words reminded me how much he cared for me. For her. And somehow, it made his absence both easier and harder.

I was growing more confident in Jayden's care. I could talk nonstop about each day's routine: every feeding, every test, every micro-milestone. She was all I could think about. I gave little thought to laundry or groceries. Soon, I'd be wearing clothes from the back of my closet simply because they were still clean.

The closest fast-food place started to recognize me. I

always ordered the same thing: a medium meal with a large Coke. No thought of nutrition. Just hot food, fast enough to fill an empty stomach. And a few extra fries for Dudley.

I poured everything I had into this little girl. To bring her home. Love became the study. Presence, the practice. The more I learned, the more I loved her.

Jayden needed more than medicine.

She needed someone to hold her.

# June 22, 2009 — Monday

I had fallen in love with a beautiful baby girl who wasn't expected to survive. Her chart read: failure to thrive.

*Just hold her.*

I tried not to think about her birth mother. The empty chair at the NICU did it for me. We had seen what was possible when birth parents were given time and support to reconnect with their children. We had learned not to judge. But these facts were hard to carry: no visits, no calls, no one coming to hold her.

Anger rose fast and hot. I hated how it felt.

People think foster parents are trained to stay detached, but that isn't how this works. The line blurs between blood and prayer and sleepless nights. Loving her like she'll stay, even when she won't. Attachment isn't a risk. It's the treatment plan.

What I give her now will stay in her body as memory...

held, safe. When love comes again, she'll recognize it. We don't guard our hearts. We pour our hearts out, knowing it will wreck us. We do it anyway. Because every child deserves to be someone's beloved. Even if only for a season.

HER SMILE FOLLOWED ME HOME... a light that wouldn't dim.

After dinner, the weight of her situation returned. My mind wouldn't rest. *Why did her blood sugar keep crashing? How could I help her gain weight?*

Something in me kept insisting that breast milk could offer healing in ways formulas couldn't. I sat at the computer long after the sun went down, the summer darkness outside my window filling with the sound of crickets.

I scrolled donor milk sites and found a breast milk bank affiliated with a hospital three hours away. The donor mothers were thoroughly screened, and the milk was pasteurized for safety before distribution. They could ship it to us for $4.15 an ounce. The mothers weren't paid. The price covered screening, pasteurizing, and packaging the milk.

Would the state ever approve that cost? I had no proof breast milk would do more than the high-calorie formula. Just instinct, intuition, and hope.

In that late-night search, I found another possibility: a powdered breast milk product. It was easy. Just scoop and mix like formula. I printed the brochure, knowing it was intended for hospitals only. Still, I hoped it might help, enough to open a door.

I prayed sleep would come easily, but my mind kept spinning. I wasn't just gathering research. I was preparing to plead her case, to push against protocols, and to ask doctors to reconsider what they knew, all for a child they didn't expect to survive.

I believed in my gut and in this child. And if no one else was going to fight for her, I would.

---

I ARRIVED at the NICU ready to advocate. I approached Jayden's pediatrician and asked about using breast milk. He explained how the formula made it easier to monitor caloric intake, but I wasn't convinced.

Next, I asked the dietitian about the powdered processed breast milk I'd found online. She didn't even look up.

"I've heard of it. It's not cost-effective."

That was it.

Babies with someone to speak for them got options: breast milk advocacy, lactation support. Babies without got protocol. Jayden and I had a spiral notebook. It felt like the beginning of forgetting... before anyone had learned her name.

---

THAT NIGHT, when John called, I let it all out. Every frustration. Every argument. Every unanswered question. He listened to the fire in my voice. He didn't try to cool it. He knew. We both knew. This baby needed a fighter, and I had already decided that fighter would be me.

There was little he could do from overseas. But his

support released the pressure inside me, and for the first time in days, I fell into a deep sleep.

I woke the next morning with renewed energy and a sharper sense of purpose. My determination to provide breast milk for Jayden didn't fade. It had only grown stronger.

I reached out to friends who understood the kind of work I was doing. My friend Terri immediately came to mind. We started fostering around the same time, both learning the system and comparing notes over coffee and playdates.

I remembered one of our first conversations. *What should they call us?* I had told Terri that since the State of Michigan referred to us as foster parents, John and I had decided we would be just that: parents. Every child deserves to know a Mama and a Papa. So we became Mama Judy and Papa John. Terri wholeheartedly agreed. She became Mama Terri.

A decade later, our lives had changed in countless ways, but she remained one of my dearest friends. So when John and I began our second week of training, Terri offered to step in as our hospital-required support person. She drove ninety minutes to join us for the CPR refresher course, a final step before bringing Jayden home.

I expected her to rush in and scoop Jayden from my arms. But she didn't. She stood there for a long moment, taking her in. Maybe the fragility stopped her. Maybe she was guarding her heart.

I sat still, my mind looping through everything I'd learned: breast milk and formula, calories and nutrients, protocol and instinct. Terri found a nearby stool, and I turned so Terri could see Jayden's cherubic face resting against my chest. Her eyes filled with silent tears.

Finally, she reached for Jayden and covered her with kisses.

I explained Jayden's medical needs. Her blood sugar, her weight, and feeding complications. Then I told Terri about my hopes for breast milk. How strongly I believed it could give this little girl a better chance. How the pediatrician had brushed me off. How the dietitian had dismissed me with the phrase: "It's not cost-effective."

Terri listened intently. She helped me see that what mattered most was learning how to care for Jayden so she could come home with us.

Jayden was gaining weight on the new high-calorie formula. So maybe now wasn't the time to push. Maybe now was the time to stay the course.

Through silent tears, Terri nodded.

After she left, the NICU grew quiet. I held Jayden tighter, pulling her body close, as if to make up for all the things she couldn't have.

JOHN and I had been visiting Jayden in the NICU for nearly two weeks and each day brought something new: doctors, tests, results.

We learned how to place the apnea leads, to read the blinking numbers and interpret what they meant. John focused on the training about the oxygen tanks: an eight-liter tank that would sit in our family room, and a smaller one for travel. We received additional CPR training. Just the two of us now, without Terri.

It felt more serious. More personal.

Jayden had a sizable umbilical hernia. But strangely, it was one of the few issues that didn't rattle me. I had seen this before. I knew what to do: gently press on the hernia-tion a few times a day to make sure nothing inside was twisting. But I also knew: if I ever couldn't get it to reduce, if I felt it trapped beneath my fingers, we were to go straight to the ER.

Every day, Jayden's care became more familiar. More hands-on, more real. Little by little, we stopped being visitors. We were becoming her parents.

# June 25, 2009 — Thursday

Miss Jayden was finally home.

Dudley approved. He greeted her with a fluffy pink ball he'd found behind the sofa cushion. His version of a grand gesture. Jayden was oblivious, but Dudley seemed to understand. He always knew when a baby needed him. Welcoming babies was his job, his purpose. Often his curls became the first thing fingers reached for.

Our time at the hospital kept us away, leaving Dudley home alone. Now Dudley was a big brother again.

Our first night at home was chaotic, as they always were. But chaos usually didn't come with medical equipment taking up residence in our family room. We positioned the oxygen tank so the seven-foot tubing could reach the rocker and the changing table. The oxygen hissed incessantly.

I kept the extra apnea monitor leads within reach. Bottles, sterilized and sorted, sat in the colander. The changing table held diapers and wipes in a warmer. The shelves carried what we needed most: the glucometer, syringes, alcohol wipes, and cannula tubing. Every surface was arranged with purpose.

The path between stations was tight. Deliberate. Just enough space to pivot, prepare, respond.

Among all the supplies, the wipe warmer was the only thing that looked familiar. Comforting, even.

Then there was the musical mobile, part of every baby's setup. One last touch to make it a nursery. I clipped it onto the changing table. Jayden couldn't see it. She couldn't hear it. It didn't matter.

It was tradition. It was love. It was our way of saying:

You belong here. You are wanted. You are home.

John stocked the fridge with salads and fresh-cut fruit, filled the pantry, brewed tea, sliced lemons. He knew what I needed, and what I might forget. In a few days, he'd be leaving. And I'd be here. Her caregiver.

I prepared bottles. I had two-ounce portions of nursery water and formula within reach. Anything to avoid putting her down. I knew I'd be dozing off here and there, day and night. I propped pillows beneath both arms, creating a cradle so Jayden could rest securely on my chest. Contained. Comforted. Close.

The apnea alarm blared often, piercing like a fire alarm and continuing until Jayden started to breathe again.

Each time the alarm split the silence, I moved on instinct. I lifted her from my lap, pressed her to my shoulder, patting and rubbing until her body remembered breath. Twenty seconds without a detected breath triggered the monitor.

Every three hours, a new cycle began.

Diaper first. I laid her down on the changing table and rushed to the bathroom. When the monitor screamed, I raced back from the bathroom, heart pounding, only to find her still and silent. I picked her up. Held her close, bouncing and rubbing until the monitor went quiet. Then I placed her back on the changing table, hoping to finish our routine: applying ointment, and securing her preemie diaper before the alarm sounded.

After I pricked her heel and read her glucose, I wrote the numbers in my spiral notebook. I checked the hand-written scale for the corresponding amount of insulin and carefully measured that amount into the plunger.

I pinched the skin on her thigh. As the needle went in, I pushed the medicine slowly, then rubbed the injection site to help absorption.

Feeding was next. I picked up Jayden and a bottle and sat in my chair, holding her propped upright in my lap. I leaned her head back. Jayden started eagerly and then gagged and struggled. I burped her and let her rest. Then I sat her on my lap, tilted her head back and started again. Each time she would drink almost ravenously for some time before gagging. I repeated the cycle for thirty minutes before returning her to my chest.

The first twenty-four hours were spent learning a rhythm.

Diapers. Readings. Injections. Feedings.

And then, trying to sleep in the rocking chair with Jayden curled on my chest. Jayden adapted with surprising ease. I did not.

Sleep escaped me. Even as my eyelids threatened to fold shut, even as my mind drifted for a moment into nothing before snapping back to her.

The alarm when her breathing stopped terrified me. Each time I feared she might not start breathing again.

The stress fueled a desire to document everything. I grabbed the spiral notebook and used a ruler to create columns. Clean lines. Legible numbers. I logged her glucometer readings, insulin doses, bottle times, ounces, wet diapers, dirty diapers, oxygen levels, every apnea event and exactly what was happening. I needed to understand, to anticipate, to protect her.

My mind raced. I second-guessed myself. I was always afraid I might miss something that could keep her alive. All this charting and searching for clues while Jayden slept quietly, curled up against my chest in the rocker. Comfortable. Content. Home.

John was home for our first night with Jayden. He went to bed upstairs but came down to check on us more than once. Each time the alarm sounded, it woke him too. We weren't ready to say what it might mean. All we could do was hold her.

Every three hours, on the hospital schedule.

Diaper. Reading. Injection. Feeding.

THE VERY NEXT DAY, we had a visitor. Not friends or family. Not yet. Jayden's condition made any exposure risky. Even a common cold could be dangerous.

Nicole arrived, Jayden's caseworker from the foster agency. She was here for her required initial visit for a baby in care to complete paperwork and sort out logistics. It took everything in me to focus while monitoring Jayden's medical needs. Nicole needed the details. All of Jayden's medical conditions. Our care responsibilities. What would be expected of us going forward.

"I... I don't know," I said.

None of it felt familiar enough to explain. Not with confidence. Nicole could see I was tired. Worn out. Maybe even a bit overwhelmed.

"Maybe this visit is a bit too soon," she admitted. "Given the circumstances and all."

Still, she wanted to document what she could.

"Can we just start with what you do know?"

Because what she knew, what we all knew, was that Jayden's time wasn't promised. No one knew how long she would live. Every moment was a gift.

A blessing.

"What's on your schedule so far?" Nicole asked. She didn't want to miss her chance to get everything in writing.

She explained that Michigan's foster care system used different "levels of care" to assess a placement, and Jayden would likely qualify for the highest. This meant increased compensation. Not as a bonus, but to offset the very real costs of caring for a medically fragile infant. This wasn't just about diapers and bottles.

Nicole needed to know how many doctor visits were scheduled. How far we'd have to travel. How often I'd be taking glucometer readings, monitoring oxygen levels, documenting every apnea event. How often we might have to perform CPR.

As she continued through the list, it finally sank in. I didn't even know the full scope yet. I had been handed a list of follow-up appointments at discharge. But I hadn't really looked at it. All I knew was that nothing was scheduled for today.

Nicole encouraged us to continue Jayden's care with the same medical team that treated her in the NICU. She said continuity mattered, especially in a case like this. A one-in-a-million case. Complicated. Likely terminal.

It would mean more travel. More time. More stress. Time on my chest was when she was comfortable with no alarms. Being transported in her car seat for forty-five minutes each way would not provide the comfort she needed. But starting fresh with doctors who didn't know her history felt too risky. Our current pediatrician had refused the case. Too complex. So we agreed it had to be done. We would do whatever it took, because even though she was "one in a million," she was also just one.

One little girl.

One fragile life.

And she needed everything we could give.

---

NICOLE HAD ALREADY CONTACTED the county and arranged for a visiting nurse and a dietitian to come three times a week. Knowing trained medical professionals would be in the house supervising Jayden's care, even briefly, felt like a lifeline. The hospital had also assigned a separate visiting nurse to check in weekly for the first two months. We weren't doing this alone.

Well, except for the twenty-three hours a day when the house went quiet again, and it was just me with Jayden. Still, their visits meant she'd be weighed and measured regularly, helping me track her progress or catch signs that something wasn't working. That gave me comfort, a sense of accountability, and the feeling that maybe we could do this.

Nicole worked for our private agency, Ennis Center, but she would also be coordinating with the state case-worker assigned to Jayden's case. She reassured me she'd begin the paperwork right away and return soon to update it, once our routines were more clearly established.

We were deep in conversation when Jayden stirred awake and the rhythm of caregiving quickly took over. I laid her on the changing table, changed her diaper, then checked her glucometer so I knew how much insulin to draw.

The infant syringes finally arrived, ordered just for her. They were half the size of the syringes I used at the hospital, and the insulin we'd picked up at the specialty pharmacy had been diluted with sterile saline. Ten parts saline to one part insulin. This made dosing safer. Instead of drawing up a "1" on the adult syringe, I could draw "10" on the infant syringe, giving me more room for precision. The trade-off: a little more fluid in her fragile thigh. But far less risk of overdose.

Nicole stood nearby and watched as I administered the insulin. She admitted she couldn't do it. She flinched when the needle pierced Jayden's skin. I explained how I did this for each feeding, every two to three hours. That I couldn't use the same injection site twice. "So I picture a grid," I said. "Top to bottom. Left to right."

"It's a Sub-Q injection, subcutaneous," I said. "Just under the skin."

It sounded simple. It wasn't. I adjusted the cannula, the clear tubing looped behind her ears and into her nostrils and taped across her cheeks. The word was new a week ago. Now I reached for it instinctively.

Nicole leaned closer, watching my hands. She understood why I needed a system. Why every detail mattered. Why this wasn't just care.

It was precision.

It was presence.

It was survival.

***

I liked Nicole right away. There was something comforting in the way she showed up for me, how she recognized the weight I was carrying. The unspoken reality.

Nicole excused herself with a quiet goodbye and closed the front door behind her. Sitting back down to feed Jayden her bottle, I realized Nicole hadn't even asked to hold her. She later admitted she didn't bother putting Jayden's paperwork in a folder. She didn't think there would be a need.

I COULDN'T WRAP my mind around the past two weeks. But now, with Jayden finally home, I felt the slightest shift. A rhythm began to form.

Diaper. Reading. Injection. Feeding.

I could exhale... just a little.

We reserved a section of the refrigerator for Jayden's two types of insulin, each diluted by the specialty pharmacy. The colander on the kitchen counter held sterilized Dr. Brown's four-ounce bottles and level one nipples, tucked neatly under a baby blanket.

I stole a breath between moments.

Then I got back to it.

I replaced the medical tape on Jayden's puffy cheeks, holding the oxygen cannula in her barely visible nostrils.

I resumed the rhythm.

Diaper. Reading. Injection. Feeding.

I logged the numbers in the notebook.

I choreographed my quick breaks like a dance: Dudley out, bathroom, bottles ready, sprint back before the alarm. This time, I even managed to grab soda crackers and a glass of iced tea, setting them beside my rocker.

Just in time.

As I stepped past the oxygen tank, the apnea alarm

began to sound. I moved quickly, reaching for my Deedle girl. Her body melted into my chest as I tucked the baby blanket beneath each arm, securing her against me. Head beneath my chin. Skin to skin. Heart to heart.

I hoped she could begin to recognize this.

Warmth. Rhythm. Safety.

That my arms, my heart, would always return for her.

Once she settled, I cradled her for a bottle. It felt good. Natural. But within seconds, the alarm wailed again. So I shifted her onto my knee, supporting her jaw with my pinky, holding the bottle between my thumb and forefinger, her head resting in my other hand. She struggled. Gagging. Choking. Trying.

All I wanted was to make it easier for her. To make her feel safe. After thirty minutes, Jayden had only managed an ounce. I made a decision right then: feedings every two hours. Not three, as the NICU required. Less formula, more often. She couldn't take much, so we would give her more chances.

She wore herself out trying. I bundled her again, easing her into the familiar curl against my chest, encouraging a tiny burp before she drifted off. I nibbled a cracker. Sipped my tea. And felt the pull of sleep. We both needed it.

Still, my mind spun, reworking feeding plans, solving problems, trying to keep this delicate little girl safe. But my body had nothing left. I started to nod off. Her breath settled into mine. For a moment, nothing else moved.

# June 30, 2009 —
# Tuesday

The sun was still low, spilling light across the driveway as John loaded the car. Today was a big day. Jayden had three doctor appointments, her first since coming home. I was grateful John was here to drive, steady me, and stay beside me. All her specialists were in the same building, forty-five minutes away, so we packed them into one long day.

Jayden slept in her car seat, her breath soft beneath the cannula taped across her cheeks while the oxygen tank hummed behind her. I bathed her in the kitchen sink that morning, holding her as the warm water ran over her skin. The scent of lavender filled the room. Now her curls caught the sunlight through the rear window. Her preemie outfit still swallowed her; even her socks slipped off, no matter how I tried. Beside her sat a pacifier and a bottle of sterilized water, ready for a scoop of formula when she began to stir.

John had packed the stroller and my favorite diaper bag, the one with the little duck appliqué on the front, heavy with supplies: diapers, clothes, burp cloth, insulin on ice, syringes, formula. The scent of vanilla creamer warmed the cabin. He sang the whole way to the hospital, classic rock softening into lullabies that carried us through the miles. I watched the road unfold ahead of us and tried to believe this was an ordinary drive.

---

WE ENTERED the medical building with our baby's head snuggled deep under the plush blanket draped across my shoulder to shield her from the coughs in the waiting room. John followed close beside me, with her life-saving equipment and the diaper bag and spiral notebook in the seat of the stroller. After checking in, we were shown to a private room. When the door closed, he wrapped his arms around us both and whispered, "Everything's going to be alright."

I unraveled. The tears I'd been swallowing all morning finally rose. My knees trembled. My heart hammered. What were we about to hear? Had I missed something critical?

I was trusted with a life I didn't know how to keep. All I had was availability. Available to go to the hospital. Learn her routine. Bring her home.

*Just hold her.*

No one asked me to save her. I fell in love with her. That was enough.

We would do everything asked of us. But I wasn't ready to let her go. It felt as if grief had already begun. How could anyone ask that of me?

A knock at the door split the sterile air. The pediatrician entered briskly. I laid Jayden on the paper-covered table, still wrapped in her blanket. Diapered. Small. The leads from the apnea monitor rested in the stroller beside us.

The pediatrician washed his hands and began the exam, tracing her blotchy torso, checking her thighs for scars, her raw heels worn from glucometer tests. When he clipped on the pulse ox, his expression changed. Her oxygen reading had dropped too low. He told John to increase the flow, here and at home.

Then a flicker of grace. The scale beeped: four pounds fourteen ounces. Seventeen inches. She'd gained weight.

I didn't wait for him to ask. I slid the notebook across the exam table, columns and arrows: smaller amounts, more often. I bit my lip and waited. One nod. My hand loosened on her blanket. I exhaled.

Then the pediatrician made an unexpected decision: Jayden would receive the standard immunizations given to a two-month-old. Yes, Jayden was ten and a half weeks old. But was she healthy enough for all those shots?

I was her foster mother. She belonged to the state. And the state required us to follow the schedule. Only a doctor could say otherwise. So I deferred. I prepared Jayden's bottle and fed her while we waited for the nurse to return with the injections. Three shots. Into her thighs. Of course.

The pediatrician also ordered labs and handed us referrals for eye, bone, and ear specialists, along with a developmental assessment through Early On. He handed us disabled parking paperwork because of the oxygen tanks. The pediatrician phoned the endocrinologist down the hall to review the readings I had logged in my spiral notebook. One less visit today. New insulin instructions followed.

John scribbled into the notebook: "Return weekly."

An infectious disease doctor added to the lab orders, but offered no encouragement for her recovery.

Jayden's lab work was scheduled at the hospital next door, but she just had three immunizations. As we stepped out of the building, John and I paused to talk through our options. Should we push through to the hospital lab, or spare her another needle? We decided she'd had enough for one day. We'd come back later in the week.

Our first real outing, and we were completely spent. I could only imagine the toll it had taken on her. All four pounds of her. We packed up the stroller, apnea monitor, portable oxygen, and diaper bag. I placed Jayden gently into her car seat and climbed in beside my little girl. As we pulled away, John and I spoke quietly, still trying to absorb everything we were told. A few miles later, he pulled into a drive-through and, without asking, ordered burgers with pickles, lettuce, and mayonnaise. While we waited, I kept my eyes closed and let his soft songs carry the rest, the same ones he'd sung on the way there.

The fries were hot; the Coke cooled my throat, sore from holding back tears. We had made it through our first outing with Jayden, and for the first time, we had professional validation for the care we were providing. Feeding her smaller amounts, more often, helped her gain weight. That progress was ours.

THAT EVENING, after the immunizations, Jayden changed.

She wouldn't take the bottle. Each time I touched the nipple to her lips, she let it sit there, then pushed it out with her tongue. No protest. No cry. Just refusal.

Her eyelids fluttered but didn't open. Her arms,

usually tucked close beneath her chin, lay loose against her sides.

I kissed her forehead. Too warm. I slid the thermometer under her arm and held it in place, watching the seconds blink by... 102.9ºF. I took her core temperature. 103.9ºF.

Our ten-week-old preemie. She wasn't even five pounds yet.

Her skin had lost its tone, turning ashy, almost gray beneath the tape that held her cannula in place. A bead of sweat gathered at her temple and slipped into her hairline. When I lifted her, her body sagged against me, heat radiating straight into my bare chest. Each breath pulled from somewhere deep.

"John."

He was already standing beside me.

"Go get gas," I said. "Fill it all the way."

He nodded and left without a word.

The house felt too quiet.

I changed her diaper. Her eyes stayed closed, breath rising slow.

I pricked her heel. The click sounded louder than usual. A slow bead of blood surfaced. I watched the meter count down, recalculated her dose.

I tried the bottle again. She turned her face away. Her lips trembled once, then went still.

John came back with a full tank and burgers I never opened. We kept our clothes on. The hospital directions lay on the table. Shoes by the door. Diaper bag packed. Portable oxygen ready.

I held her skin to skin through the night. Her heat settled into me. My own skin damp beneath her. Now and then she let out a low exhale, not quite a cry. I checked her temperature.

103.9ºF.

103.8ºF.

103.9ºF.

It didn't move.

Around two in the morning, I asked, "Do we go?"

John watched her breathe for a minute.

"We wait."

We sat in the dark. I could feel the slight beat of her heart against my ribs. Too fast. Too hot.

They told us to expect a mild fever.

Morning came thin through the windows. And then, suddenly, she stirred. Her mouth opened. She turned her head toward my chest, searching.

I laid her on my lap and reached for the bottle. One scoop of formula added to two ounces of water. I held the bottle to her dry lips. She gulped. Swallowing fast and desperate. Relief flooded me so quickly it hurt.

Then it happened. Her chin jerked up. Her back arched. Gagging. Choking. The apnea alarm screamed.

I pulled the bottle away, rubbed her back, rocked her back and forth, counting under my breath. One, two, three...

She sucked in air. Just a small breath. The alarm stopped.

I looked down at her, her small body trembling in my hands, and understood it in a way I hadn't before. It wasn't just that she was fragile. Every effort cost her.

We had been awake all night watching her struggle in my arms.

---

BY MID-MORNING, the worst of it felt further away. I

felt her breathing settle against my chest. A small relief, but it held.

John was back at work by afternoon. The house was quiet except for the alarms. This was our new life.

We were scheduled to meet a state-appointed legal caseworker, along with the county dietitian and our visiting nurse. I laid her on the changing table, knowing I had only a few minutes before the alarm. I threw on some clean clothes, washed my face, and poured iced tea while I mixed Jayden's formula. The basket of folded laundry John had hidden away in the downstairs bathroom had everything I needed. Except a shower. Showers had become rare. I was almost done putting on a clean T-shirt before Jayden's alarm sounded.

I raced back into the family room, forgetting my half-poured tea and her bottle, and found a very still baby. I rubbed her chest with my knuckles until finally, she raised her arms. Her eyes opened, and only then could I breathe.

I changed her preemie diaper. Her bottom was red and raw. I dabbed some ointment and whispered an apology. In the margin of my spiral notebook next to the columns for diapers, readings, injections, and feedings, I logged the irritation: red bottom, rash starting.

THE DIETITIAN, Ms. Chase, was due at 10:30 a.m. She came in with a small metal scale swinging against her leg and asked if she could set it on the kitchen table. After a quick pat for Dudley, she washed her hands at the sink and stepped over to the changing table where Jayden lay.

Ms. Chase silenced the apnea monitor and undressed her, peeling away the leads from the dry skin of Jayden's torso. She lifted Jayden's hands gently, testing her reflexes, then settled her onto the scale.

As the numbers flickered, she began asking questions.

"What formula is she on?"

"How many ounces?"

"How often?"

I answered quickly, the numbers already living in my head. Then I told her about the apnea alarm screaming during feedings, how often it happened.

Ms. Chase nodded. "That's why I'm here."

I realized I'd been holding my breath.

A professional was overseeing Jayden's care. Someone who understood the numbers and alarms that ruled our days. She asked to see my spiral notebook. I handed it to her. Page after page of neatly organized columns: diapers, readings, injections, feedings. She studied it for a moment and said she was impressed with the organization. But when she reached the columns where I tracked the apnea alarms, she paused.

"That's a lot of events," she said quietly.

She asked when our next pediatrician appointment was. Working through Oakland County, she hadn't heard of this particular doctor. We scheduled the next few visits, and I added them to the calendar on my phone and wrote them down in the notebook.

When she gathered her things to leave, she paused at the door.

"Carry on," she said. "Do the best you can."

Then she added, "And remember to take care of yourself, too. I'll be back."

She slipped out quietly, closing the door behind her.

TWO DAYS LATER, John and I drove to the hospital clinic for Jayden's labs. At check-in, we asked for a private room and they took us straight back. I fed her a bottle while we waited.

In the draw room, I laid her on the crinkled paper. The tourniquet looked too big on her arm. Alcohol. Cold. The first vein collapsed. Then the second. They called another tech.

Jayden screamed until her voice broke.

Four techs. Thirty minutes. 4 cc. Just enough.

Bandages wrapped both arms. The tape tugged at her skin. She was too worn out to cry another tear. I swaddled her and walked quickly to the car, singing into her curls. She was asleep before we pulled away.

On the drive home, we made a plan: warm packs before the stick. The smallest draw the lab would allow. One attempt per arm.

Next time, we'd ask sooner. Next time, we'd push.

Our Deedle girl didn't take her next two feedings. The night was long.

BY WEEK'S END, the agency sent a worker to go over Jayden's intake paperwork. Every knock meant putting Jayden down, risking another alarm just to answer. Dudley greeted every guest with loud barks and joyful pouncing, then darted outside so we could talk.

I let him back in after they left, before rocking Jayden back to sleep.

Because Jayden was medically fragile, the agency worker said my compensation was slightly higher. I wrote it next to her feeding notes, as if it mattered. Eighteen dollars a day.

# July 6, 2009 — Monday

Over the past few nights, I learned to cover the rocker with a bedsheet and wedge pillows under my arms, like the walls of a crib keeping her close even if I doze. The sheet lent the night a familiar comfort.

She rested on my chest; her breath warmed my collarbone in small, damp puffs. When she inhaled, I inhaled. When she exhaled, I followed.

Safe. For now. Until the next alarm.

This wasn't according to the handbook. Babies on oxygen weren't meant to sleep like this. But the apnea alarm had taught me that sometimes love chooses quiet breathing over perfect form. Sometimes survival looks like improvisation.

With the other babies, things had been simpler. A small fuss. A bottle warmed. A body gathered close. Feed, burp, lay them down. Twenty minutes. Back into bed and sleep. With Jayden, nights never ended. They only reset.

Every two hours: diaper, reading, injection, feeding.

Every two hours, whether she had slept or not. Whether I had slept or not.

My timer buzzed. I set her down on the changing table. My heart was already racing ahead of it, because the apnea alarm sounded at nearly every feeding, often when I stepped away. Each time, I was certain it was the end. That her small body decided it had enough.

I let the dog out and ran to the bathroom before starting. It was the only chance I had because the seven feet of oxygen tubing restricted Jayden to our sitting room. Then, to the refrigerator for the insulin. Back to the changing table before the alarm sounded.

I changed her diaper and cleaned her up, reassuring her with a hand on her body as often as I could keep one there.

I pricked her heel, no bigger than my thumb. Waited for the blood to well. Pressed the strip to the bead of red and held my breath until the meter beeped.

The reading was always too high or too low. Never simple. I consulted the chart and calculated the dose. Drew insulin into the half-size syringe, hands steady only because they had to be. Slid the needle into her thigh. Watched her flinch. Rubbed the spot in slow circles, whispering apologies she couldn't hear. I logged the reading and dose in my spiral notebook. Back to the rocker. Back to the sheet and the pillows and the blanket wrapped around us both. I positioned her upright, chin tilted just so, one finger bracing her jaw. I couldn't cradle her. Nor could I relax. If her chin dropped even slightly, the formula spilled down. If her chin was too high, the formula pooled in the back of her throat, and she choked.

Thirty minutes to feed her two ounces. She latched onto the bottle with urgency. For a few seconds, it worked. Swallow, swallow, swallow. Then the shift. Her throat tightened and the rhythm faltered. She coughed. I paused. She tried again, a desperate suck. And then a violent gag with her tongue thrust forward. Formula flooded her mouth faster than she could swallow and it spilled from the corners of her lips, warm against my fingers. Her body stiffened.

"Breathe," I whispered. "Come on, Jayden. Breathe."

The monitor numbers began to fall. 92. 88. 84.

The room felt smaller. My pulse throbbed, counting down the seconds before the alarm.

I patted her back. Then harder. Her chest heaved but no air moved. The apnea alarm split the dark. High-pitched, mechanical, merciless.

She was still. This is it, I thought. This is the one.

I rubbed her back firmly. Tilted her forward. Counted under my breath. One. Two. Three.

And then a ragged inhale tore through her. A thin, wavering pull of air. The monitor climbed. 86. 92. 94.

I didn't exhale until she did.

Reset. Head back. Chin up. Back arched. We had already lost five minutes. She tried again, hunger and hope in the same motion. She wanted to live and her body simply did not cooperate. This wasn't a feeding. It was a negotiation.

Sometimes we made it through both ounces. Often we didn't. When the timer buzzed again, thirty minutes gone, I would look down at the bottle, measure what remained, and write it in my spiral notebook. I reclined slowly, careful not to sit on the oxygen lines or to let them catch under the chair. Then, I held her against my bare chest, feeling the rise and fall of her breath, the pulse of her heart. I counted her breaths until my own slowed to match. In an hour and fifteen minutes, it would begin again.

If I slept, it was shallow and fractured. Ten minutes, maybe twenty. Not the full hour. My body couldn't find rest. One ear tuned to her breathing, the other to the low electrical hum of the monitor.

I studied the rise and fall of her chest as if it were language I might learn to interpret. *Was that pause too long? Was that inhale weaker? My mind would not slow down. Is this hospice? Is there hope? Am I helping her? Is there a better way? Why can't she eat?*

It was maddening. It was relentless. The cycle refused to loosen its grip. It only tightened, night after night. When my timer buzzed again, I did not feel rested. I felt summoned. Every two hours, I began again.

She was failing to thrive, the doctors said. I was learning to hold her without promise.

<hr>

MY MORNING ALARM sounded at 8:30 a.m. I was still in the rocker, Jayden asleep on my chest. I don't know when I dozed off, only that exhaustion still held. Usually by midday I longed to close my eyes, if only for a moment. There wouldn't be time for a nap today. Today was her appointment with the infectious disease doctor, pediatrician, and pediatric endocrinologist, forty-five minutes away.

John drove us. I grabbed the spiral notebook of Jayden's readings and insulin doses for review. Our first stop was with the infectious disease doctor who first diagnosed Jayden with congenital syphilis. No weight gain. Eyes yellow. Scaly skin. No promising words. I gathered her closer. Not healed. Held.

John put his hands on my shoulders. He bent and kissed Jayden softly on the forehead, whispering, "My

Deedle, Deedle girl." Then he gathered our supplies and followed me down the hall to the pediatrician.

I needed to speak up for this fragile little girl. I wasn't sure how that would be received.

To our surprise, the pediatrician entered the exam room followed by four residents. Jayden's case warranted a teaching moment. Something to be seen.

As they filed in, I stood and spoke, sharing everything I'd just discussed with the infectious disease doctor. The recent complications, the fever, the exhaustion, and the way Jayden's fragile body struggled to recover. Then I said plainly, "No more immunizations. Not right now." No one argued. In that moment, I felt validated. For the first time, I didn't feel like a visitor in the room.

The pediatrician glanced through my notebook, then shifted into educator mode. He turned off the lights. Each resident stepped forward to shine a light into Jayden's eyes. Each repeated the same movements: side to side, up and down. And each of them saw the same result.

Jayden's eyes did not follow the light.

At home I believed she was gazing toward the window, sure she could see the light. In this darkened room, it was clear.

My heart sank.

Our final stop was with the pediatric endocrinologist. He beamed when he saw her. He had already connected us with the specialty pharmacy that diluted Jayden's insulin. Most of her doses were only two or three units of that delicate solution.

He traced the highs from a few days ago, then looked up, concern in his eyes.

"Immunizations followed by a fever there," I said. "Labs that day."

He nodded. I asked to pause anything traumatic until she was stronger. He agreed.

He scanned her chart and shook his head. Still four pounds fourteen ounces. No gain. Not even an ounce. He wished us well as he left the room. I closed the notebook; the number settled in my palm like a stone.

The nurse lagged behind. Her smile widened as she kissed Jayden's cheek. She was overjoyed to see that Jayden was still here. Still fighting. Still alive.

She thanked us for the care we were giving and handed me her number, in case we needed support. She made the sweetest fuss over Jayden's outfit, the lavender scent of her freshly bathed skin, and the bow slipped into her curls. The way her preemie clothes, just a bit too big, framed her frail face.

I loved dressing her up and showing her off.

My Deedle girl.

---

DUDLEY WAS THRILLED when we came in from the garage.

We were gone longer than usual since bringing Jayden home, and sensing her importance, he seemed to take it as his duty to make sure she was okay. After a quick sniff of each of us, John opened the patio door and Dudley ran into the yard.

I laid Jayden down, changed her diaper, tested her blood sugar, prepared and injected her insulin. John offered to feed her while I ate the sub we'd picked up. He watched my routine and now mirrored it. He held Jayden upright on his knees, letting the formula touch her lips... a dribble to encourage her mouth to open. Soon she was sucking on the softest nipple we could find. His mouth moved in sync with hers, focused, tender.

I offered to help around the house while he fed her, but he shook his head and pointed me back to the chair. "Sit," he said quietly. "You keep her breathing. I'll keep everything else moving."

He meant the house. The bills. The bottles. The floors. The food.

He meant me.

For a few minutes, he held her. I closed my eyes.

I tried to schedule Jayden's away-from-home appointments for his days off... not just for the help, but because we were stronger together. Sometimes I thought work, flying across the country and overseas, might be easier than what waited at home. But I never doubted his commitment. We always said, "Family first."

Later, lying in the rocker with Jayden asleep on my chest, I thought about the way he held her... sure as breath. As her breathing settled against my chest, I felt it again. Presence. Enough.

# July 13, 2009 — Monday

Jayden's routine finally settled.

Nights quiet. Feedings rhythmic.

For the first time, I could almost breathe.

Yet beneath that calm, something uneasy stirred.

John was scheduled to leave Sunday for two weeks of recertification on an aircraft he already knew by heart. He asked if I wanted him to postpone. Cindy, who managed his schedule, had already done everything she could, booking "out-and-backs" instead of overnights whenever possible. His crew picked up extra shifts so John could be home more. Their way of saying, *We've got you.* Even his co-pilot, Carey, had stepped up. He gripped John's shoulder and said, "John, it would be my honor." The weight of his hand said more than the words.

All of it had helped until now. The training in Charlotte was mandatory. Two full weeks. I almost asked him to stay. I could manage... for now.

But *for now* felt fragile. When would it end? When would she change? When would I reach the edge of what I could do alone? Still, it seemed wiser to get the training behind us before things got harder. If time would be so kind.

John prepared for his trip. He sat with a yellow legal pad in hand, pen ready, and we started a list of the things I might need if something went wrong while he was gone. First, I prepared the case details and address for the paramedics. If I called, I wanted no delays. I had glucose tablets for emergencies, or a can of frosting in the pantry, if it came to that.

"Just rub a little on the inside of her cheek," the doctor had explained during NICU training.

I knew how. What I didn't know was how to handle the overwhelming emotions that could come if I ever had to.

I also had the emergency number for Ennis Center. They promised someone would answer, day or night. The NICU had shared its direct line, too. They had been with us from the beginning. There was always someone available to talk to whether I needed assistance or comfort. I programmed those numbers into my phone, labeling each "ER" so I could find them fast.

John wrote the same numbers, along with notes, on the last page of my spiral notebook. A lifeline, in more ways than one. His handwriting was firm, intentional. Each line pressed deep into the paper, as if he could hold the plan in place by writing hard enough.

The biggest problem we had to solve was transportation. Jayden had multiple appointments, but I couldn't drive her there alone. It wasn't the distance. It was potential emergencies. What if a cannula slipped or she needed to be held and rubbed to restart her breathing? Our foster friends wanted to help, but each had children. Jayden wasn't allowed around other kids.

I couldn't ask them to find childcare. It was too much. I needed to expand our support network.

Before Jayden arrived, I trained as a postpartum doula. It was a four-day session in Ann Arbor, focused on "mothering the mother." We learned about postpartum care, breastfeeding, and the everyday practicals of parenting. I had connected with some incredible women. Women who shared my heart. Since Jayden arrived, I hadn't had time to follow up on those friendships. But maybe they could help. *Maybe I could have a postpartum doula.*

While Jayden was sleeping on my chest, I sent a few emails. I explained our situation. I asked for help. Within days, two women responded, not just willing, but honored that I reached out. They offered to drive us to appointments. They offered to hold Jayden while I did things around the house. Things John usually handled. They asked how they could support us.

We mapped coverage on our calendar. Someone would be with me the day after John left until he returned.

For the first time in days, maybe weeks, I felt a wave of relief. There was help and a plan. And maybe, just maybe, I'd be able to take more than the sponge bath I treated myself to during the few days he was away. Knowing a trusted friend could hold Jayden would allow me to take a real shower.

John filled the freezer with meals and stocked the fridge with vegetables. He placed a basket of fresh fruit beside the changing table and a stash of cookies and peanut butter crackers next to my chair. He checked Dudley's new auto-fill food and water station, leaving notes for refills next week. He made sure the laundry was washed, dried, folded, and put away. Jayden's clothing, blankets, and burp cloths were folded away in the bins beneath her changing table.

My own clean clothes were stacked neatly in a basket next to my chair. Sometimes, I'd hide the laundry basket in the bathroom to make the family room look tidy when I knew a nurse or caseworker was coming. Sometimes I didn't.

I was quickly running out of energy. And I had to reserve what I had left so I could give Jayden everything she needed.

* * *

THE NIGHT BEFORE JOHN LEFT, it finally happened. The big conversation. The question we had both avoided until that night.

"What will you do... if Jayden dies in your arms... and you're alone?"

The moment he said it, tears filled my eyes. My mind spun.

*What had I been thinking when we said yes to this?*

*How was I supposed to let her die?*

Jayden was fading. The deep tone of her skin gave way to pale blotches. Her bottom was so raw there was blood in every diaper. Her heels, punctured again and again for glucose tests, bled constantly and her thighs hardened with scar tissue from the endless injections.

She slept every minute that wasn't feeding time, and even then her eyes stayed closed. When was the last time she opened her eyes? Oh, dear Lord. What was happening?

My chest ached. My heart pounded. John saw my panic and wrapped his arms around me.

When I finally lifted my head, his chin was quivering. Silent tears spilled down his cheeks.

Selfishly, I wanted John with me when she left us. Would his trip interfere with that? Or would he be home in time? He loved his Deedle girl.

He loved me, and we'd been a team from the start. I was surviving this through the strength of his arms around me. And I needed us to finish it together.

It was as if I'd been dropped into a new reality. Until now, my heart had been guarded, protected by the constant adrenaline of survival mode. One task after another. Everything required to keep her alive.

Meanwhile, my head never stopped. While Jayden slept on my chest, I was always thinking, always solving.

*How can I help her suck? How can I protect her skin? How can I heal her bottom and her heels? Her hair was thinning. Her complexion fading. What if I tried this? What if I stopped doing that?*

I was all in. One hundred percent. I hadn't really talked to family or friends since we brought Jayden home. Despite this, we were losing her. We just didn't know when.

I didn't want her to struggle, but now, it didn't even seem like she realized she was struggling. Her oxygen remained constant. She didn't cry. She lay quiet. She almost seemed content if the apnea alarm didn't still scream daily. The monitor told a different story than her face. Every time it blared, I feared it would be the last time until her little lungs breathed again.

I held her closer, felt the faint rise of her ribs against my chest. Holding her was the most important thing I had ever done. It was also the most terrifying.

JOHN HAD to leave early Sunday morning. On Saturday evening, I asked him to hold Jayden while I took a quick shower. He maneuvered the oxygen tubing and the apnea monitor wires, then settled into the recliner with Jayden on his shoulder.

I let Dudley outside on my way to the upstairs bathroom. The shower lasted only five minutes, but it felt like heaven. That night, I decided to try sleeping in pajamas. Real pajamas, not my shorts and T-shirt.

I came back downstairs with my wet hair wrapped in a towel and heard a soft voice singing a familiar lullaby.

As I stepped into the room, I saw John rocking Jayden, using a tissue to wipe his eyes. While I had taken the shower I so desperately needed, John poured his heart into Deedle. I knew that image would live in my heart forever.

When John's alarm sounded early the next morning, he showered, dressed, and carried his suitcase out to the car. Then he came back in for goodbye. He helped me up, keeping Jayden safe in my arms. We held each other in silence, tears blurring everything but love. John kissed us both, over and over, his face pressed against ours. He turned the doorknob, then looked back to find my eyes. Then I watched the man I love turn and walk away, and I slowly lowered myself back into the chair.

Dawn broke soft and pale through the blinds. The faint scent of vanilla creamer lingered in the room, a small comfort in the morning air. Jayden stirred, a small breath, then a sigh. For a moment, the room filled with golden warmth.

*Dear Lord, please keep her alive until he returns.*

# July 20, 2009 — Monday

The morning John left, Lorene planned to assist me. We met months earlier at a postpartum doula training. Two women drawn together by newborn care, shared stories, and the kind of conviction that doesn't need words. We connected instantly, so she was one of the first people I had thought of. Lorene didn't hesitate.

Jayden had an appointment with her pediatric endocrinologist at 11:00 a.m. I peeled off the apnea monitor wires and bathed her under the warm kitchen faucet. Her body fit neatly in the crook of my arm, her delicate limbs still unsure in the water. Wrapped in a hooded towel, I carried her to the changing table and smoothed lavender gel across her chest, avoiding where the leads would go. It didn't help her flaking skin, but it smelled like hope.

I slipped on the first outfit I grabbed and added socks and a headband. Her skin was dry enough, so I pressed each pad into place. Then I tucked her into a pink swaddle. One leg peeked free, awaiting her blood sugar check. I pricked her heel, my hands barely steady. The glucometer blinked. I ran my finger down the chart. At the fridge, I drew the insulin into the half-size syringe, checked it twice, and returned to the table. The needle slipped into her thigh. She didn't flinch.

I reached for the soft-bristled hairbrush. Lorene walked in. It was her first time in our home. She washed her hands at the kitchen sink, then stepped into the family room, smiling. Her eyes were fixed on the tiny bundle on the changing table.

*"Deedle, Deedle girl,"* I heard John's voice echo in my mind, as if he were there to introduce her. I lifted Jayden and placed her into Lorene's waiting arms as she handed me a gift bag with pink curls of confetti. Jayden's very first gift. The first visitor in three weeks who wasn't on the clock.

I helped Lorene into my chair, threading the tubing and wires clear of the changing table. Once she was settled, I taped the cannula to Jayden's cheeks.

Lorene snuggled Jayden close. "My little girl, three months last week," she said softly, her voice catching, "she's fifteen pounds."

Jayden was three months old.

She weighed five.

Lorene marveled at her dark curls and dainty fingers, her eyes full of wonder. I smiled, then shifted my attention to finish the rest of my routine. Everything was done except for the paperwork. I logged the time, glucometer reading, insulin dose, and her pre-bath diaper.

Then I turned to the gift bag. Inside was a pink-and-white striped swimsuit with a ruffled neckline. I hung it on the changing table, a reminder to dress Jayden in it so Lorene could see it when we got back.

I had to get Jayden fed because I had already given her

insulin. It would take the rest of our time. I made her bottle, then packed the extras and the can of formula. Gathering Jayden into my arms, I sat down to feed her.

Lorene and I talked through how we'd load up, so the move to the car would go smoothly. I was mid-sentence, explaining how I would disconnect the tubing from the eight-liter oxygen tank and attach it to the portable one, when Lorene stopped listening.

She watched Jayden arch with her chin up, clucking softly as the formula dripped in. Jayden choked. The alarm cried on cue.

Lorene jumped from her seat before I could warn her.

"This happens nearly every time I feed her," I said. Her eyes filled.

I asked Lorene, "Could she be allergic to the formula?"

I was doing exactly what the dietitian and pediatrician had prescribed. She started the high-calorie formula five days before we received the initial call. Those calories got her weight over the discharge threshold.

I knew the high-calorie formula was supposed to help her. But every bottle felt like a fight. Her feeding position matched the NICU's. No one there raised a red flag. But the gagging had worsened within days of bringing her home.

I brought it up with her pediatrician, but he brushed it off as if to say, *"Isn't this what we should expect? This baby is dying."*

Lorene stayed silent, watching. We were both breast-feeding mamas. We believed, wholeheartedly, that mother's milk was best for our babies. But not for this baby. Not without the mother she didn't have. I had so few options.

I told Lorene how I asked the NICU dietitian about

ordering processed breast milk formula, the kind only available to hospital NICUs.

"It isn't cost-effective," the dietitian said.

Lorene didn't speak. She grabbed a tissue from her handbag and held it against her eyes.

---

LORENE WAS A HUGE HELP, carrying Jayden and her equipment into the doctor's office while I parked the car. We were quickly ushered into the exam room, and I undressed Jayden. I set her on a soft blanket to protect her from the cold, crinkly paper that covered the exam table.

The pediatric endocrinologist entered. Nurse Amor followed, wrapping me in a tender hug. She knew. She knew what it meant, day after day, to keep Jayden comfortable.

*Just hold her.*

The doctor's nimble hands moved from the top of Jayden's head downward. He gently circled her neck, listened to her heart, tapped her tummy, one side and then the other, pressed lightly on her umbilical hernia, then moved down her legs. He held Jayden's hands, pulling her slightly off the blanket, which cradled her. He let her fall back the inch he had lifted her, checking her startle reflexes. Sluggish.

When he finally looked up, his expression changed.

"Based on appearance alone," he said cautiously, "this baby shows signs of malnutrition."

As he continued his exam, he found more. An enlarged spleen. An enlarged liver.

He ordered labs in five weeks and a follow-up visit in six.

I barely heard the rest.

When he finished, I asked, steadying my voice:

"Would it be possible to start her on donated breast milk?"

He met my eyes.

"I can't tell you not to," he said.

It was the closest thing to permission I'd had since the day I met Jayden. Until now, the answer had been no. Jayden wasn't mine. Not legally. She belonged to the state of Michigan, and there were rules. I couldn't act without permission. Maybe now I could ask the caseworker to check with the state authorities again.

He didn't open the door, but he didn't close it either. Through that sliver, light found its way in.

LORENE HELPED me to the car. In the back seat, she held Jayden's hand. We kept talking, wondering if mother's milk might help in ways formula hadn't. My phone interrupted us.

It was Terri, my dear friend and fellow foster mom. I hadn't seen her since her required NICU visit, when she served as my "extra support person" so we could bring Jayden home. Terri asked if it would be okay to stop by that evening.

She'd been on my list to call. Now here she was, offering herself without being asked.

"I can be there around four," she said.

I exhaled.

"And one more thing," she added casually. "Would

you like me to bring some of my daughter-in-law's frozen breast milk?"

Had she remembered how desperately I asked for that option in the NICU? How I'd clung to it like a lifeline, only to be told it wasn't cost-effective?

"Yes," I whispered. "Yes, please."

In the rearview mirror, Lorene's eyes brimmed. I hung up and sat in the stillness. It felt like the first crack of daylight after a long night.

THAT EVENING, after our visit with the visiting nurse, Belinda, I got on the phone. I called my doula contacts for guidance on getting state approval to feed Jayden human milk.

Terri suggested a pediatric practice she used for her foster babies, no small feat since Medicaid-accepting providers were scarce. She told me about a pediatrician there, Dr. Sonja Earles, who focused on complex endocrine kids and was known for taking on complicated cases. I called the office that day and booked the earliest available appointment, six weeks out.

It wasn't soon, but it was something.

Closer to home. Closer to possibility.

A new path. Maybe a better one.

BY MORNING, whatever hope we found felt fragile in my hands.

The county dietitian, Ms. Chase, returned for her assessment earlier than required. She expressed her anxiety over Jayden's decline. Jayden had lost two ounces since her previous visit. Her expression changed. Her eyes narrowed. The room went still before she spoke.

"We may not need to come back next week," she said. "Jayden may not be alive much longer."

The air thickened. Her words stayed. Through the haze of panic, I told her I'd found a new pediatrician, Dr. Earles, but the first opening wasn't until late August.

Without hesitation, Ms. Chase responded. "Call back," she said firmly, "tell them it's urgent. Dr. Earles needs to see this baby now, while there's still a baby to see."

I called Dr. Earles's office while Ms. Chase held Jayden in her arms. If I couldn't speak, she could take the phone from my hands. The office manager, Sophie, came on the line. I took a deep breath and explained, as clearly as I could, that Jayden had to be seen right away.

"Or we may not have a baby to bring," I said.

She placed me on hold to speak with Dr. Earles. When she returned, her voice carried something I hadn't heard in a long time: reassurance.

"Come in tomorrow morning, before office hours. Dr. Earles will see Jayden then."

She made room. From the moment she said yes, Dr. Earles was already showing up for Jayden.

---

IT HAD BEEN a couple days since I spoke with John. When he called that evening, I ached for his strength. I couldn't hear anything he said. I just spoke until I needed to gasp for air. Everything poured out: the endocrinologist's concern, malnutrition, weight loss, enlarged spleen, enlarged liver, listless, sluggish, a new pediatrician recommendation, the dietitian's demand to call for an immediate appointment because we couldn't wait. All signs of failure to thrive.

I told him the new pediatrician would meet us before office hours tomorrow morning. 8:30 a.m., July 22. I don't know what he said. I just kept going. I don't remember saying goodbye.

I was writing the date for tomorrow's appointment in the spiral notebook when my pen caught.

*Today...*

*today was my birthday.*

# July 22, 2009 — Wednesday

Permission. A slot before hours. John still away.

Just Jayden and me. A new doctor. The office, fifteen minutes from home. I could get her there and ask for help.

Terri came over the night before so I could shower and get ready. I still laugh when I think about how many days passed between showers back then. Turns out, even if you're sitting in a chair nearly twenty-four hours a day, you still need to shower.

I read through my notes before the appointment. The NICU entries were sterile: facts, protocols. Now, my heart was all in.

Her decline felt heavier by the day. I was holding her together and falling apart myself. Still, I held on to hope. Maybe this new doctor would recommend a path that would make a difference.

One note from the NICU almost made me laugh. I'd asked a young resident about Jayden's raw bottom, hoping for help. He'd tilted his head. "Have you considered switching diaper brands?"

Kind, but so far off.

I loaded Jayden and her equipment into the car, then backed out slowly, after checking her cannula one more time.

*Please sit beside her, Lord.*

The drive was peaceful. A small plaza, an easy space. I hung the handicap tag John had left for me. One more way he was still here.

Just as I opened the trunk to grab the stroller, Sophie came out to greet us. Seeing her brought an unexpected sense of relief. They were ready for us.

I clicked Jayden's car seat into the stroller and slid the oxygen tank and apnea monitor into the basket below. Sophie closed the car doors behind me, then held the office door open as we made our way inside. She led us into the first exam room. The walls were lined with pink-and-blue teddy-bear wallpaper, and a bright rack of children's books just inside the door.

I lifted Jayden into my arms and wrapped her snug in her blanket.

Sophie held a clipboard thick with paperwork, but instead of handing it to me, she asked me the questions. It took me a moment to realize she was filling it out for me so I could keep Jayden in my arms. With each line she completed, Sophie offered gentle reassurance.

"You're right where you need to be," she said.

She told me Dr. Earles was relentless when it came to finding medical solutions. Tenacious, in the best way. I asked again if their office supported breastfeeding moms. Sophie placed a warm hand on my shoulder.

"You're in capable hands," she said.

Then Sophie peeked down at the baby bundled in my arms.

She whispered, almost to herself, "Oh, how small."

A soft knock. Dr. Earles was here. She tapped again, asking permission before entering. The moment she stepped through the door, the air shifted. She brought with her a new energy. Purpose. Compassion.

Dr. Earles reviewed the paperwork Sophie had prepared, then went straight to questions. I answered as best I could. I told her everything I remembered, from the first time I heard about Jayden's case in the NICU five weeks ago to every moment since. I explained how her oxygen levels were unstable, how the apnea alarm screamed six to ten times a day, mostly during feedings. How we had to hold her around the clock because lying her flat caused her heart rate to plummet. I gave her the facts. Then my eyes filled. The only thing on my mind spilled out:

"I've been wondering if donor breast milk might help her."

Her face said yes before she spoke. But first she wanted to examine Jayden herself. To see what other options might be possible. Dr. Earles examined Jayden methodically, noting the loss of pigmentation across her body. The swollen, bubblegum-pink cheeks. The yellow tint in her bulging eyes. The rawness of her bottom.

"This baby is struggling to survive," she said, her voice catching slightly, just enough to reveal a warmth I hadn't heard from any other physician.

She collected a stool sample with a small swab and left the room.

A few minutes later, Nurse Melissa entered and guided us to the scale for an updated weight. Jayden was five pounds one and a half ounces, and measured eighteen and a quarter inches. In the four weeks she'd been in our care, feeding every two hours, day and night, Jayden gained eleven ounces. It wasn't enough.

I could feel Melissa watching me as she led us back to the exam room. Then the door flew open. Dr. Earles burst in, eyes wide.

"There's blood in Jayden's stool," she said.

A clear sign she was reacting to the high-calorie formula. The primary ingredient: corn syrup solids. My heart dropped. No wonder she gagged halfway through every bottle. I felt sick. I had worked so hard to keep her alive. But the truth was unbearable. Her body was fighting the very thing meant to sustain it.

Dr. Earles sat on the edge of the desk, eyes warm and unshakable.

"I think your idea about breast milk," she said, "might be the very thing that saves this little girl's life."

Tears came fast. Weeks' worth.

I thought of those early NICU days, asking if breast milk was an option, even the powdered kind.

*Why hadn't I fought?*

Then... gratitude. Dr. Earles had given Jayden a chance.

I closed my eyes.


*Thank you, dear Lord. Thank you.*


Finally, someone listened.

I knew that having a doctor recommend breast milk was only one part of it. Jayden was a ward of the state of Michigan. I would still need permission from the state before I could act on Dr. Earles's recommendation. I explained this and asked for a clear letter to the caseworker explaining the allergy to the formula, Jayden's diagnosis of failure to thrive, and the medical need for breast milk. We agreed it needed to happen today.

Dr. Earles explained that breast milk is typically a twenty-calorie-per-ounce food. Healthy, but not high enough in calories for a baby like Jayden. She suggested I go to the health food store next door and buy some coconut oil. Adding it to the breast milk would boost the calories, and as a fatty acid, it would also support Jayden's pancreas, one of the root causes of her insulin dependence.

Then she glanced down at my notebook, the hand-written records of Jayden's glucometer readings. Her eyes widened. Jayden's blood sugars swung from 38 to 545. The range expected by her endocrinologist? 100 to 225. We weren't even close.

Dr. Earles asked me to request a full copy of Jayden's hospital records. She knew I had explained all that I could, but she wanted more. There was a lot I didn't know.

The NICU nurses shared only the basics. Just what I needed to care for her. They hadn't told me about her birth mother or about the day Jayden was born. Those things weren't considered "appropriate" for me to know. I promised Dr. Earles I'd request the records right away. I hugged her, tears streaming as I whispered, "Thank you, Doctor."

She gave us what no one else had: a path forward.

Once she stepped out to begin seeing her scheduled patients, I dressed Jayden, placed her in the stroller, and walked straight to the store. My legs shook and my mind raced. I had no idea what the process of state approval even looked like. I only knew a few breastfeeding mothers, and the milk bank in Kalamazoo charged $4.15 per ounce for pasteurized breast milk. Would the state cover it? If not, who would?

Still, coconut oil in hand, I couldn't wait to tell John.

———

THE FIRST THING I did when we got home, after feeding Jayden, was call our caseworker, Nicole. She had already received the faxed letter from Dr. Earles and immediately forwarded it to the Department of Human Services. Jayden's case had been assigned to an administrator in Lansing.

While Nicole waited for a response, I waited with my stomach in knots. The food Jayden was eating was hurting her and the breast milk Terri brought was waiting in my freezer.

By the time Jayden woke for her next feeding, I had a three-ounce bottle of breast milk thawed and ready. What could it hurt to give her just one bottle before the official call came?

The phone rang. It was Nicole.

"Do what you have to do," she said. "I've got you covered."

She moved fast. She knew what was at stake. The tension in my neck eased. I pulled my Deedle girl close.

I settled into the recliner, burp cloth in hand, the bottle warm in my hand. I prayed it would strengthen her and soothe her struggling body. Prayed that it would hold her heart. That it would be mercy, in liquid form. I touched the bottle of breast milk to her lips.

A few drops touched her lips. Jayden chewed and swallowed. She swallowed again and again.

I felt her small body soften against my hand, her weight settling onto my leg. She was still.

I pulled her close and leaned back, cradling her. She sucked and swallowed. Not once did Jayden gag, not once did the apnea alarm blare. I lifted her to my shoulder and rubbed her back. She burped. Then her tiny hand found my neck and stayed. She fell asleep holding me.

I didn't move. I couldn't. It was the first time she reached for me. The first time her body felt peaceful. I wept.

Not from fear, but something new. Hope. Gratitude. Grace.

It came quiet. Like breath returning.

I thought of the friend who led me to this doctor. The one who filled my freezer. The women who listened. Who acted.

I picked up the phone and called John. He had to know. It rang seven times before he answered, his voice tight, bracing for the worst. Our last conversation had been filled with fear. I'd told him I thought we were losing her. So my call now, in the middle of training, could only mean one thing.

"What happened?" he said. "Is she...?"

I stopped him.

I told him everything. Dr. Earles. Nicole. Breast milk. Peace.

And then, silence. A long, beautiful silence.

<hr>

THE NEXT FORTY-EIGHT hours brought slow, steady changes. By the second day, with no complications, I added five milliliters of coconut oil to every other bottle.

She wiggled and pushed her head beneath my chin, pressing her forehead to my shoulder. I felt her head slide from beneath my chin to the edge of my shoulder. Her head tilted back slowly. I wondered if she was losing consciousness. I turned my head to look at her.

Jayden's eyes were open. She was staring at me. She seemed to be studying my face. She found my eyes and held them.

I moved my head slightly right, then left.

Her eyes followed... right, then left.

I moved her to my lap, her weightless head cradled in my hands. Now our faces were inches apart. I turned my face again. Her eyes followed.

I brought her back to my shoulder. Tears fell.

I didn't say anything. I wasn't ready to say it out loud.

*She saw me.*

# July 24, 2009 — Friday

Jayden's eyes remained focused and clear. I held her and marveled. Today, the nurse would return to a different child.

Nurse Belinda arrived on schedule, placed the baby scale on the kitchen table and took the seat across from me. I walked her through the last few days. She listened, wide-eyed, then asked about the apnea monitor.

"Just once yesterday and once the day before, only when she's lying unattended."

My voice cracked. "She can see."

Nurse Belinda's eyes welled. She laid Jayden on the fluffy blanket on the kitchen table, the best lighting in the house, and examined her. She couldn't believe the change. The yellow gone from her eyes, her bottom healing, heart rate and breathing strong.

Days ago, at her last visit, Nurse Belinda had said, "Jayden's system is giving out." Now she was thriving.

Nurse Belinda suggested short intervals off oxygen, about twenty minutes at a time, just walking around the house. Freedom from the fourteen-foot tether. My shoulders softened before my mind caught up.

I asked for a photo of Nurse Belinda holding Jayden so the name would have a face. For the first time, I could picture it: Jayden hearing this story, knowing she'd always been loved.

Nurse Belinda's smile stayed as she left.

I logged the visit and exhaled. No more appointments today.

Still, my mind spun. Jayden was improving and I had to keep it that way. I had trained as a doula just a few months before the call came for Jayden. Certification required a resource list: lactation consultants, support group leaders, breastfeeding network organizers. I'd even attended La Leche League meetings locally, so I could stand behind my recommendations to new mothers. The women I met while exploring my resources had stayed with me. Capable. Generous. The kind you trust when things get hard. And now, I realized I needed them.

Bottom desk drawer. There it was. My list.

Back in the rocker, with Jayden curled on my chest, I scanned the names. One stood out: Courtenay, a doula, midwife-in-training, deeply connected. I dialed her number. That evening, she arrived with a cooler of surplus milk from a preemie's overproducing mother. Two freezer shelves of breast milk, no longer needed. One mother's surplus became my baby's chance.

Courtenay watched as I fed Jayden the bottle of human milk. She saw the weak, uncoordinated suck-swallow. I cupped Jayden's chin and pressed her cheeks to help her latch. Then Courtenay tried a few techniques she had learned while working with other babies. She shifted Jayden to her side, tapping the bottle to pace the flow.

Jayden still struggled. Even so, she was here. Alive. Drinking. Seeing. Enough to celebrate, quietly.

Before she left, I asked Courtenay for help finding more breast milk. Our hands were full and the supply was thin. Without hesitation, she agreed. She lingered in the doorway, radiant, then slipped away.

---

JOHN HAD LEFT ON SUNDAY. Terri came Tuesday to hold Jayden while I sterilized bottles. By Thursday, the list hadn't gotten any shorter.

Before he left, John set the baby bouncy seat in the corner. Now, I pulled it close. After the bottle, I burped her, swaddled her, and eased her onto her side, elevated to spare her heart.

The moment she settled in, I ran to the kitchen. I washed and sterilized twelve bottles, thawed bags of milk, then ran to the bathroom, door cracked to listen. I prayed she'd stay comfortable enough for just a little longer.

The alarm pierced the quiet. I had her in my arms before I could think, bouncing until the beeping stilled. When her breathing came back to her, I sank into the chair and exhaled. I missed John.

As I rocked, the routine replayed itself. Wash, sterilize, thaw, bathroom, alarm. Too much, too fast.

Next time I'd break it into smaller parts. A new plan.

And a quiet word of thanks. The bouncy seat had worked for a few minutes. Enough to remind me I didn't have to do it all at once.

One thing at a time.

One moment. One bottle. One breath.

THREE DAYS INTO BREAST MILK, the freezer and cooler were full. I began adding coconut oil to every other feeding. Jayden was up to three ounces every two hours.

I was mid-diaper change, just about to check her blood sugar, when the doorbell rang. A familiar face from a La Leche League meeting stood on the porch.

"Murielle," she said with a smile and a bright French accent. "Courtenay told me your sweet Jayden needed milk."

Her toddler son, Elias, peeked around her legs. Murielle explained that Elias was nearly at the end of his nursing days, but she'd managed to pump an ounce and a half that morning.

"Would you like it?" she asked generously.

Tears filled my eyes.

I invited her in. "Perfect timing. We were just about to make a bottle. Will you feed it to her?"

She beamed.

She washed her hands and followed me into the family room, where Jayden waited on the changing table, wrapped, changed, and ready. I pricked her heel. The glucometer beeped. I showed Murielle the chart I'd kept since we brought Jayden home from the NICU. She ran her finger down the columns, pausing at the most recent, tightly clustered numbers.

"She's doing so well," she said softly.

I nodded. Healing had begun. Her body was learning to trust the world again, one mother's gift at a time.

Murielle and Elias sanitized their hands to hold Jayden. I secretly held my breath. She wasn't supposed to be near toddlers, but Elias's tenderness disarmed me. I whispered a prayer and placed her in his mother's arms. As they settled in, I poured the ounce and a half into a fresh bottle.

Elias sat beside his mother, watching with wide eyes as she cradled Jayden. He listened as Murielle told him who Jayden was and why her story mattered. Murielle lifted the bottle to Jayden's lips. The gift she'd brought now sustained the little girl in her arms.

Murielle and I talked while Jayden drank.

I told her the diagnoses: blind, deaf, insulin-dependent, failure to thrive. Then I explained what had changed.

"After just two days of breast milk, she could see."

Murielle's eyes lit. We celebrated with soft claps and wide smiles.

Then a bark. Jayden startled. The smallest answer to Dudley's sharp warning at the window.

My teeth rattled. My palms shook. I looked at Murielle.

"On the fourth day of breast milk, she heard."

Not imagined. Real.

Jayden was listening now. The world whispered its welcome.

---

JAYDEN GAVE me small stretches of twenty minutes off oxygen, just enough to breathe. The baby wrap's stretchy seven feet of fabric held her to my chest; skin to skin, her temperature settled into mine. Our hearts beat together. In those small pockets of time, I moved swiftly: rinse a dish, switch a load, stare out a different window. Grateful for the weight of her. For the simple rhythm of being alive, together.

But I was running on six weeks of broken sleep. Jayden was now taking nearly three ounces every two hours. Her body was behind, but working hard to catch up. Each bottle still took thirty minutes to finish.

John had been gone for six days. I was fading. Help wasn't optional anymore. My doula class still hadn't finished the required practicum hours. I opened the list. With Jayden asleep on my chest in the baby wrap, I scrolled slowly and chose three names. Warm, committed women I remembered. I didn't need a newborn lesson. With a medically fragile infant fighting to survive, I needed another pair of hands. It would count for their training and maybe, just maybe, carry me through the week.

I sent an email to each of the women I selected, explaining the situation: what I needed, what Jayden needed. Cressie wrote back almost instantly. She lived over an hour away and worked full-time. "Can I come this weekend and stay the night?"

*Yes, please.*

We'd connected in training. She was new to the work, but wise in all the ways that mattered and sacred in the way she listened. Now, she'd meet my little girl. See what I'd been living, carrying, praying through.

Saturday finally came. I was at my edge, stretched thin, clinging to routine, running out of breath. Cressie burst through the front door with food, gifts, and a grounding presence that brightened the room. She wrapped us both in a hug that stole my breath, then settled on the floor, eyes full of wonder. She asked questions, one after another, shaking her head as she listened, trying to comprehend all Jayden had endured. She studied Jayden as if her face held a secret only love could unlock.

Cressie radiated a confident, maternal stillness. She didn't just show up. She arrived. Like I'd known her forever. In her presence, even in my exhaustion, I didn't feel alone anymore.

Cressie served a full chicken dinner with sides, and warm slices of homemade banana bread. She fed me like someone who knew what I hadn't let myself need. Then she cleaned the kitchen while I gave Jayden her bedtime insulin injection. I laid a clean sheet on the recliner for Cressie, checked the oxygen tubes, the apnea monitor wires, then slowly climbed the stairs to bed.

*My bed.*

Before I could second-guess it, I was out. I slept for four straight hours in one position and without interruption.

When I stirred, I tip-toed downstairs. 3:00 a.m.

Cressie sat in the recliner, Jayden asleep on her chest. Her hand moved slowly along that tiny back, the same way mine did.

I stood motionless. Cressie smiled tenderly, like she'd always known how to do this. I thanked her again and again, then sent her upstairs to rest.

"Sleep as long as you want. You've got to take care of me again tomorrow."

By the time she left the next evening, order had returned. A full supply of clean sterile bottles. I'd showered and put on clean clothes. Ate real nutritious home-cooked food. I almost felt like myself again.

We hugged at the door. Quiet gratitude, the kind that keeps showing up. Today, mercy showed up as a woman with a chicken dinner and a way of seeing exactly what was needed. Not to rescue. Just to support.

Somehow, it was enough.

# July 28, 2009 — Tuesday

Our follow-up with Dr. Earles was Tuesday morning. I couldn't wait to show her Jayden's progress. She was no longer blind. No longer deaf. Her blood sugar had stabilized. Her skin, once pale and paper-thin, had deepened into a rich ebony. She was drinking three ounces of breast milk with five milliliters of coconut oil every two to three hours. She was thriving.

At least, I thought so. The clinic staff greeted us at the office door and ushered us straight into a private exam room. First on the list: Nurse Melissa. She stripped Jayden down, carried her across the hall, and placed her on the scale. I stepped back, certain she would surprise us all. Nurse Melissa leaned in, squinted. "Five pounds, two and a half ounces." Last week, she weighed five pounds, one and half ounces.

Only one ounce? I felt the hope drain from me. One ounce.

When Dr. Earles stepped into the exam room and glanced at the weight Nurse Melissa had recorded, I saw it, the shadow that passed through her eyes. But before I could spiral, she offered the gentlest reassurance.

"With everything else we're seeing, you absolutely made the right decision starting her on breast milk."

She explained how severely Jayden's body had failed in those early weeks, how much internal repair had to happen before her weight would start to climb.

"Right now," she said, "her energy is going toward healing. Not growing. But it will come."

Her conviction steadied me.

"Be patient," she said. "We're figuring her out."

Then she reached for the growth chart and plotted Jayden's numbers. Each dot she placed was lower than the last, until she paused and smiled.

"Well, she's not even on the chart yet," she said, tapping the paper, "but that just means we get to help her write her own curve."

Then she asked how often the apnea alarm sounded. I sat up straighter, smiling.

"Seven times," I told her. "All week."

A full-body gasp escaped her, and she danced. Joy for a baby who finally knew how to breathe. After a few more notes, Dr. Earles stepped out of the room. When she returned, she was holding a can of supplemental formula.

"This is a 24-calorie formula. It should pair well with the breast milk and coconut oil."

She scanned the label.

"This might be just the boost we need to help her gain weight."

She turned back to Jayden on the crinkled exam paper. She leaned in for a closer look. The film over her eyes was almost gone. Her skin was rich, smooth, and healing. Nothing like a week ago.

Dr. Earles mumbled, "Her heart and lungs sound good." She smiled and called out to Nurse Melissa:

"Let's get a pulse ox."

Nurse Melissa returned with the small device and slipped the sensor onto Jayden's finger. The screen blinked. 73%. Melissa glanced at me, eyes wide. She reset the device and tried again. 75%. That's when Dr. Earles stepped in, calm and focused. She looked at Jayden's tiny hands and feet and shook her head.

"We can't use these," she said softly.

Jayden had been born without skin on her hands and feet. Even now, the skin was too thin, too compromised to allow an accurate reading. Dr. Earles wrapped the pulse ox around her wrist instead.

She waited. The screen held. 94%. Better.

I adjusted her oxygen tank so many times. I was bouncing from 0.03 to 0.12, then back down to 0.06. Trying to follow the readings. All those numbers. All that stress. Had it all been wrong? I kept blaming her fragile body, assuming it was just another sign of her decline. But maybe it wasn't her. Maybe the problem wasn't inside her at all.

Relief and anger tangled in my chest. I grew leery of her prior care. But Dr. Earles? She steadied me. So did that number.

"Let's try taking the oxygen cannula off for thirty minutes," she said. "Belinda suggested twenty, but I think we can stretch it. Let's see how she does."

And she stayed right beside me while I fed Jayden. No clipboard. No rush. The whole thirty minutes.

Just presence.

When Nurse Melissa returned, she wrapped the pulse ox probe around Jayden's wrist. We waited. Still at 94% even without oxygen.

Dr. Earles smiled. "Let's keep the oxygen on at night, but during the day she's free."

*Free.*

No more tubes tethering her to the wall. No more tape across her cheeks. Breathing on her own.

Jayden and I left Dr. Earles's office with hugs and warm smiles from the entire staff. Everyone there already knew her story and already loved her. She wasn't just a chart. She was a fighter.

As I loaded Jayden and all her gear into the car, I heard footsteps behind me. It was Dr. Earles jogging into the parking lot.

"Would you mind if I faxed her glucose log to a pediatric endocrinologist I have worked with?" she asked. "Dr. Jeremy Sinclair. I'd love to get his eyes on this."

I said yes, of course. Grateful she cared enough to chase us down.

WE HAD a short window at home before it was time to head out again for Jayden's next appointment. That afternoon, we drove to the medical complex attached to Dr. Earles's hospital. With a new pediatrician, we were switching Jayden's specialists too. Today, we were seeing a retinal consultant that Dr. Earles trusted.

The waiting room was packed with dozens of babies and young children crowded into every chair. At check-in, I asked if they had a private room I could wait with Jayden. Something away from the germs and potential risks. They didn't. So I told the front desk we'd be in the hallway.

"When you're ready," I said, "please come find us there."

Thankfully, I already wrapped Jayden securely in the baby wrap before leaving the parking garage. She was snug, sound asleep, and protected from whatever might have lingered in that waiting room. So I walked back and forth for forty-five minutes. Then a staff member stepped out to place the dilation drops in Jayden's eyes.

"About twenty more minutes," they said.

So I kept walking, bouncing, and singing. Each breath its own kind of prayer. Doing everything I could to keep her safe.

Thirty more minutes passed. Finally, nearly two hours after we checked in, we were escorted into the exam room. I was irritated. The doctor who entered wasn't even a doctor yet. Still a resident. My guard went up immediately. After everything we endured at the first clinic, I had little trust left for residents. This was Jayden. She deserved a real specialist. But this young resident surprised me.

His handshake was firm, his eyes kind. I took a breath and felt my shoulders drop. He asked me to hold Jayden on my lap, her head resting in his as he sat across from me. He reached for the light switch, darkening the room, then turned on his instrument, a bright magnifying scope. He leaned in. Gently opened her eyes and began the exam, moving the light across every angle, every visible surface.

He already knew her story. I could hear him murmuring the details as he worked, "Born premature at thirty-one and a half weeks. Blind when discharged from NICU."

He was slow. Respectful. Then he looked up, met my eyes, and said, "Her eyes look healthy."

I nodded politely, but didn't let it sink in. He was only a resident. We were here for the retinal consultant. So I held his conclusion lightly, and I waited for the real answer. Fifteen minutes later, the ophthalmologist entered the room.

She reviewed Jayden's chart again, out loud: "Born prematurely at thirty-one and a half weeks. Three pounds fifteen ounces. Diagnosed blind upon discharge at nine weeks old."

I was already holding Jayden in place when the doctor dimmed the lights and took her position across from me. Another bright light. Another exam. She stretched Jayden's eyelids as wide open as they'd go and looked deep into both eyes, searching. The lights flicked back on. I braced myself. But instead of giving me a diagnosis, she asked me a question: "Why are you here?"

I blinked. My heart stuttered. I repeated what she just reviewed: Jayden's NICU stay, the discharge papers, the blindness. She listened, then smiled.

"There is no sign of damage from syphilis," she said. "Both eyes are perfectly healthy."

She offered to see Jayden again in two weeks, just to be sure. But from what she could see today, there was nothing wrong. I stared at her eyes. Jayden blinked once, twice. Unafraid. Air left me like a prayer I hadn't known I was holding. Light stayed in her eyes.

---

PEOPLE PROBABLY STARED. I walked the long hallway crying, Jayden asleep in the baby wrap. Tears streamed down my cheeks as I bounced her, snug against my chest, walking through the parking garage.

By the time we got home, both of us were completely spent. Jayden passed out on my chest. I sank into the comfort of our rocker.

John called that evening to check in. He wanted to

hear the updates about the pediatrician visit and the ophthalmology results. I tried to explain it all, but halfway through, I paused. I was so tired. Every muscle in my body ached. John waited. Then assured me that he would be home the next evening. Relief flooded my soul. I had only one more day to hang on.

Jayden lay curled on my chest, breathing peacefully. I picked up my cold, untouched sandwich and took a few bites. And suddenly I was crying. The tears flowed and flowed. I began to share the fear, frustration, gratitude, exhaustion, and hope.

I DECIDED to take it easy the next day. No appointments. No phone calls. No charting or Googling or trying to outguess the future. I had to take care of myself because I was all Jayden had.

That evening, as I settled in to feed Jayden, the phone rang. Courtenay. We talked about Jayden, the day, the waiting rooms. She listened the way she always did, saying the small things that keep a person going.

"There's something I've been meaning to ask. Have you ever considered naturopathy for Jayden?"

She told me what had helped her. She'd already spoken to her naturopath, Dr. Nancy, and said she could help. Non-invasive, low-risk. Nothing that could harm her. And no payment. Another hand extended, just when I didn't know I needed one.

I wasn't sure how the state would feel. In foster care, free rarely means simple. Another approval. Another chance to be told no. Still, after what corn syrup had nearly done to her, how close we came to losing her, I couldn't dismiss a gentle path just because it wasn't conventional. I agreed to a consultation, mostly to listen and understand what we'd be asking Nicole to approve.

After the feeding, I spread the sheet over the rocker and eased Jayden onto my chest. The phone face-down on the table. Her breath warm on my neck. Enough quiet to feel like mercy. By 6:30 p.m., the day was done.

***

JOHN CAME HOME to an exhausted version of me. He took one look at me and he knew I was spent. But awe overcame worry when I placed Jayden in his arms. He stopped mid-breath. He cradled her close and just stared.

The skin that had been gray and paper-thin now shone with rich, brown warmth. The cannula was gone and her breathing calm and even.

When he left two weeks earlier, we were making funeral plans. Preparing to say goodbye. But every call since had carried life. Hearing about it was one thing. Seeing it? Feeling her weight in his arms, alive, was something else entirely.

Then John whispered, "Deedle, Deedle girl."

The same words he murmured into the phone night after night.

Jayden tilted her head up and found him. She saw him. His chin trembled. His eyes filled.

For a long, quiet moment they stayed like that. Papa and his Deedle. No tubes. No monitors. Only the hush of breath. The soft weight of light.

# August 2009 — Part One

We were up early again for another big day. Jayden was in a great mood, eyes bright and curious, blowing slobber bubbles. That only slightly reduced the scramble to get ready. She needed a bath, a bottle, insulin, and a bag packed. Bath time had gotten easier lately. She fit perfectly in the little pink dishpan we brought home from the NICU. The water lapped against her knees. She blinked up at me. No fuss, just the slow flutter of toes testing the edge.

That morning I dressed her in a newborn-sized onesie for the first time. It fit her just right, nearly six pounds of chubby-cheeked proof that she was making progress. I let her go barefoot and slipped a pair of socks in the diaper bag, just in case.

We pulled into Dr. Nancy's before her regular hours. It was an early start, an easy ride to a small, converted house on a quiet side street. It felt more like visiting a friend than a clinic. The waiting room was cozy. The air held lavender and rosemary from a humming diffuser, soft lighting, trailing plants. Jayden's mood stayed light.

Dr. Nancy knelt to meet Jayden's gaze.

"Precious girl, I've been thinking about you all week."

Her voice was smooth, her presence calm. The quiet confidence of someone who already believed. We sat together at her desk while I told her what we knew so far. She listened intently, nodding, never interrupting. Then she turned to her computer and filled in Jayden's profile.

"This will give us a look at her lifelines," she said.

As the data loaded, a graph appeared: a jagged tangle of lines.

"This is Jayden's system right now," she said, pointing to the screen. "There's no regulation. No calm."

I didn't need the graph to tell me that, but seeing it mapped in restless spikes made the chaos harder to ignore. She spoke about carefully waking the nervous system. Letting the body meet what frightened it and learn not to resist.

"It's a reset," she said. "Teaching the body to remember calm."

Dr. Nancy worked to desensitize her to the allergens attacking her fragile body. It sounded like allergy shots, without the needles. Could healing really be that simple?

She treated Jayden at least once a week, and with a silent intensity. I still don't understand how it worked, but I understood this much: Dr. Nancy believed in the work, and she believed in Jayden. That was enough to keep coming back.

She was, as she put it, "balancing her energy."

It was unlike anything I'd known. But it felt right. It felt kind.

After our visit with Dr. Earles and her quiet yes to feeding Jayden breast milk, our days had found a new rhythm. Jayden could see and hear. Her glucometer readings held. The irritation of her skin had begun to fade. It wasn't easy, just enough.

John was home again, watching with me. Every morning, he woke up eager to check on her, leaning over and kissing her forehead, and then mine, before heading into the kitchen to make coffee and breakfast. He loved her with an unspoken intensity, as if the world had narrowed to her.

But in the past week, something felt off. Jayden was irritable, gassy, and restless. The color in her skin seemed to be fading again. A pale ring had formed around her eyes, like a mask, and her bottom was red and raw again.

As I sat there feeding her, my mind kept considering what had changed. The only thing I could think of was the high-calorie supplement Dr. Earles had given us to boost her weight. Jayden had done so well on breast milk. Even coconut oil agreed with her. But the supplement made her miserable within hours.

Then the alarm screamed. Jayden arched her back and began to gag. My stomach dropped. She hadn't done this since the switch to breast milk. It had to be the supplement. No more. Not until we saw Dr. Earles again.

It wasn't even a hard call. Everything pointed in the same direction: the swollen tummy, the sudden cries mid-feeding, the scream of the apnea alarm.

I lived on edge, always watching, always bracing.

If Jayden got too stressed, her blood sugar soared. If she slept longer than two hours, it crashed. If I adjusted her feedings, her tummy revolted. There was no off switch. Only me. Listening. Measuring. Guessing.

I had agreed to care for Jayden. *Just hold her.* But now that she was still here, was I prepared for the endless work it might take to keep her alive? Or worse, would she die in spite of everything we did?

The doorbell rang before I spiraled any further. John went to answer it and a moment later, he walked into the family room carrying a cheerful floral arrangement in a yellow smiley-face mug. It was from my sisters, Sonya and Doreen. I didn't even need to read the card to know it meant *we see you, we love you, we're with you.*

Still, I read it, aching for their words. Their love never wavered, even when I had no time, no voice left to call. I missed them.

For a moment, the house fell still. The machines, the numbers, the charts faded, and it was just love, unseen. This small surprise felt like a hand on my back, lifting me just a little.

And then I realized... there were warm hands at my back. John stood behind me, rubbing my shoulders as I stared out the window, tears slipping onto the open card in my lap.

He set the flowers on the shelf beside me so I could breathe in the sweet scent. As the fragrance filled the room, something else rose too. A smile. Tentative. Surprising. Like an old friend.

We didn't have long to soak in the comfort of it. There was just enough time to prepare for another car ride, another appointment. While I fed Jayden, John packed the diaper bag and filled a few bottles. Then we were off to meet the new pediatric endocrinologist, Dr. Sinclair.

Dr. Earles had already been in touch with him, faxing over Jayden's glucose readings and notes. He'd even started making adjustments to her insulin doses. But this week, her numbers weren't as consistent. Not like they had been.

———

WALKING into Dr. Sinclair's office brought all the staff from behind their desks. Everyone wanted a glimpse of the baby in my arms. After smiles and greetings, we were ushered into an exam room.

When Dr. Sinclair arrived, he didn't hold a clipboard or dive into questions. He gathered Jayden from my arms, lifted her to his shoulder, and swayed, humming an unrecognizable tune. Only after a few moments did he place her on the exam table. The nurse stepped in to draw a small vial of blood to check Jayden's A1c. Dr. Sinclair began the physical exam. He pressed her thighs, then paused.

"These little legs are already building up scar tissue," he said.

I explained how I was using an imaginary grid on each of her thighs so I didn't inject the same spot twice in the same day. He shook his head. "Too many injections for too small an area."

Dr. Sinclair walked us through the critical realities of infant diabetes. Very severe or prolonged low blood sugar levels can cause long-term problems with brain development. Dr. Sinclair began calculating. He adjusted her insulin dosage and handed me a revised chart to follow. He also switched her syringes, prescribing a finer needle to reduce trauma. He left us with a clear plan: start the new dosage right away, call in a week with her updated readings, and return in one month for a follow-up appointment.

After the exam, the nurse helped dress Jayden again. Not because I couldn't do it, but because she wanted to. She was smitten, cooing and easing each sleeve into place. In rooms like this, kindness is its own medicine.

***

THE NEXT MORNING, when John walked into Dr. Earles's office for the first time, he couldn't help but laugh.

"She's exactly how you described her," he said, grinning.

Watching her move was different.

Swift and certain, she didn't just command the room. She carried it.

John already held enormous respect for her. I watched as he stood there, chin trembling, trying to find the words that captured his gratitude and admiration for saying yes to breast milk, giving Jayden a real chance, saving this Deedle girl's life.

Dr. Earles saw it all in his eyes. She gave John a warm welcome, then turned her full attention to Jayden. And wouldn't you know it, Jayden entertained the whole room.

She smiled at everyone who peeked in, charming them one by one. She was a content, bright-eyed, impossibly small girl. But even as Jayden smiled, Dr. Earles's exam revealed a few new concerns. She found patches of eczema behind Jayden's knees and in the folds of her elbows. Her tongue was coated with white again, the same way it had in the NICU. Her skin looked more irritated than before. Despite stopping the supplement two days earlier on my gut feelings, there was still blood in her stool.

Dr. Earles agreed. It was an allergic reaction. She scanned the supplement's ingredient list, eyebrows knitting, and frowned.

"58 percent corn syrup," she said.

Then she reached for her massive three-ring binder, packed with printouts and product data for every formula and supplement on the market. She flipped through page after page. Corn syrup. Corn syrup. Corn syrup. Jayden would likely be allergic to all of them.

A knot rose in my throat. What would've happened if we hadn't started breast milk? The thought knocked the air from my chest. And still, beneath the ache, I felt gratitude and relief.

We had found at least one answer. Real breast milk. Liquid gold. It wasn't just nourishing her. It was saving her.

Dr. Earles pulled out Jayden's growth chart again, the thin paper crinkling as she traced the line. Jayden was still below the preemie curve. At almost four months old, her height and weight didn't even register. But her head circumference had grown.

"That's the most important part," Dr. Earles said. "If the brain doesn't grow, nothing else matters. If the brain grows, we have hope."

I asked her about Jayden's white tongue. Was it thrush again? She paused.

"Maybe not," she said. "It's quite possible that each time her tongue was white it could have been an allergic response to the corn syrup."

If that was true, then the weeks of medications, the forced doses, the struggle to get each milliliter down was all unnecessary. I winced, heat rising in my cheeks. But I had to let it go. What mattered now was forward.

As we packed up to leave, a nurse at the back station called out, "Five pounds thirteen ounces, baby!"

The whole room erupted in cheers.

John laughed, shaking his head. Part disbelief, part relief. We had found our pediatrician. The one who saw our Deedle girl the way we did.

On the way home, John pulled into another fast-food drive-thru. There wasn't time to cook, not with one appointment behind us and another less than an hour away. When we got home, we unloaded the car, let Dudley out, and barely had time to settle before the doorbell rang.

Nurse Ann and dietitian Ms. Chase stepped inside carrying the baby scale and Jayden's ever-growing folder of medical notes, pens already clipped to their pockets.

They hadn't seen her since that day everything nearly fell apart.

Ms. Chase squealed, then quickly covered her mouth, realizing how loudly she'd reacted.

"Oh my! This can't be the same baby!" she said, eyes wide.

They took turns holding her, marveling, laughing, completely stunned.

Jayden just snuggled into their arms, smiling and cooing like she knew exactly what she was doing. She sighed and tucked her face into the crook of Nurse Ann's arm.

For once, what they saw matched what I'd been feeling. She was changing. She was here.

EARLY ON, John and I promised each other this: one of us would always show up for court. Every single time. We agreed that someone had to be there for the child. Someone who wasn't being paid to attend. Someone who cared for no other reason than love.

So on August 6, John got up at the crack of dawn and drove forty-five minutes to court to stand in for our little girl. The judge was expected to decide whether the case would move forward with reunification or if parental rights would be terminated. Nicole, our caseworker, was adamant. The agency was moving to terminate parental rights, and she supported the recommendation. The medical circumstances at birth had been too severe; Jayden's survival too uncertain.

When the birth mother didn't appear, the judge granted the request and terminated her parental rights. Then the judge ordered a DNA test to determine paternity.

When John told me, I didn't speak. I just gripped the phone and listened. I couldn't tell if I was holding still or just holding on. What if a father came forward? Would he want custody? Would he be ready for a medically fragile child? And if he wasn't, would his extended family?

We'd already been told that no one on the birth mother's side was available or willing to take the baby. Now the unknown shifted to his side of the story. It was one of the hardest truths of foster care. We're chosen to be the interim. We love these children with our whole hearts. We show up for them, we fight for them, we fold them into our families like they were born there. But in the end, we don't get to decide where they land.

Seven weeks ago, this wasn't a concern. Now, hour by hour, feeding by feeding, prayer by prayer, our Deedle girl was still here. I loved her. I had fought for her when it felt like no one else would.

*How could I let her go?*

---

WHEN JOHN GOT HOME from the courthouse, we sat for a moment to take in what had happened. We prayed the only prayer that made sense now: *Thy will be done.* If this was Jayden's chance to know a father who would love and care for her, then we had to open our hands.

*Dear Lord, please take care of my little girl.*

That evening, Courtenay stopped by with fresh and frozen breast milk. More of her midwifery clients had stepped up, eager to help. She came prepared with every bag labeled and sorted by date. She put each one in the fridge or freezer, then joined us in the family room.

The moment she saw Jayden, she froze.

"She looks... completely different," Courtenay said, her eyes wide. I filled her in quickly on Jayden's progress, the dramatic changes, and the brief setback with the corn syrup supplement. I admitted I was still discouraged by how slowly she was gaining weight.

Courtenay nodded, then reminded me, "Breast milk is healing first. Growing comes later."

We both knew how much damage had been done early on. The congenital syphilis and NICU formula had taken a toll. Rebuilding would take time. Again we chose hope and patience.

Courtenay also updated me on the network she was building. She had set up multiple "drop sites" for milk donors across the area, organized by day and location.

She'd already recruited trusted friends to gather the milk and deliver it to us. She'd thought of everything. Jayden would have the milk she needed. And I wouldn't have to rearrange my already overflowing schedule.

Courtenay was more than a midwife. She was the village at our door.

---

JAYDEN WAS ONLY DRINKING ABOUT three ounces every two to three hours. We were freezing breast milk that could last for months. But I had no idea where we'd put all the milk being delivered. Then an email landed in my inbox: the neighborhood newsletter listed a deep freezer for sale just down the street. I called immediately. Our neighbor offered to deliver it that day. Free of charge. John cleared space in the garage, right outside the kitchen door. It fit like it had always belonged there, close enough for a midnight run in my socks.

Now we could safely store the growing supply, each bag dated and labeled. Enough to last through setbacks and seasons. I stood there that night, the freezer humming, rows of donated milk neatly stacked. Women I'd never met, new mothers themselves, had filled these bags with care and trust. Courtenay had gathered them, our "Pumpin' Mamas."

Generosity. Love. The very best of them flowing into our little girl, drop by drop.

---

I SAT in the recliner late that night, reviewing the spiral notebook. Her trends over the past few weeks told the story better than I could. Line by line, the numbers traced the difference between barely surviving and beginning to live.

These were Jayden's numbers on her last day on formula, compared with her numbers after three weeks of breast milk.

|  | Last Day on Formula | One Week on Breast Milk |
| --- | --- | --- |
| Eating | 14–16 oz per day | 20–24 oz per day |
| Spitting up | Every feeding | Rarely if ever |
| Dirty diapers | 12–14 per day | 4–6 per day |
| Apnea monitor | 6–10 alarms per day | 0–1 alarms per day |
| Glucometer | 36–468, no pattern | 100–200, normal variance |
| Insulin cover | 12 doses per day | 4-5 doses, as needed |
| Eyes | Cloudy coating, no tracking | Shiny, focused, tracking |
| Whites of eyes | Yellow | White |
| Hearing | Failed test, no response | Responsive |
| Skin | Flaky, raw, discolored | Rich, smooth, hydrated |
| Awake/Alert | 1.5–2 hours per day | 4–6 hours per day |
| Feeding | Gagging, choking, thrashing at each feeding | Calm, cradling, gagging rare (about once a week) |
| Nasal congestion | Thick and yellow | Clear breathing |
| Condition & Care | Malnutrition | First fingernail trim (at 3½ months old) |

I closed the notebook. The numbers didn't guarantee anything. But they told me we were moving in the right direction.

# August 2009 — Part Two

Balancing Jayden's needs with my own basic care took everything I had. Most days, I forgot to eat.

John noticed before I did. He'd appear beside me with a plate balanced in one hand. "Eat," he'd say softly, setting it down within reach while I held Jayden against my chest. Sometimes a cold glass of iced tea would find its way into my hand before I realized how thirsty I was. Condensation beading down the sides. The first sip woke me up again.

He took Jayden so I could slip away for a shower. Folded the laundry before I remembered there was laundry. Tossed the ball for Dudley in the backyard until the dog collapsed happily in the shade. He drove everywhere. He loaded the stroller, buckled car seats, and hummed off-key to whatever song came on the radio while Jayden blinked up at the passing light.

Having him home felt like breathing again.

That morning, we sat in the audiologist's waiting room, Jayden cradled in my arms. Initial testing showed

Jayden could hear clearly in her left ear, but only partially in her right.

A tech led us down the hall to an exam room for further testing with a neurophysiologist. They attached probes to her forehead, behind her ears, and on each earlobe. A machine sent rhythmic pulses through the sensors while a graph traced lines across the screen.

The results confirmed something remarkable: Jayden's brain was sending signals to her ears. The problem, they said, might be mechanical, not neurological. Possibly something as simple as a fluid buildup behind her right eardrum. It sounded like good news, but I didn't let myself relax. They recommended a more thorough two-hour exam with a team trained to measure brain-to-ear responses like this.

We'd have to schedule it for a time when Jayden could sleep through the entire procedure, like she had today. Still and silent. We made the appointment for three months later and kept going.

THE NEXT MORNING started with a storytelling session with Miss Jayden. She made eye contact and cooed, lips pursed into a little O. I spoke softly to her.

"Hey Deedle, Deedle," I whispered through a big smile.

"The cat and the fiddle, the cow jumped over the moon."

She flailed her arms like a drummer, tiny limbs bursting with joy.

Full of life. Full of story.

I held her on my lap, her head resting in my hands. Her cheeks, once hollow and pale, had filled out with softness. Dimples deepened, echoes of the smile her body was learning to hold. She was beginning to settle into the life she'd fought so hard to keep.

And just like that, the morning turned back toward the work of keeping her alive. It had been five weeks since our visit with the infectious disease doctor. He'd ordered more bloodwork before our six-week follow-up. I dreaded putting Jayden through that again. The last time had been awful.

So John and I tried the lab associated with Dr. Earles's office, hoping it might be different. But the moment the lab technician saw Jayden, her expression changed. She looked nervous, but said she'd try. She had a backup plan if it didn't work.

Simmer down, mama bear, I told myself. After two failed attempts, I asked for the backup.

We were escorted downstairs to another pediatric clinic in the same building. Three pediatricians studied Jayden's damaged veins, quietly talking through options for nearly thirty minutes. Before proceeding, they called the lab to confirm the absolute minimum amount of blood required.

They wrapped the tourniquet around her arm. Tighter this time. They inserted the needle into her wrist. Then again. Yet again. Fifteen minutes of screaming and trembling as her fragile body tried to flee the pain. Tears streaked her cheeks.

Finally, they drew 2½ cc. Just enough.

It took less time, but still too much.

---

LATER THAT WEEK our occupational therapy sessions began. Dr. Earles believed that if we could help Jayden calm her frantic sucking which burned calories, she might begin to gain weight. During our first session, the therapist carefully observed Jayden's feeding and then recommended creating a pattern. The therapist explained that babies exposed to cocaine in utero often struggle with rhythm. Their bodies can't regulate the patterns that come so naturally to other infants.

We would turn her feeding into a metronome. Count her sucks.

*Count to ten. Nipple out.*

*Count to ten. Nipple in.*

*Remove the nipple. Reinsert it. Repeat.*

Over and over for thirty minutes. It was exhausting, but it worked. That day, Jayden drank four ounces in a single session.

JAYDEN TURNED four months old on August 17, a day I didn't expect to see with her. We left the NICU seven weeks ago with warnings and one ominous request:

*Just hold her.*

But now, she was still here. She was smiling, cooing, content. Her small body was heavier in my arms than it had been in June. Her color was better. Her eyes followed the light across the room.

She lived at the center of an orbit of adults: a pediatrician, pediatric endocrinologist, infectious disease doctor, occupational therapist, audiologist, ophthalmologist, naturopath, reiki therapist, county nurse, county dietitian, and a cluster of caseworkers.

Most days, we were in someone's office. Some days, they came to us.

Nurse Kay practiced reiki therapy, a gentle way to quiet the rhythms of Jayden's body. I didn't understand how it worked, but I was open to anything that wouldn't cause harm.

Once a week starting at the beginning of August, Nurse Kay settled in at our kitchen table while I laid Jayden on the changing pad. Jayden didn't fuss. Maybe she sensed the calm. Nurse Kay would place her hands above Jayden's body, eyes closed, her breathing slow and deep.

She said little. Just moved with quiet intention, holding space, sending healing, shifting what she could. I couldn't explain it, but in her stillness, I could finally breathe. A reminder that we were not alone.

Nurse Kay wanted nothing in return. She donated her time, stopping by on her way home from twelve-hour hospital shifts.

Our days were predictable. We followed a simple routine. Every two hours, we repeated the same pattern: diaper, reading, injection, feeding.

Nights still found us in my chair, Jayden on my chest. Sometimes she slept longer stretches.

My sleep came in fragments, if at all. I waited for her to open her eyes. Just to be sure.

---

WE TOOK Jayden in for imaging that would show how she swallowed in real time. The radiologist wanted to see if a structural reason made feeding hard for her.

Jayden was placed upright in a small infant seat. A technician mixed her breast milk with a safe barium solution, so her swallow would show clearly on screen. As I fed her, a live image of her swallowing flickered on the screen behind us. The beeping of monitors marked each second.

I turned to look and gasped. Her jaw was straining furiously but nothing was coming through. She wasn't sucking at all. She was swallowing only what dripped slowly from the nipple. It looked more like chewing than drinking.

Maybe it explained those earliest days, when she pushed away from the formula and flailed in frustration. Protecting herself.

She wanted to eat. She just didn't know how.

As I stood holding Jayden, her body warm against my shoulder, the radiologist began to speak. His voice was deep and deliberate.

"For the first three months of her life," he said, "Jayden was being fed something her body couldn't tolerate. To her, it was poison. She learned to avoid it."

My eyes filled as he spoke.

"To satisfy her need to suck without actually drawing anything in, she trained herself to survive by swallowing only what dripped passively from the nipple."

He called it food by default. In those earliest weeks, when nourishment should have brought strength, each bottle taught her to endure it, to shut it out. It explained her straining jaw.

She was so tired. She fought every feeding. It wasn't stubbornness or immaturity. It was survival.

The radiologist recommended we begin intensive occupational therapy at the hospital right away. There was a path forward, but before we went anywhere, I took a moment to be right there and hold her.

I was heartbroken that her first instinct had been to

protect herself from us. But I was also grateful we were finally feeding her something her body could receive, something that said, you're safe now, you can grow, you can stay.

A few days passed. The swallow study stayed with me, but the routine didn't stop for grief. Diapers. Readings. Injections. Feedings.

Something began to shift. No alarms overnight. No urgent calls. Just a Tuesday. I was holding a happy Deedle girl. Calm and alert, she looked up at me with a grin, like she was ready to take on the world.

We headed to Dr. Earles's office for our regular weekly weight check. Today, it was paired with her four-month well-baby visit. I had just finished undressing Jayden when Nurse Melissa whisked her across the hall. A few moments later, her voice echoed back toward us:

"Jayden weighs six pounds three ounces!"

Then came the cheers. Nurse Melissa carried Jayden out to the nurses' station, snug in her fuzzy blanket, and announced her weight to anyone within earshot. Everyone clapped. The staff, the patients, the parents. An entire waiting room of strangers celebrating for her. It was a moment.

Melissa returned to the room just as Dr. Earles walked in, hips swaying, a little shimmy in her shoulders. She called it her "happy dance." We grinned at each other over Jayden's head. We both knew it wouldn't last, but for once there was no emergency to chase, nothing urgent to fix.

And then came the best news of all: Jayden no longer needed the apnea monitor. Her respiration and heart rate were strong. There hadn't been a single alarm in over a week. The last one came during the high-calorie supplement trial, when we confirmed her corn syrup allergy.

But since we'd switched back to breast milk and coconut oil? Zero alarms.

Under normal circumstances, this would be the time for Jayden's second round of immunizations, Dr. Earles said. But knowing her history, she chose to wait until Jayden had a bit more weight on her before restarting the process.

We still needed to fine-tune her insulin levels, keeping her blood sugar as close to 100 as possible for optimal brain growth.

Jayden's pulse ox reading looked great. Still, Dr. Earles recommended we keep oxygen on hand, just in case. We no longer needed it running through the night, a big step back from the "always on" hiss and hum. I made her walk me through exactly when to use the oxygen, so I'd know if the time came.

And with that, Jayden and I left the office, grateful.

Life was getting a little easier. Fewer alarms. Fewer wires between her and the world. A little more room for breath. A little more room for grace. A little more room to hold her.

---

LATER THAT EVENING, Courtenay arrived with the weekly breast milk delivery. She placed several labeled bags of fresh donor milk on the second shelf of the fridge, lining them up by date.

"These will need to be used within six days of the pumping date," she explained. "Fresh breast milk is always more beneficial."

I nodded. She would definitely benefit.

We wanted to start using it right away. But I already

had bottles prepped, so we decided to wait until the next morning.

The first bottle of fresh breast milk went down beautifully without a pause.

The second... not so much.

Jayden turned her head and refused it. She just flat-out would not drink.

Why?

This was supposed to be the better option, the one I'd fought for.

I couldn't think of any reason she'd know the difference between frozen and fresh breast milk. But something had changed.

I'd seen this before. Jayden's body knew how to protect itself.

Clearly she sensed something she didn't want.

I called Courtenay.

"If the donor mom drinks a lot of soda," I asked, "could the corn syrup make it into the milk?"

Could Jayden really be *that* sensitive?

If she reacted so strongly to corn syrup in formula, could traces of it in breast milk hurt her too? Or other ingredients passed through the mother's diet?

And what about the freezing process? Did it neutralize something? Did it change the composition in a way that made it more tolerable?

Courtenay was stunned that Jayden could tell the difference, but she didn't dismiss it. "I'll find out," she said.

I hung up the phone, looked at Jayden, squirming in my arms, and gave in to what she already seemed to know.

I put the fresh breast milk into the freezer.

I thawed the frozen breast milk, warmed it, and offered it to her.

She drank it without hesitation.
She knew what her body needed.
And I was just learning to listen.

---

THE NEXT AFTERNOON, Nurse Ann arrived for her monthly home visit. She couldn't stop marveling at Jayden. "She's a miracle," she said, again and again.

Jayden weighed six pounds ten ounces on her scale. Nineteen and a half inches long. A full inch of head growth. I logged the numbers in my notebook.

I handed Nurse Ann a few printed photos to take back to her office: one from those first weeks on formula, and a few from now. In the early picture, Jayden was all tape and tubes, bubblegum cheeks and hollow eyes. In the new ones, her cheeks caught the light, round and sure.

Ann slipped the older photo into a manila folder and laid the newer one on top, tracing the edge with her thumb, as if she could feel the difference. She shook her head, smiling. "I can't wait to show the others," she said. She used that word again, the one she couldn't quite let go of.

After she left, I pinned a copy of that same smiling photo to our fridge, just above the rows of donated breast milk.

The house settled back into its hum. I sat in the stillness and felt Jayden's chest rise and fall. Ann's word still hung in the room, but I didn't say it. I just watched my Deedle sleep.

J AYDEN WASN'T herself the next morning. She hadn't eaten much overnight. She seemed like she wanted to sleep, but instead she squirmed. I didn't sleep at all. I spent the night retracing every routine we'd learned since she came home. The feedings, the medications, the monitor checks, the specialists carrying us through. I spent the night trying to soothe her tense, twisting body. I spent the night missing John.

But morning came, as it always did, whether I was ready or not.

When Miss Pam arrived, I recognized her immediately. She was part of Jayden's initial evaluation team, and I'd been impressed by her calm professionalism. I also remembered the way she effortlessly wrangled our friendly, thoroughly neglected dog, Dudley, while she completed the developmental assessment.

Now, she sat at our kitchen table reviewing the official paperwork. An Individualized Family Service Plan was in place. It outlined specific goals and teaching strategies designed to bring Jayden "on target" for her age. Miss Pam explained what skills they'd begin with, what milestones they were aiming for. I nodded, but inside I was confused. Jayden only weighed six pounds. How could she possibly participate in *any* of this?

Miss Pam didn't seem concerned. She simply spread a blanket on our family room floor and got started. I sat nearby and watched. In her hands, therapy looked like play.

She encouraged Jayden to track a brightly colored toy, eyes once blind following every move. Then she shook a soft rattle on either side of her head and waited for Jayden to turn toward the sound with ears they'd once called deaf.

She took Jayden's hands in hers and slowly guided her

into a sitting position. Her head lagged only briefly before she could control it; her gaze locked on Miss Pam's face the whole way up.

But the moment that undid me came at the end of the visit.

Miss Pam reached into her quilted blue bag and pulled out a brightly colored board book. She settled into the rocker with Jayden nestled against her chest and read to her in a slow, melodic voice. With each page, Jayden turned her head, watching as if she were following the story. The whole world moved a fraction of an inch.

I couldn't ignore it. For more than two months, Jayden had lived on my chest, held close and protected. But now, from across the room, I really saw her. Not just as my medically fragile baby. But as a child.

A little girl with curiosity in her eyes, and rhythm in her body. With possibilities I hadn't dared picture stretching out ahead of her. She was still impossibly small. But she was capable, of learning, of connecting, of *becoming*.

---

MISS PAM KEPT ADJUSTING her visits to fit Jayden's schedule. The times shifted, but she still came twice a week.

I was struck by how naturally she treated Jayden like a four-month-old. Never smaller, never less. Watching her work was like a master class in motherhood.

Her hands taught what my heart already knew but hadn't dared practice. Inspired, I pulled picture books from the toy shelf and held Jayden upright in my lap, just like Miss Pam did. Together, we met the barnyard, the cows, pigs, ducks, and dogs in the pictures. Jayden leaned into the pages, wide-eyed and focused.

But even as I settled into this new pattern, something in me wouldn't rest. Yes, Jayden was four months old, but she was still only six pounds. And yes, until a few weeks ago, she hadn't fully arrived.

Still I wondered why I hadn't read to her sooner. Why hadn't I thought to treat her like a baby who might grow and learn, rather than one I was trying to keep alive?

I'd been in survival mode, counting breaths, ounces, and glucose readings. Chasing alarms. Fighting formula. No, I didn't have time for guilt. I was doing my best.

# August 2009 — Part Three

The sun was low on the horizon when we merged onto the highway. It was just Jayden and me, heading back to the courthouse.

Over time, I picked up a few tricks for solo drives. I rolled receiving blankets to tuck around her tiny body to keep her from sliding and to help her feel snug and secure. I wedged a teddy bear between the seat and her head for support. Her pacifier was clipped to a burp cloth so I could find it by feel. She couldn't hold it in her mouth on her own, but if I kept it in place, she would stay calm.

Every trip carried its own risk. Keeping her calm wasn't optional. Even a little crying could aggravate her umbilical hernia. The pressure was dangerous.

We had our system. My first line of defense was musical. I would belt out *Old MacDonald Had a Farm*, twenty-seven verses. If the trip was longer, I would make up animals as I went. Jayden had opinions. Some animals got big smiles. Others earned squeals. Every car ride was a negotiation.

When my greatest hits ran out and she still fussed, I

had a backup plan. My left hand on the wheel, right reaching back, feeling for that pacifier. I'd guide it to her lips and hold it until she settled.

I missed John. He wouldn't be home until tonight, so this one was on me. We always show up for court. Today was no exception. It wasn't technically court, but it was a court-ordered DNA test, held at the courthouse. So basically, court.

I left the oxygen tank in the car, parked in a handicapped space, close enough to reach if needed. As we entered the building, I felt a wave of nerves. We joined the security line, just one more set of bodies moving through the metal detectors and bag checks.

I had to unwrap Jayden from the baby wrap so the guards could see we weren't a threat. They scanned our things, then pointed me down the hall to the designated testing room. None of this was unfamiliar. We'd done it before, with other placements in our care. But this felt different. A different weight pressing against my chest.

Unlike our local court, where we'd always been the only family carrying in a baby, this room was full. Rows of adults and children. Paperwork clutched. Eyes down. We were just one more case. I moved quickly to the check-in counter, voice low, asking if there was somewhere more secluded so I could protect a medically fragile baby from unnecessary exposure. After a few hushed conversations behind the desk, a staff member nodded and waved me toward a side room with a long table, mismatched chairs, and a smudged dry-erase board. I was grateful.

While we waited, I changed and fed Jayden, and then rocked her against my chest. The barnyard animals had lost their magic. Today it was the fuzzy pattern on her blanket that held her gaze, her fingers tracing shapes only she could see. After forty-five minutes, Jayden's name was called.

I followed directions to a small room at the end of the hallway. Inside, a technician sat behind a desk, paperwork stacked in front of her. No greeting. No smile. Just a glance up and a quick wave toward the chair in front of her. She flipped through the forms, reading the court order aloud as if reciting a grocery list. As if it were routine. I suppose it was. I confirmed everything.

Then she pulled out the long cotton swab. She stood up, leaning her body over the table between us. She rubbed the swab along the inside of Jayden's cheek, firm and fast, rougher than I expected. Jayden flinched. I instinctively pulled her closer.

Then the woman looked up and really looked at Jayden.

"She reminds me of my mother," she said, almost to herself. "So beautiful. You know, I think I'd adopt a baby like this."

I froze. The words didn't land, they lingered. I wanted to say something, anything. But nothing came.

She kept talking. Told me about the children she'd already adopted. How they managed while she was at work. How she was a good mom. "Even at my age," she said with a half-laugh.

She asked what agency we were with. Before I could answer, she flipped a page and nodded. "Oh, I see it here."

She kept talking. As if none of it mattered. Not Jayden's case. Not her prognosis. My hands trembled.

*She didn't know.*

Didn't know about the oxygen tank in the car, the insulin, the two-hour cycle that never stopped. About the charting, feeding, and decoding language most parents didn't have to learn. About caring for a baby who couldn't cry without consequence.

She didn't know what it took to keep Jayden alive. She hadn't asked. All she saw was a beautiful baby. A doll, maybe. A fantasy.

But this wasn't hypothetical for me. It wasn't aspirational. This was a child I held through the night. A life I guarded, every hour. A truth I held without words. Only presence.

I took a breath.

Then I said, softly but clearly, "A lot depends on this test. There may already be a family waiting."

That quieted her. She nodded and turned back to her paperwork. No apology. No more talk.

I gathered Jayden into my arms. Then we left. I held her tighter.

---

ON THE DRIVE HOME, the technician's words echoed behind me. But so did the dozens of others who had stopped to admire her, not realizing what they were seeing.

I knew Jayden was adorable. People stopped in their tracks to look at her at least once a week, usually more. When we walked into a doctor's office or down a clinic hallway, someone would pause, point, or lean in just to get a closer look. I'd learned to leave twenty minutes early for appointments because of the walk from the parking garage.

"Is that a doll?" they'd ask, peeking into her carrier. "Is she real?"

I'd laugh politely, sometimes joking that I was too old to be toting around baby dolls. But mostly, I just smiled.

Because they were right. She looked like a porcelain doll, petite, pristine, impossibly delicate. The kind of baby people picture in dreams, not the kind whose life depends on how closely you watch her breathe. Almost too precious to be real.

And yet, here she was. Warm. Wiggly. Breathing softly against my chest, her sweet, milky breath warming the space between us.

People saw a doll. What they didn't see was the fight beneath that beauty. The alarms. The long nights. The prayers I whispered while watching her chest rise and fall, pretending not to worry.

Not porcelain. Not pretend. She was real. Delicate. Determined. Undeniably here. Impossibly alive.

And not mine to keep.

My mind drifted to the possibility of Jayden transitioning to a new home. A permanent, forever home. Her home. One I might never see.

New doesn't always feel safe, even when it's good. But not every home is good. And not every goodbye is peaceful.

With Jayden, there was no room for error, no time for delay. Even a well-intended disruption could be life-threatening.

We'd seen it before: healthy babies faltering during transitions. Some lost weight or slipped in ways we couldn't always explain. We tried to make sense of it, to talk ourselves through each setback.

I carried it all in silence, one arm wrapped over her car seat, tapping her pacifier as we drove. Once we got home, I changed Jayden's diaper, checked her blood sugar, injected her insulin, and began feeding her the prepared breast milk with coconut oil. One hand held the bottle; the other reached for the phone.

I called Nicole to confirm the DNA test was done. I told her the results would take ten to twelve business days, expected well before the next court hearing. Then I paused and told her about the technician. How she'd talked about adopting Jayden. How it caught me off guard. I said I understood the process, if the DNA results pointed to a biological father, family placement could be considered. If not, the court might move to terminate parental rights and prepare for an adoption plan.

But I asked her, "Could we please request that Jayden remain in our care until she's physically strong enough to handle a transition?"

Nicole listened. She agreed. She promised to bring the request to the court. It wasn't a guarantee. But it was something.

A simple ask, but one that could mean everything for a Deedle girl whose world depended on those small, relentless routines. Depended on the promise that arms would return and on the mercy of being allowed to stay.

---

JOHN GOT HOME LATE that night. He spotted his little girl, still awake.

"Deeeeeedle!" he called, his voice bright with wonder, loud with love. She lit up. Eyes wide, arms flailing, a squeak so small and bright it sounded like joy, unfiltered.

"Deedle, Deedle, Deedle, Deee…" he sang, as if he'd been waiting all day to give her that song. As if the whole world narrowed to her name. He lifted her high above his head, grinning up at her like he was seeing the sunrise for the first time. She kicked her feet in the air, delighted, uncontainable. The way babies love when someone really sees them. Then he drew her close, pressing her to his chest, wrapping her in one of his best hugs. The kind that said: *You're safe now. I've got you.* John sat beside me, cradling her in one arm and me in the other, a trace of aftershave in the air, familiar and warm. Home.

"How was today?" he asked, voice low, deep with care.

And I did the only thing I could. I cried. Cried until the weight of the day finally let go. Cried until my shoulders dropped and my breath slowed. Cried until I remembered I wasn't alone.

NURSE BELINDA HAD BEEN ASSIGNED to us for just sixty days of home visits after Jayden left the NICU. That was all we were allowed.

Today was her last visit.

She lifted Jayden from my arms and studied her for a moment, the way she always did, one hand cupping the back of Jayden's head.

"I can't believe this is the same baby," she whispered.

Now this Deedle girl watched her, eyes bright, cheeks full and warm against Nurse Belinda's hand.

Nurse Belinda moved through the familiar routine one last time. She checked Jayden's color, counted her breaths, listened with her stethoscope. Jayden squirmed when the cool metal disc pressed against her chest, then settled again.

Nurse Belinda laughed under her breath. "That's what we like to see."

She wrote a few final notes in her chart at the kitchen table, the scratch of her pen filling the quiet. Her bag sat open on the chair beside her, supplies neatly packed inside. When she stood to leave, she gathered Jayden into her arms again and held her a little longer than usual. Her cheek pressed against Jayden's curls.

"You keep fighting, little girl," she whispered. "And you're going to be just fine."

She handed Jayden back to me, her hand lingering for a moment on Jayden's soft curls. Then she picked up her bag and walked out the door. No fanfare. Just the click of the latch behind her.

I sat in the quiet, Jayden warm against my chest, wishing I'd found the right words to thank her. But maybe some moments aren't meant to be spoken.

Maybe they're meant to be felt. Held.

# September 2009

She was still here. Still trying. Still learning how to do what came naturally to other babies.

The next step in caring for Jayden was introducing solid foods because eating from a spoon might help her gain tongue control, which could support her swallowing. I poured a few teaspoons of rice cereal into a small bowl, propped Jayden in her bouncy seat, and offered the first careful spoonful to her lips. It was delicate, hopeful work. John watched beside me, part coach, part baby bird, his mouth opening with every lift of the spoon. It made me smile.

Most babies would instinctively suck the cereal in. Jayden didn't have the coordination for that yet. Her tongue pressed outward against the spoon, pushing the cereal back out, her lips slow to close around it, unsure how to hold it in. Eventually, we found a rhythm. Spoon, wipe, smile, repeat... until the bowl was empty. Jayden loved it. John loved watching.

It took nearly thirty minutes to get two teaspoons

down that afternoon, but if the therapists thought it would help her, I was all in.

Later that evening, Jayden began squirming, arching her back, and crying. Gas.

I ran to check the rice cereal box and found the likely culprit: soy lecithin. I was furious with myself. I should've checked the ingredients. Every label mattered now, every line of fine print. John had chosen a brand marketed as high-quality. Truthfully, we had no way of knowing if Jayden ever had soy before or how her body would react. But I knew better. A baby this sensitive needed simple ingredients. Nothing hidden. Nothing extra.

That night, John and I took turns walking the floors, comforting her as she tried to pass the gas that upset her sensitive tummy. I grabbed my spiral notebook and scribbled a note:

*Rice cereal: not tolerated. Wait before reintroducing.*

For now, we would stick with breast milk and coconut oil, even if we had to push her to take more. Jayden needed the calories to grow. She also needed calm.

John was enjoying his time with Jayden now that she wasn't tethered to the family room. I think it helped that she no longer looked like she might die in my arms. That mattered more than he could say.

His favorite thing was walking her around the house, her tiny body leaning against his chest, legs curled up as he cradled her with one arm. He would point out the windows, narrating the whole world to her with wide-eyed hope.

"Someday, I'll take you for a walk in your stroller and we'll see all the puppy dogs," he'd whisper.

Then he would point to the framed pictures on the walls and explain each one. "This one? I think Mama Judy likes it because of the colors."

Room by room, he bounced and narrated, singing softly as he went.

"Deedle girl, Deedle girl. Daddy's Deedle Girl."

I loved watching him fall for her.

And with Jayden in his arms, I finally had a few minutes to myself. Not to clean, definitely not that. To organize.

I went to the basement and pulled up the bin labeled "Newborn Girl — Fall." I washed what might fit. Swapped out the preemie clothes in the changing table drawers. Made room.

John and I worked with many children over the years, and we had our own ways of helping. He washed bottles. Folded laundry. Ran errands. Made sure I always had something nourishing. Held the baby when I showered.

He never changed a diaper. Not once. And that was fine. We were a good team. The babies could feel it.

***

By mid-September, Dr. Earles finally received the paperwork from the NICU that we requested back in July. At our next visit, she began by sharing Jayden's APGAR scores.

APGAR: Appearance, Pulse, Grimace response, Activity, Respiration. A standard scoring system used to assess a newborn's condition at one and five minutes after birth, rated on a scale of zero to ten. My own four birth children were all strong. Rated nine at one minute, ten by five.

Jayden's scores?

Two at one minute. Seven at five.

*She was a 2.*

I could hardly take it in. A score that low meant full

intervention: oxygen, stimulation, maybe resuscitation. It explained the jump to seven by five minutes. But still... she was a 2.

Dr. Earles went on, now reading through Jayden's full NICU history. The NICU nurses had told me some of this three months ago, but still hearing it spoken in stark, clinical terms struck deeper than I expected. It bruised something tender. In her first week of life, Jayden had battled pneumonia, brain bleeds, rickets, chlamydia, collapsed veins, sepsis, insulin dependence, and congenital syphilis.

Although she was born at three pounds fifteen ounces, her weight had dropped to just two pounds eight ounces in the weeks that followed. There were nights the NICU staff hadn't expected her to make it. I could hardly believe this was the same Deedle girl now sleeping on my chest.

With the new information in hand, Dr. Earles wrote orders for fourteen lab tests. But she told me to hold onto it, just until after our upcoming appointment with the new infectious disease doctor, Dr. Matthias. She suspected he'd want to add a few of his own.

After that intense visit with Dr. Earles, we had good news: Jayden weighed seven pounds eight and a half ounces. She had gained more than an ounce a day. We were all thrilled. We had our Pumpin' Mamas to thank. Their dedication kept Jayden alive. Thriving.

One mama lived in Ontario, Canada. Whitney wanted to donate her breast milk, but crossing an international border added a layer of complication. She called U.S. Border Control for permission to bring frozen breast milk into Michigan. When they approved, she updated her passport, rented a car, and found a friend to ride along.

She borrowed a commercial-grade insulated cooler from the paramedics in her town. Something sturdy enough to transport three hundred ounces of frozen breast milk. She shared her plan with her local parenting support group. They surprised her with a gas card, paid for with donations collected among themselves. She drove five hours to bring Jayden her milk. She arrived at our home on a Saturday afternoon. John met her at the door and helped carry the heavy cooler into the kitchen.

The moment she saw Jayden, she stopped, covered her face, and fell to the floor, sobbing. I spoke gently, reassuring her. And when she was ready, I placed Jayden into her arms. Jayden looked up at this tearful stranger and reached out to grab the sparkling necklace at her neck.

John began unloading the milk into our deep freezer while I thawed a single bag. In just a few minutes, I had a fresh bottle ready. Whitney, still weeping, fed Jayden her own milk. Jayden gulped it down, then nestled into her arms. Only then could Whitney speak. Through tears, she told us how honored she felt, to do something that mattered.

***

THE PUMPIN' Mamas became a reminder that we were not alone. Some days, the sight of a cooler waiting on the porch was enough to carry us through the afternoon. One family drove from Chicago to visit relatives nearby and brought a cooler in their trunk, packed full of frozen breast milk for Jayden.

There was a Pumpin' Mama who no longer nursed her own children, but offered to serve as a transport hub, driving donated milk from out-of-state moms or those who lived too far to come themselves.

Then there was Carrie Ann. She hadn't breastfed her own children, but after hearing Jayden's story, she wanted to do something. So she organized a network of moms in her town, ninety minutes away. She picked up breast milk from each home, packed the coolers herself, and delivered them to our doorstep. She would slip the bags into the oversized cooler on our porch, careful not to disturb our day. Then she'd drive away. No need for thanks. No interruption. Just grace in motion.

There was a breast milk bank in Kalamazoo, nearly three hours away. They charged $4.15 per ounce for milk that had been tested and pasteurized. It was good milk, safe milk. But it wasn't *this* milk. This milk, Jayden's milk, came from women who asked for nothing. Women who gave what they could, whenever they could.

I reached out to a few companies that sold milk storage bags and bottles for breastfeeding moms. Within weeks, one company donated a full case. 205 four-ounce bottles, delivered to our door. All for Jayden's Pumpin' Mamas. The next day, more boxes arrived: another company had sent hundreds of breast milk storage bags, samples of nipple cream, and a stack of coupons. We started sharing these supplies with our donors, hoping to thank them in some small way. Many declined. "Pass it on," they told us. "Give it to another mama who might need it more."

Their selflessness staggered me. They weren't just part of Jayden's story; they were part of her survival. They will always hold a piece of my heart.

---

It was the second week of September when we returned to see Jayden's infectious disease doctor, Dr. Matthias.

And just like Dr. Earles predicted, he wanted more tests. But before ordering anything, he examined her thoroughly. He moved her tiny limbs with slow precision, listening and observing closely. Every motion showed how aware he was of her fragility.

Jayden didn't make a sound. She just lay there, watching him work. Her eyes studied his, as if she were curious about what he might find.

After several minutes he ordered a full ultrasound panel: her heart, fontanel, liver, spleen, and kidneys. He requested X-rays of her chest and legs. He reviewed the fourteen labs Dr. Earles had already prescribed and added seventeen more of his own.

I remembered his early commitment to her case. How he drove across town to meet with Dr. Earles before ever seeing Jayden, just to read through every page of her NICU records. He wanted to be ready. He wanted to understand. John and I were both impressed. Maybe even a little relieved.

Progress. Small, but meaningful. We'd done our part. We'd carried her this far. Maybe now this new team of doctors could shoulder some of the weight. Jayden was in good hands. And for the first time in a long time, she didn't feel like ours alone.

---

I FINALLY FELT free enough to make a few phone calls. Friends. Family. From the start they had supported our decision to say yes to care for this fragile baby. They understood why I didn't have the time or energy to talk. John had done his best to keep everyone updated. Quick calls between flights. A few lines over dinner while I rocked in my chair, balancing baby and plate.

Our youngest daughters, Casey and Emily, had recently graduated from college and moved out of state. I called them first. I wanted to hear about work, their apartments, what they were cooking for dinner. It comforted me just to hear their voices.

Our oldest daughter, Kelly, and her husband were preparing to move from Denver to Portland. They'd planned to stay with my son Andy while they made the transition. They were excited. I was... trying not to hover. They were grown.

Andy was still in Milwaukee, the city we'd called home for fifteen years before moving to Detroit. He invited us to visit for Christmas. He wanted us to see his new place.

I missed them. All of them.

And I would've loved to spend the holidays together, hot cocoa in hand, babies on laps. But with Jayden, I didn't know what the future held. She had started rolling over, a beautiful, delayed triumph. But she was still fragile, still insulin-dependent, and still a mystery. I was afraid to hope she'd be strong enough to travel by Christmas.

Still, those calls refilled a part of me I hadn't realized was running empty. I loved being their mama. And somehow, being a foster mama felt like an extension of that same love. Some days, the sound of their voices was the closest thing to rest I knew.

My mom and Aunt Ethel were thrilled to hear my voice sounding steadier. They'd been worrying about me, just as I'd been worrying about Jayden. Back when things felt most dire, I'd made tearful, frantic calls to both of them, calls I feared might be our last about Jayden. Now, with her doing a little better, I reached out again.

My mom reminded me of something I said during one of those early calls. I told her I was scared I might end up in jail, because I was ready to start feeding Jayden donated breast milk even without the state's permission. She said I'd sounded panicked. Torn.

"I just didn't think we had time to wait for approval," I admitted.

We shook our heads and laughed, grateful it hadn't come to that. Before we hung up, I asked her to keep praying. For wisdom. For strength.

For Jayden.

A FEW DAYS after receiving the lab orders from Dr. Matthias, I called Nicole to begin the process of scheduling appointments and getting state authorization for the next round of procedures.

The bloodwork didn't require an appointment, but it would require guts. Just the thought of putting Jayden through another blood draw made my stomach turn. We knew what we were up against and requested special handling again.

When we arrived at the lab, the pediatric team who'd drawn her blood last time refused to try again. Her veins were too delicate. It had been too difficult. But one of the techs had a different idea. "What about the PICU chief nurse?" she suggested. A quick call confirmed the chief nurse from the Pediatric Intensive Care Unit was in a meeting, but would be available in an hour.

When the nurse finally arrived, she didn't waste time. Within minutes, she had a stretchy band around Jayden's little head.

"The scalp vein," she explained. "It's our best option for her."

I squeezed John's hand. I knew the NICU nurses often

used this method, because when babies were this sick, other veins just didn't hold. But it seemed so violent, so desperate. Were we slipping back? PICU nurse? NICU care? Was this where we were headed again? I took a deep breath.

John pulled me close, his arm around my back. "It'll be okay, honey." I felt his words more than heard them, soft and warm in my ear. "We can do this. She can do this."

I blinked away the panic and stepped back toward the exam table, leaning over Jayden and giving her a big, upside-down smile. Carefully pinning her arms beneath mine as instructed. It still felt extreme. Then, with sure hands, the nurse slid the needle into a prominent vein in Jayden's scalp. I closed my eyes.

"All done," she said.

It didn't even take a minute. A clean, successful draw. No blown veins. No repeated pokes. No screaming. Then the previous blood draws flashed in my memory, every botched blood draw since we left the NICU.

Why hadn't anyone done this before? Maybe it was extreme. But so was her condition. I knew right then this would be our go-to method from now on. Even if it made me queasy, even if it broke my heart to watch. What other choice did we have?

---

THE APPOINTMENTS for Jayden's imaging were scheduled for that same afternoon. I stayed with her through the ultrasounds and X-rays, lead apron secured across my chest. The exam table was cold and hard, but I kept her calm by singing softly and stroking her arm. I scooped her up to snuggle between scans.

It was a long, brutal day. By evening, her glucometer read 425. Her body was reeling from the stimulation, and we had to give her higher doses of insulin to bring it back down. Another reminder of how unstable she still was and how little it took to tip her.

Not long after completing the labs, Dr. Matthias's office called with the results. Jayden was asleep on my chest when I answered. I shifted the phone to my shoulder and grabbed my notebook. Parts of what he said were encouraging.

"The echocardiogram looked great," he said. "Her heart is functioning beautifully."

I pulled her in, cheek to hair, and breathed in her soft lavender scent.

"And her urine is normal too," he continued. "But her stool sample shows she's not absorbing nutrients properly. That may explain the slow weight gain." He paused, then added, "Something isn't working the way it should. Either her body isn't breaking things down, or it's not getting what it needs from what she's taking in."

It shouldn't have surprised me, but hearing it spoken aloud felt sharper than I expected.

"I'd like to move forward with a lumbar puncture and an MRI," he explained. "Both would require general anesthesia."

He said the lumbar puncture was to confirm that the congenital syphilis had cleared, that the early antibiotics had done enough.

After *anesthesia,* the rest slipped past me. His next words blurred into a distant hum. Everything went still. I realized I wasn't breathing. I thanked him, then immediately called Dr. Earles. She listened closely, then responded with calm certainty: "I want her to gain a bit more weight first," she said. "Let's give her a better cushion before we put her under."

I agreed completely. She relayed the recommendation to Dr. Matthias, and thankfully, he was on board. They were working together now: listening, weighing every step, fully invested in the same fragile child. A team we could trust.

People who saw what we saw: a little girl worth fighting for.

Dr. Earles also had an idea to help with the nutrient absorption. She suggested digestive enzymes.

"They're simple to administer," she said. "Open the capsule and sprinkle the beads on her tongue before she feeds."

It sounded simple. But giving them to her? Not so much. The moment the granules hit Jayden's tongue, she gagged. I followed with the bottle nipple as fast as I could, hoping it would help her swallow. At best, half the dose went in.

By day two, she was vomiting after feedings. And then she stopped eating altogether. For ten hours, she refused the bottle. Panic set in. No food meant dehydration and weight loss. Setbacks we couldn't afford. And then the color changes started. Her face and her bottom turned faint at first, then darker just like in July during the corn syrup reaction.

I called Dr. Earles again.

"She's vomiting after the enzymes," I said. "And now she's refusing her bottles."

She paused, then exhaled slowly. "I was afraid of that," she said. "It's not unheard of." She sounded disappointed, but not surprised. We were running out of options, and she knew it.

We had to find a way for Jayden's body to absorb

what it needed to live. We just hadn't figured out how. I turned to Dr. Nancy, our naturopath. I showed her the rash on Jayden's bottom. The shadowy circles around her eyes. She studied Jayden's face closely.

"Like a mask," she said, gesturing around her eyes. "A masquerade mask, the kind that covers just here."

I nodded. "Yes, exactly." I told her about the vomiting. The feeding battles. The enzymes we still couldn't give her.

Dr. Nancy listened attentively. She agreed that Jayden's system was still far too reactive. Her plan was to begin slowly, to start by desensitizing Jayden to sugar-based allergens.

"One day," she said, "her tiny body might accept the enzymes. But first, we have to help her body feel safe."

We left the appointment with no magic fix, no sudden breakthrough. Just a fragile plan, and a fragile little girl.

Just us. Still here. Holding on. Holding her. Showing up. One bottle, one breath, one impossible day at a time.

---

JAYDEN CONTINUED DRINKING DONATED breast milk every two to three hours. Some feeds barely reached an ounce. Others climbed toward three. Each one kept her here.

Diaper. Reading. Injection. Feeding.

Ten counts. Nipple out. Ten counts. Nipple in.

She had regular Early On sessions, with Miss Pam visiting three times a week for an hour at a time. Her visits came at different times of day, but she was always on time. I could set my watch to her light knock on the door, her warm greeting. Some days, if her visit fell at the end of her workday, she lingered a bit longer, sharing a bit more play and a few more stories, for Jayden and for me.

I welcomed it. Especially on the days John was gone. His new schedule now included more overnight flights, and those stretches felt too long. Some days, she was the only person who saw how hard we were trying.

Miss Pam would tell me about her college-aged son, her twin daughters, their family vacations. Small stories from a life that still included restaurants and road trips and college move-in days. When there were no appointments, I craved adult conversation.

Miss Pam tracked Jayden's progress: the small arcs, the tiny victories, the way her eyes followed a toy across the room. But she noticed other things too: the dark circles under mine, the stack of dishes, the weight of it all. And she stayed.

As she spoke, the room seemed to widen. The air lifted. Jayden watched her closely, often reaching for her hand, her scarf, her smile, kicking her legs in a rhythm all her own. It was a small window into the outside world.

Some days, I wasn't sure who needed her more. Some days, it was everything.

# October 2009

Jayden received weekly treatments from Nurse Kay, our reiki therapist. I wasn't sure they made a noticeable difference in her day-to-day health, but I understood the concept and appreciated Kay's commitment.

Dr. Nancy continued her weekly naturopathic treatments. I held Jayden on my lap while she slid vials into Jayden's sock and began her work. She tracked a long list of variables, some familiar to me, many not. But there were no side effects, and Jayden stayed calm in my arms. That was enough for me to keep going.

Healing would be slow.

Jayden was no longer on oxygen or the apnea monitor. Without the hiss and beeping, our days felt lighter. We no longer had to lug equipment to every appointment, and the family room was finally free of machines and cords. I could move freely, grab a bottle from the fridge, and let Dudley outside without stepping over wires or checking monitors.

Dudley, for his part, was thrilled. Every time I laid

Jayden on her blanket, he perked up, like he'd been given a job. He always seemed to protect her in his own doggy way, but now he listened to her coos and watched her kick. And whenever I squeaked her rainbow-colored butterfly, his ears shot up, waiting to see if I'd toss it his way.

Jayden was doing better with me leaving the room for a few minutes at a time. She no longer struggled when I laid her down. I'd prop her in her bouncy seat so she could see me while I rushed around finishing what needed two hands. For everything else, I slipped her into the ring sling, and managed with one.

Nights were the same. I continued doing as much skin-to-skin care as she seemed to need. Bedtime was still the two of us. Sometimes three, if Dudley joined, curled up with us in the recliner, a sheet beneath us and pillows under my arms, the chair creaking whenever I shifted. Jayden would rest on my chest, just as she had from the beginning.

The only difference now? She insisted on burrowing her face into the crook of my chin, her arms cinched tight around my neck. She held me. I patted her bottom and sang *"You Are My Sunshine,"* until her breathing settled into sleep.

All night long, I pricked her heel, tested before every feeding, then gave insulin according to the chart in my spiral notebook. Jayden's glucometer readings still spiked when she was stressed, especially at her appointments. But her times with Dr. Nancy and Miss Pam? She loved those. She was becoming sociable, lighting up whenever she saw a familiar face.

The occupational therapist made the call to pause Jayden's therapy for the winter, concerned that germ exposure wasn't worth the small gains we were seeing so far. I agreed. One cold could change everything.

But that didn't mean our schedule got easier. Jayden still had a full slate of specialists; nearly every day brought someone new, something critical. Between appointments, breast milk deliveries arrived. Jayden still needed to eat every two hours, day and night. I was tired. A constant, grinding tired that settled beside me, blurring the edges of each day.

I didn't mind the exhaustion or the constant appointments. Not even the ever-present worry. I was in love. Somewhere between the feedings and appointments, the early mornings and long nights, I realized something extraordinary was happening right in front of me. This little girl had changed my life.

I had always believed. I had heard stories, the ones passed along in waiting rooms and late-night calls. I believed them. I just never stood this close. I had been given so much already. A good husband and four healthy kids with remarkable spirits. More than I ever thought to ask for.

And now, with Jayden, something unexplainable was happening. Quiet, but unmistakable. She was changing people. Softening them. Stirring something they hadn't felt in a long time. Even people who hadn't met her. Friends of friends who only knew her as a name on a prayer list. And the handful of people who found themselves in my kitchen, backs against the counters, asking to hear her story and not really knowing why.

I shared what I could, what I was legally allowed to share, because they deserved to know what their kindness was making possible.

And all the while, Jayden simply lived her small life. Every coo. Every squeal. Every kick of her little legs. Her spirit was vibrant. Exuberant. Somehow it reached past the charts and diagnoses, cut through the noise of people's lives, and touched something that hurt when they listened.

Watching it all unfold around me changed me, too.

I had heard the saying all my life:

"Good things come in small packages."

Now I knew some of the very best ones do.

---

JAYDEN HAD her very first pediatric ophthalmology appointment today, with a new doctor in a new building. Since we weren't familiar with the location, John dropped us off at the front. I had Jayden snug in the ring sling before stepping out of the back seat, and I handed the diaper bag to John to carry after he parked.

Jayden and I started down the long hallway toward the suite. As we walked, an elderly couple approached me and asked again if I was carrying a baby doll. I smiled and pulled the sling cover back a bit so they could see her adorable face.

Jayden quickly caught their gaze. First, the woman's, then the man's. She smiled at them, eyes twinkling, then kept switching her gaze between them, grinning each time. They oohed and aahed over her, charmed by the way she locked eyes with them, as if she were in on the conversation. I wished them a good day and made my way toward John, closing the last few steps between us just as he held the door open for us.

The front desk staff welcomed us warmly and led us to a private exam room, away from the waiting area and other children. There were the usual anatomical charts on the wall, illustrations of eyeballs and tear ducts. But most of the room was cheerfully decorated. Big Bird, Bert, and Ernie plushies sat on shelves. A bright rubber ball rested in the corner. A small stack of children's books lay neatly in a bin.

John and I exchanged a quick glance.

"How in the world is this doctor going to figure out what she can actually see?" I whispered.

He nodded, smiling. "I guess we'll find out."

An earlier eye exam had confirmed her eyes were structurally healthy, that much I understood. But how well could she see? I didn't know.

Jayden sat on my lap as the doctor examined her eyes. He gave her a stuffed Elmo to hold, then leaned in, the brightness of his headlamp catching the sparkle in her gaze. After several minutes, he sat back and said, "Her eyes are healthy, but she is farsighted and she has an astigmatism."

I nodded, trying to absorb it. It wasn't blindness. It could have been worse, but it was still hard to hear. Our nine-pound baby girl needed glasses.

Finding glasses that small proved to be its own challenge. The state only covered a handful of approved frames, none of which were remotely suited for a baby who had just started rolling over. I worried about nose pads digging into her eyes, miniature screws working loose in the metal hinges, the weight of them pressing on her tender face.

Eventually, I found a pair online: pink, soft silicone frames designed for newborns. I submitted the request to our agency, asking if they could cover the cost. To my surprise, they agreed. Jayden had her first pair of glasses before Halloween. They were bright, flexible, impossibly small. Just like her.

In our home, milestone birthdays are cause for celebration. Three months, six months, nine months. We mark each one with professional photos. It's always been our belief that every child deserves to have pictures from their earliest days. Tangible proof that they were loved and cherished. When a child left our care, whether reunited with their birth family or adopted, we made sure to send those photos along. A gift for their forever story.

We missed Jayden's three-month session. Her condition had been far too critical. But I was determined not to miss her six-month milestone. I called ahead to explain her medical fragility and requested the earliest appointment possible, before the store even opened, so we could avoid crowds and minimize exposure.

One of my small joys was taking foster babies shopping, hunting the clearance racks for the cutest outfits. Several salesclerks knew me by name. They'd fuss over each baby I carried in my sling, and I'd happily let them. But I hadn't been to the store for months.

So I called my next-door neighbor, Amy. Her daughter was two months older than Jayden, so I asked if she had anything I could borrow. She kindly pulled out a bin of retired baby clothes and found the perfect thing: an adorable leopard-print dress with a ribbed knit shirt underneath. I laid it across Jayden. It was perfect. I packed it in the diaper bag, planning to dress her once we got to the portrait studio.

John and I arrived early, Jayden snug in her carrier. We waited outside until the lights flickered on and the door unlocked.

This was more than a photo session. It felt like a declaration: Jayden is here. Jayden is loved. Someday, when someone asks where her story began, there will be something to show them.

The time came to get Jayden dressed. I started with the shirt. Then I pulled the dress over Jayden's head, watching as it slipped off her tiny body. It was much too big. I checked the tag again: 0–3 months.

Jayden was six months old.

I looked at the photographer and smiled sheepishly. "Do you think we could just do a close-up with the shirt?" She agreed, but her loud voice startled Jayden, who burst into tears.

Out of nineteen photos, I chose one. Tears clung to her lashes, her expression somber. Yet her cheeks were soft, her ebony skin glowing, her gaze holding the camera without fear.

Eyes that could see. That was enough.

---

I FINALLY HAD a moment to sort through the bin of fall clothes. Newborn sizes still fit Jayden perfectly.

To document the month, I propped her in the corner of the sofa for a quick picture. Before I could settle on the floor across from her, Dudley jumped up and nestled beside his little girl. There were no studio lights, just our worn sofa and the afternoon sun. I snapped a few as Jayden leaned toward him, her small hand reaching for a fistful of his curls. I clicked again just in time to catch the connection. One more frame for her forever story, right before Dudley decided he had enough and hopped down.

Later, looking through the pictures, something caught me off guard. Dudley weighed just twenty pounds, but in the photo he looked nearly three times her size.

Sometimes the truth in those pictures hit me harder than any lab result could.

I'd grown used to caring for Jayden. Used to her slow progress. But then I'd hear it again:

*Just hold her.*

The words from that first call didn't let go. Was that still our mission?

Jayden was doing better. Her body was no longer gray, no longer limp. She looked healthy. Her skin was vibrant, her limbs waking up to the world. But then I'd weigh her, watch her sleep just a breath too still, see her startle without warning. A flicker of doubt would rise. And I'd wonder, was I holding on to hope or ignoring a truth I didn't want to face?

# November 2009
## — Part One

Lately, I caught myself wondering something I wasn't ready to say out loud: *What if she stays?*

Jayden had begun sitting with more stability, her back slightly straighter, almost rolling over. Hope crept in on small milestones like that. Each visit from Miss Pam felt like a celebration: stacking rings, trading giggles, watching Jayden sneak glances toward the blue quilted bag, waiting to see what treasure Miss Pam might pull out next.

I always looked forward to her sessions. Miss Pam was quick to offer support and made space for the harder things: the unspoken worries about Jayden's future, the ache of not knowing how this would end, the fear that loving her this much might break me later. She admitted, more than once, that Jayden was stealing more of her heart each time.

Sometimes, after the hour-long session, Miss Pam would feed Jayden while I snuck away to the kitchen for a quick dinner. Other times, she stayed longer, helping me prepare for the next day or just listening when the emotions got tangled. She became part of our rhythm.

Occasionally, Miss Pam brought other specialists to support Jayden's development. It took time for Jayden to warm up to every new person. She was afraid to trust anyone, clinging to me, begging for reassurance. She'd been hurt by new faces before and counted on me to tell her when someone was safe. I learned to read her: the worried brow, the way her breathing grew shallower whenever new situations stirred her anxiety.

These new Early On specialists gave Jayden a chance to learn to trust others. Especially when she saw Dudley lapping up attention from the women sitting on the floor. If Dudley approved, she usually did too.

Miss Sarah worked on her oral coordination, coaxing small movements from Jayden's mouth with a patience that felt almost playful.

Miss Marsha came once a month to work on large motor skills, a phrase that made us both smile when we looked at Jayden. Marsha showed me how to use props to help Jayden lift her tummy into a crawling position. She encouraged me to try the jumper to strengthen her legs and build a sense of independence.

Marsha coached me through each step. We wrapped a blanket around Jayden's torso, tucked stuffed animals beside her so she wouldn't slip through the wide leg openings, and eased her into the jumper. She went still, wide-eyed. Once she realized she was safe, she opened up. She bounced. Then she jumped. Her eyes locked on mine as if to ask, *Am I still okay?* I nodded, clapped softly, and she kept going. She bounced for both of us.

As we celebrated Jayden's small victory, we kept our promises. We showed up for court. John drove to the hearing while I stayed home for Jayden's session with Miss Sarah.

She brought silicone bulbs with handles and showed me how to help Jayden grasp them and bring them to her mouth: small, playful movements meant to strengthen her tongue. It was a quiet milestone, a hint at progress. Miss Sarah wanted us to practice several times a day.

When John returned, I searched his face. He exhaled slowly. "The judge had the DNA results," he said. "She terminated all parental rights." I nodded. We'd expected this. But the finality still felt heavy. From then on, the case would be reviewed every three months by a referee. It sounded like more paperwork, but that wasn't the moment that stayed with John. It was what happened at the end.

Jayden's case worker, Nicole, made a plea, asking the judge not to rush Jayden's placement. She explained how disruptive transitions can be, especially for fragile children like Jayden, who was still labeled "failure to thrive" and remained insulin-dependent. John said Nicole's voice cracked with emotion, and the judge listened. She agreed and had it entered into the court record. John's voice trembled as he told me the rest. He said the judge looked directly at him and smiled.

That was it. That was the moment we hadn't dared imagine. Someone in power finally saw what we saw. Not a case. Not a diagnosis. A child. A life worth protecting. Our Deedle girl.

BACK HOME, the world returned to our routine. Jayden's feedings were still entirely donated breast milk. I cradled her, eyes locked with hers, rocking as I sang the same silly songs she'd come to expect.

*"Hickory Dickory Dock."*

*"Hey Deedle Deedle, the cat and the fiddle."*

I kept time by patting her bottom and rocking the chair. Sometimes, mid-suck, she'd pause to flash a smile.

John joked that she was laughing at the old woman singing nursery rhymes as if she were onstage. But I believe it was something more. She knew we were connected. Knew I was hers. That this slow rocking and these silly songs belonged just to us. Whatever the reason, those mid-suck grins melted me every single time.

Feeding her was still painstaking work. With Courtenay's help, I discovered Jayden refused milk high in lipase. There was no simple way to test for it at home. Jayden was the measure. If she pulled away or struggled, I knew. I started passing those bags back to Courtenay so the milk could help other babies. She once explained how to scald the milk to deactivate the lipase, but I didn't have the bandwidth. We were blessed with more than enough. If that ever changed, I would reconsider.

For now, Jayden was fed. She was content. During those feedings, she looked at me with her sparkling eyes, and I felt it again. Chosen. Honored. Loved.

---

LIFE MOVED FORWARD THROUGH QUIET, tender visits. Murielle and Elias stopped by with some home-made pastries. I figured they were there mostly so Murielle could hold Jayden again. I hadn't realized Elias specifically asked to see Dudley.

Jayden perched calmly in Murielle's lap, eyes fixed on me the whole time, doing her best to be brave. Meanwhile, Dudley was in heaven, chasing the ball Elias kept tossing into the kitchen.

When they got up to leave, Murielle handed Jayden back to me. She nestled into my shoulder and snuggled closer than she had in days. But when I laid her on the changing table for her bottle and insulin, her lip trembled. Her blood sugar was elevated. Her body had worked hard to make it through that visit.

I rocked and sang to soothe her as her breathing slowed against my chest. Holding her, I realized that what felt joyful and lively to us might have flooded Jayden's sensitive nervous system. Next time, I would let her lead.

THAT AFTERNOON, we turned our attention to logistics. I was grateful to Miss Pam for staying after her session. It was a rare window for me to shower and tackle the stack of paperwork on the counter.

Half-distracted, I flipped through the bills until I saw it. It was the form from Jeannette, our adoption worker. She'd left it on her last visit and I'd set off to the side. I hadn't forgotten it. It was simple on the surface with just one question.

*"Now that Jayden is legally available, do you want to adopt her?"*

Both birth parents' rights were now terminated. Now it was our turn. Our choice. John and I prayed and talked, turning it over again and again. He was sixty-two. I was fifty-six. Our four kids were grown. The youngest was twenty-three.

We loved Jayden so deeply we knew we had to let her

go. She deserved a future unburdened by our age and limits. Parents who could crawl with her, chase her, and show up with the energy her growth demanded.

John had already signed the form without hesitation. I picked up the pen, my hand shaking slightly. I added my name beneath his, then paused. In small, careful handwriting, I added a line:

*"Unless she has no permanent home by the time she is two years old."*

If no family chose her, if her needs kept her from being adopted, I didn't want her drifting through the system. If she needed us, we would still be here.

There was no ceremony. Just ink and paper. As the envelope sealed, something in me settled.

Not peace. A pause. In that pause, just enough room for hope to breathe. We hadn't meant to fall in love. We hadn't meant to imagine the future. Still, we did.

We told the truth: we couldn't adopt. We meant it. That didn't mean we knew how to say goodbye. So we held her close. Rocked her through the night. Waiting for the answer to a question that kept rewriting everything:

*What if she stays?*

# November 2009 — Part Two

Thanksgiving paused the appointments, but not Jayden's progress. She accepted her glasses, and Miss Pam believed they were helping her respond better during their sessions. I kept a basket of toys and books beside my chair so that learning could continue all day. Jayden embraced every new discovery. Everything went straight into her mouth, a milestone I recognized and quietly celebrated. By mid-month, she sprouted her first tooth, gnawing on anything I handed her, clutching toys on her own, even shaking a rattle.

Miss Pam had made real progress helping Jayden roll over, but we were eager for her to sit on her own. Miss Pam used an infant support seat to mimic a classroom, Jayden propped up like a tiny student at her desk. But the support seat had room for two of her, so she kept sliding sideways. A few burp cloths rolled up around her helped keep her more upright, freeing Miss Pam from catching her every few seconds.

Around his Deedle girl, John's pilot precision gave way to soft eyes, a light voice, and effortless laughter. He sat cross-legged on the floor, gently rolling Jayden back and forth on a beach ball, her little body wobbling with each pass. It was therapy to strengthen her neck muscles, but she didn't know that. To her, it was just fun with Papa John. He read her books in a singsong voice that made every page feel like a lullaby. Then he took her hand to point at every brightly colored picture.

"Here is Deedle's ball. And this is Deedle's duck."

Jayden was mesmerized for minutes at a time. John could've stayed there for hours.

He told everyone about her, sharing her tiny triumphs like front-page news. The pilots he flew with knew every update, reciting her quirks and progress with the kind of affection usually reserved for family, even though they hadn't met her.

Cindy, the dispatcher, tried to keep John based at home when she could. Whenever he called in with another Jayden update, her jolly laugh crackled through the receiver.

Everyone loved Jayden.

---

By mid-November, fall fully settled in; cool air drifting through the house, colorful leaves rustling on the porch. The Thanksgiving season had always marched to a well-practiced cadence of family, food, and football.

We were big Michigan fans. Saturdays had been reserved for football since we moved here, when Kelly, our oldest daughter, transferred to the University of Michigan. I'm pretty sure John was just as excited as she was. He took her to a game that first year and never looked back, keeping the tradition alive every fall of her college career.

When Emily, our youngest, followed Kelly to Michigan and joined the marching band, our fandom rose to another level. We weren't just parents anymore; we were season ticket holders, tailgaters, band parents who knew the pageantry by heart. John took anyone he could to every home game, pointing out Emily on the field, "That's my girl."

I stayed close behind the scenes, packing snacks, planning routes, joining them at games when it wasn't too cold. It wasn't a stretch for us. We'd been doing this for years, cheering from high school bleachers as each of our four kids marched across the field. Kelly and Casey even rose to be drum majors. We loved football, sure. We loved the marching band more. But mostly, we loved showing up.

And the Michigan Marching Band? That was something else entirely. Back then, our Saturdays began before sunrise: watching rehearsals, catching the percussion step show, eating hot sausage sandwiches from the cart near Revelli Hall. Then the energy inside the Big House wrapped around us. And of course, after the game, we stayed for the Fifth Quarter. The band played on as the crowd lingered, the stadium still buzzing.

Now Emily was living in Madison, working on her graduate degree, and our Saturdays looked different. We still watched the games. We still cheered. The fight song drifting through the TV carried years of memories.

*"Now for a cheer they are here, triumphant!"*

I curled up on the couch beside John, grateful for the rhythm of it, something familiar in a life that had become anything but. By the third quarter, I usually dozed off, Jayden cuddled against my chest, as always.

But as we watched that Saturday before Thanksgiving, soaking in the comfort of the ritual, my mind wandered.

This Thanksgiving would be different. No clatter in the kitchen, no guest room made up, no kids calling from the road to say they were almost home. The front door would stay closed: no knock, no whirlwind of coats and crockpots, no well-meaning relatives reaching for Jayden's cheeks. We loved them, but this year love meant keeping everyone away. We couldn't risk it.

I hadn't cooked a real dinner in months. Most days, I grabbed slices of ham and cheese and called it lunch. In the early weeks with Jayden, even that felt ambitious. But John made sure I ate when he was home, quietly placing a plate in front of me, no fuss.

This year, he didn't ask what I wanted to do. He ordered a turkey breast from a local restaurant, complete with stuffing and mashed potatoes. Then he made a Costco run for diapers and a pumpkin pie. It wasn't the meal that steadied me. It was the way he lifted the weight without a word.

I used to count the days to Thanksgiving by recipes and guest lists. This year, I measured it in ounces and glucose checks. The house was quieter now. The stadiums, the cheering, and the chaos of holidays past all lived in my memories. This fall brought something new. A tiny heartbeat. A new kind of cheering. A different kind of Thanksgiving.

JOHN DROVE us to as many appointments as he could, working around his flight schedule. Jayden's routine hadn't changed much, a similar rhythm, just with a bit more ease now that the equipment was gone. Sometimes she even slept a little longer at night.

I didn't.

Since June 25, I'd spent my nights in the rocker with Jayden on my chest. I got up for thirty-minute feedings every two hours. It made sense to stay close to the fridge, close to her bottles and insulin. Easier than climbing out of bed and stumbling down the hall and down the stairs.

I wondered what it would take to move back upstairs, to sleep in a real bed again. We already had a crib set up on my side of the bed, but I had questions: where would I keep the insulin cold? How would I warm the milk? Could Jayden sleep in a crib without dropping her blood sugar or struggling to breathe?

It wasn't just the logistics. I knew what happened when I didn't hold her. In those first weeks, her fragile body had shown me how quickly it could shut down without warning. No change in her face, no gasping or flailing — just pretty, peaceful, and quietly slipping in the wrong direction. The monitors told the truth long before I could see it. Her glucose climbed whenever I wasn't near her, numbers spiking while she still looked happy and beautiful in my arms. Now there was no apnea alarm to jolt me awake if something went wrong. Laying her flat in a crib, unable to prop her with blankets for fear of breaking protocol, felt less like a bedtime routine and more like a test I wasn't sure we'd both pass.

She had been off oxygen and the apnea monitor for weeks now. So I focused on figuring out the logistics, and pretended it was only that.

I decided to start after Thanksgiving, after our mini-feast and a full weekend of football. And maybe, just maybe, I'd get to snuggle with my husband again. For five months, we were in survival mode, passing responsibilities back and forth with practiced precision. We were a team. It was the only reason we made it this far. But now I wanted more than teamwork. I wanted to feel his arms around me. To finally exhale. To sleep.

---

LATE THANKSGIVING NIGHT, after the meal, after all the games, after Jayden fell asleep clinging to my chest and long after John had gone to bed, I stayed up. I reviewed my notebook from the beginning. November had brought a regular rhythm. Appointments, yes, but nothing major. No lab work, no unexplained spikes in stress, no crashes. Jayden seemed balanced this month. She was ready. And maybe I was too. It was time for the next step.

Saturday night, we went upstairs as planned. I used the same cooler from the diaper bag to keep Jayden's insulin chilled. I stocked a second, smaller cooler with breast milk on ice. I brought one warm bottle ready to go.

When she woke, I grabbed the bottle I'd already warmed. After she finished, I slipped a cold one from the cooler and set it near the heat vent on the floor. I'd lay a towel over it to trap the warmth. By the time she stirred again, the milk was ready. It was heated by the vent humming under the floorboards. It was a makeshift method, but in that room survival was the only protocol that mattered.

Upstairs, the crib sat on my side of the bed, but the rocking chair in the corner waited for us. Jayden and I settled there again and again while John slept beside us. I worried my stirring would wake him. Instead, his breathing anchored me.

---

THE RHYTHM TOOK ROOT, and so did my confidence. Each time I woke, I moved through our steps with practiced choreography: diaper, reading, injection, feeding. I'd hold her on my chest and rock her back to sleep. I no longer needed to second-guess whether this was the right time. It *was* the right time.

Could I have managed this a month ago? I honestly didn't think so. Jayden hadn't signaled her readiness. My body hadn't yet recovered enough. My spirit hadn't caught up to the demands.

But now we were here. Upstairs. In our bedroom. My hand could still reach her crib without leaving the bed. My heart hurt while learning to rest. With her so close and not in my arms, my chest felt hollow, as if my body still believed the first rule:

*Just hold her.*

It wasn't the bed. It was the small, unfamiliar hope shifting in me. This wasn't a holding pattern anymore. We were beginning to live. Not in full, not yet. But enough. Enough to hope. Enough to sleep for two-hour stretches and wake with a grace I hadn't felt in a long time.

Jayden was stable. I was settling in. And for the first time in five months, the night felt gentle. Not because anything was easy. But because we were still here, still together, and still finding a way. And for now, that was everything.

# December 2009

In our home, every little girl leaves with a "dolly" of her own. Something tender and meant for her alone, a comfort she could carry into whatever came next. By early December, I knew I wanted Jayden's Christmas gift to be that dolly. I didn't know where she would spend her next Christmas, but I knew she would have one that looked like her and fit in her hands.

Finding it was harder. Jayden was doing better, but we still had to limit her exposure. During her naps, with her tiny body curled against my chest, I searched online for a small Black baby doll. Something age-appropriate, safe for an eight-month-old who weighed only ten pounds.

I mentioned the doll search to a few of the Pumpin' Mamas during milk drop-offs, and to a couple of friends in passing. What I didn't know was that Miss Pam had taken it to heart. Of course, she was the first to find one: a bathtime doll with warm brown skin and a subtle, powdery scent. Just the right size for Jayden's hands. Miss Pam even brought a miniature baby bottle so Jayden could pretend to feed her dolly. Jayden wasn't sure what to make of it at first. She stared at the doll, touched it to her face, then pulled her close. Miss Pam beamed.

Another friend found an old-fashioned cloth doll in a deep brown, with black yarn hair and a painted face. She was soft all over, perfect for snuggling. Jayden loved resting her cheek against it, eyes fluttering as she pressed into the comforting fabric. Both dolls were lovely, but it was the way my friends saw her, and somehow saw us too, that stayed with me.

Still, I kept looking. One night, I found one on eBay: a small Black doll, seven inches tall, in white corduroy overalls with angel wings stitched on her back. Something about her felt right. The starting bid was twenty-five cents. I bid the minimum, not expecting much. But within hours, the auction closed and she was ours.

As I filled in the shipping details, I saw a box for a message to the seller. I wrote that this doll was going to a little angel everyone expected to lose, but who was still here. A baby sent to us with no promises, who now lived and loved and shifted every heart she touched. I thanked the seller for the chance to give her something special for Christmas.

The next day, a reply appeared. The seller offered me the other two dolls in the set, identical, angel-winged, and sweet-faced, each for the same small price: twenty-five cents. I had to read the message twice. I wrote back with tears in my eyes. Yes. Yes, I would love them.

When the package arrived, there were two dolls in plastic sleeves and a third wrapped carefully in Christmas paper. Taped to the wrapped doll was a handwritten card:

*Jayden,*
*Please accept this dolly as my Christmas gift to you.*
*May God continue to bless you!*

I pressed the card to my chest for a moment before

sliding it back into the package. I wrapped one of the other angel dollies and helped Jayden give it to Miss Pam for Christmas. A tender gift from a beloved baby girl to the woman whose grace lifted her, little by little, into the life waiting for her.

I slipped the third dolly into my dresser drawer, a token of this time with her, something I could hold onto long after the day we would have to let our Deedle girl go. One to send with her, and one to hold on to when my arms were empty.

---

AT HER DECEMBER PEDIATRICIAN VISIT, two and a half weeks before Christmas, our almost eight-month-old Jayden weighed ten pounds one ounce. She measured twenty-one inches long. Dr. Earles was pleased with her progress, although puzzled by how slowly Jayden was growing.

She walked into the exam room chatting about her day off, saying that while she was out running errands, she kept thinking about Jayden and wondering what might be going on. I laughed as my heart melted. More than once, Dr. Earles told us about waking in the middle of the night with a new idea. She was always thinking. Always problem-solving.

That day, she suggested we rule out cystic fibrosis. She called the lab right then and scheduled Jayden for a sweat chloride test on December 15. Jayden was still losing more nutrients than she could absorb, and Dr. Earles couldn't figure out why. There had to be a reason.

She let out a small laugh. "It's almost like she doesn't have a pancreas."

I chuckled, trying to muffle the fear rising in my throat.

The sweat chloride test wasn't difficult for Jayden. It didn't give us answers either. It ruled out cystic fibrosis. Just another door closed.

At our last appointment with Dr. Matthias, he recommended a lumbar puncture. Jayden had no immediate red flags and was finally stable enough for anesthesia. As Dr. Earles and I talked through the timing, she suggested we wait until after the holidays and use that sedation window to run every test we could. Pituitary. Pancreas. Hearing. All of it lined up on the schedule, a procession of boxes to check, one by one. For me, each test carried its own small prayer hidden inside the protocol.

Jayden was doing well in my eyes, though I still worried about her size. She was happy. Always. A calm presence cradled my arms, radiating a light that seemed to come from somewhere beyond her smallness. Her smile eased the edges of my worry.

There was so much we didn't know, and more testing was coming. But not yet. With the scans scheduled for after the holidays, and this month's medical appointments completed, I set all of it aside. I turned my focus toward Christmas.

Uncertainty would still be waiting. But we'd return with something more, a quiet strength that had been forming in us all along. For now, I chose joy. I chose presence. I chose to give Jayden a season that wasn't measured in scans or symptoms... but in music, cookies, and arms that held her close.

OUR KIDS HAD TURNED in their wish lists, and I needed to get my shopping started. Most of it I handled online, a first for me. But there was one thing my son Andy wanted that I knew I could find at the mall. I remembered exactly which store carried it and planned how I could do it safely with Jayden, who still needed to be shielded from people.

On a quiet Tuesday morning, just as the mall opened at 10:00 a.m., I pulled into a space right by the closest entrance. I slipped Jayden into my beloved baby wrap, tucking her face inward, safe and warm against my chest in her favorite curled position. I went straight to the store. No browsing. No distractions. In and out. I had just turned to leave, bag in hand, when I nearly bumped into someone.

It was Kristin, a woman we met five years earlier when she adopted one of our foster babies. She had stayed in our home back then, caring for her soon-to-be son while waiting for the state's paperwork to catch up with the bond already forming between them.

Her eyes lit up when she saw me. She reached into her purse, eager to show me a recent photo of her son. As she dug through the folds of leather, she glanced up and smiled warmly.

"And who's this little peanut?" she asked, nodding toward the small bundle pressed against me.

I hesitated. "She's very sick," I said softly. "Medically fragile. I really shouldn't have her out, but I needed to grab a gift for Andy. She's diabetic and not doing well, but she's beautiful, and she's happy."

Kristin leaned in to peek, and her eyes instantly filled with tears. She didn't ask questions. She didn't back away. She just nodded, placed her hand over her heart, and said, "Bless you. What a gift you're giving her."

We exchanged quick holiday wishes, and then she was gone, melting into the morning quiet of the mall, leaving me breathless.

I turned and headed for the car, moved by the grace of the encounter and the girl in my arms who made it all matter. Jayden slept, as if nothing in the world could touch her: not the diagnosis, not the dangers, not the days ahead that none of us could yet see.

I left the mall and stopped at the drive-through pharmacy to pick up Jayden's prescriptions. There was a bit of a wait, then my required signature. Jayden was in her rear-facing car seat. The pharmacist, who now recognized us, asked if she could take a peek at the baby girl she'd come to know. I rolled down the back window so she could see Jayden, then completed my business and made one more stop for a quick lunch at a drive-through.

By the time I got home, I noticed two large bags on my front porch. They didn't look like breast milk donations, the way most of our surprise deliveries did. In fact, they were placed a few feet away from the insulated cooler we kept out front for just that purpose. I carried the car seat inside and set it in the kitchen. Dudley trotted over and gave Jayden's cheeks a gentle kiss before I let him out. Then I opened the front door to retrieve the big, blue bags.

Inside, I found a red plaid dress perfect for Christmas. Tights. Overalls. Shirts. Socks. Decorative headbands. An adorable sweater that matched everything. And a hand-written note:

*"Merry Christmas to your little Angel!"* — *Kristin*

How? I had just seen her. We must've passed each other on the road. Somehow, in the space between two errands, she had gathered, wrapped, and delivered an entire armful of Christmas. Jayden asked nothing of the world, yet people kept finding themselves moved to answer her all the same.

---

As the holidays grew closer, I found myself aching for time with my family. It had been months since I'd seen them, and the nonstop demands of caring for Jayden were beginning to wear on me. My children have always been my priority. Some would say to a fault. Now, as young adults on their own, they were making sacrifices so I could give myself fully to this struggling baby. We still spoke regularly by phone or email, but more often than not, I was either too tired or too distracted to fully engage. They were patient and loving, always understanding.

All four children moved out of state in recent years, and I struggled with that even before we agreed to dedicate ourselves to Jayden's care. With Christmas approaching, the desire to reunite weighed heavily on my heart. Thankfully, Jayden seemed to be making progress. We were finally on steadier ground. Recently, Dr. Earles suggested reducing our visits from weekly to every other week, unless I felt she needed to be seen sooner.

At our next appointment, I asked Dr. Earles if it might be possible to travel to Wisconsin, where three of our children were living, for a Christmas visit. She thought it was a wonderful idea.

I knew it would take a lot of preparation for a six-hour trip across state lines, but I was ready. I wanted to hold my children again. I called our caseworker, Nicole, to ask permission to take Jayden out of state. She assured me she'd start the paperwork. Then I called our other daughter, Casey, who was living in New York City, and asked if she might consider flying to Wisconsin for the holiday. She happily agreed.

John requested time off work, and once it was confirmed, we began making detailed plans. We had done plenty of traveling with our four kids, ten-hour drives to visit family on holidays and summer breaks. With no relatives living nearby, the kind of everyday support most families take for granted wasn't there.

Still, when our kids were babies and I was breastfeeding, I always had everything I needed with me. Through storms, delays, or breakdowns, I had milk. Nothing to prepare. Nothing to measure. It was simply enough.

Jayden was a different story. Breast milk couldn't be picked up on the road, and she wasn't a baby who could simply be fed. Some bags she welcomed; others she rejected for reasons I never uncovered. Dates, donors, storage, none of it revealed a pattern. Now we had to pack enough for days, hoping the bags we chose would be the ones her body would accept.

Casey flew in to Detroit to help with preparations and ride with us to Milwaukee. She stayed at our home helping with Jayden as I packed for what felt like an impossible trip: a four-day Christmas celebration at my son Andy's house.

The car was stuffed with everything we needed, including two full coolers of precious breast milk packed in dry ice to keep it safe for the drive. We picked John up at the airport as his jet touched down, just in time to begin our journey west. We decided to leave that evening, hoping Jayden would sleep through most of the drive. But what we hadn't accounted for was the snow. Lake-effect flurries blowing off Lake Michigan had already begun. Within two hours of leaving the house, we were deep in what felt like a blizzard.

Without warning, Jayden threw up all over herself. John pulled into the next gas station, and I jumped out of the car, Jayden wrapped tightly in a blanket. I threw my coat over her and pulled it tight, bracing for the cold as Casey opened the door with the diaper bag over one shoulder and a clean pair of pajamas in hand.

The icy wind burned my cheeks. It was a short walk to the doors, but I found my teeth chattering by the time we entered. We rushed into the small convenience store and asked the two attendants if there was a bathroom with a changing table. They looked at each other, then at us, and shook their heads no. But they offered something better than nothing — the checkout counter near the register.

The store was empty except for the three of us and the storm pressing at the glass. Scuffed linoleum stretched toward half-stocked shelves, the air was thick with burnt coffee. Under the tired hum of fluorescent lights, we cleared a space by the register and laid Jayden on the counter, unwrapping her from her damp clothes and easing her into a clean pink terrycloth sleeper, scattered with stars.

She looked up at both of us, unbothered by the storm or the cold, her expression settling into the softest smile. Not a crib or a cradle, it was just love gathering around her. Almost like a manger, in its own strange way.

Outside, John filled the tank and walked Dudley through the knee-deep snow in the parking lot. By the time Casey and I returned to the car, they were both waiting, warmed and ready. And so, we drove on. Into the night, into the storm, and into Christmas.

WE ARRIVED at Andy's house around 1:00 a.m. Everyone was still awake, waiting to greet us and to meet Miss Jayden. Andy and my son-in-law, Adam, helped John unload the car, placing the two coolers of frozen breast milk outside in the foot of snow by the back door. Andy cleared a refrigerator shelf for Jayden's bottles and insulin.

Upstairs, I laid Jayden on the bed and began unpacking her things. Casey, Emily, and Kelly had created a cozy bedroom for us and set out a tray of freshly baked cookies. Christmas carols played softly in the background. Sugar cookie-scented candles flickered on the end tables.

For the first time in months, everyone I loved was under one roof. My husband. Our grown children. Jayden, our cherub, sitting in the middle of us as if she'd always been there.

Cookie crumbs dotted the tray. My girls' voices floated up the stairs, and Jayden's tiny hand wrapped around my finger. For a little while in that borrowed bedroom, we weren't patients or caregivers or case numbers. We were simply a family, getting ready for Christmas.

Within the joy, something stirred in me. Sacred. Still. Weeks earlier, we'd been told she wouldn't make it. We'd held her through seizures and sickness, sung to her as alarms screamed, watched her fight for every breath. Now she was awake and curious, skin rich and full of color, eyes glowing, smiling back at me as my kids took turns holding her. Admiring her. Loving her.

It was Jayden's first trip. Only the basics. No wires. No alarms. Just insulin, syringes, and breast milk. Just her. She stepped into a life we never dared imagine. She was free, if only for a moment, from all that once held her captive.

The road was uncertain, winding, and at times terrifying, but it led us here, threaded with grace and lit with love.

This was Jayden's first Christmas. I didn't know how many Christmases we would have. How many she would have. But I knew this one was to be cherished. This one was ours.

I wanted to hold onto it all. To freeze this moment, this house, this night. On the other side of it: Doctors. Diagnoses. Feeding trials. More tests. More questions. Stressful days. More sleepless nights. But not tonight. Tonight, we were here. Together. Whole in a way we hadn't felt for a long time. Jayden had come through the dark. In our own ways, we all had.

I curled up with one arm around her, the other cradling the hope slowly growing inside of me. I let the joy and fear exist together, tangled like a ribbon. I prayed, with all my heart, that every Christmas to come would find her held in the same way, surrounded by courage, joy, and the kind of love that asks for nothing in return.

Outside, the snow kept falling. Inside, we lived in that small, fragile space between fear and hope while the future waited its turn. Lying there in the dark, quiet hours as the night slowly gave way to morning, I stroked her cheek with the back of my hand. She looked up at me, warm, glowing, impossibly alive.

"Merry Christmas, Deedle girl."

# January 2010 — Part One

The holidays had given John and me a rare break. Instead of appointments and alarms, we spent our days at Andy's home, surrounded by our children. They were enamored with every little thing about Jayden.

I stepped back from the meal prep, letting the kids enjoy working together in Andy's kitchen. We played games and gathered around a keyboard to sing. Christmas carols floated in the background of nearly every activity. A few times a day, someone would bundle up and head out into the snow to retrieve bags of breast milk from the coolers.

Jayden's glucose numbers finally stabilized, but we still checked her before every feeding. She seemed more alert lately. Her eyes tracked light and shadow with intent, and she startled at sudden noises. She was gaining weight, just a bit, but enough to notice. Her thighs still felt more like folded fabric than flesh, yet a little plump began to appear at the backs of her arms, above the elbow crease. That small softness was its own victory.

Having Casey with us for a few days before and after the trip was a joy. She loved holding Jayden during naps while I focused on preparing for the weeks ahead.

Between the holidays and Jayden's hard-won gains, we coasted on a carefully held sense of progress. Thinking about the toys she might enjoy felt like a small act of hope. Even the clothes were a guess. It was surprisingly tricky to know what size to choose. Rather than guess wrong, Casey carried the bins up to the dining room, out of sight from the family room, so I could keep things close without constantly running down to the basement.

Saying goodbye to Casey was hard. After she left, it was just Jayden and me in the big, empty house. Alone. Dudley stood watch at the window, certain someone would return.

John had only been home once since we returned from Milwaukee. Only for the night, long enough to sleep, unpack, repack, and kiss his Deedle girl on the way out the door. He was thankful to have driven us to see family for Christmas. He was flying almost every day now, paying back the time they'd given him. Not out of obligation, but gratitude.

John left around 4:00 a.m., and sleep never came back. I worried about the preparation for Jayden's MRI, but more than that, I worried about the unknowns. The questions I hadn't learned how to ask yet. I sat up and watched the sun rise, a hot cup of tea in one hand, Jayden and her bottle in the other. The snow fell softly outside as the steam from my tea curled into the bright winter light. I missed him. I missed my kids. I didn't enjoy being the only one holding all of this.

WHEN JANUARY ARRIVED, I wasn't less afraid, just a little more determined to keep looking for answers. Jayden saw Dr. Earles the day before her scheduled MRI and lumbar puncture. There was a lot we needed to do to prepare. Most importantly, we had to manage her insulin carefully to keep her stable during the scheduled two-and-a-half-hour procedure.

Dr. Earles performed a thorough exam to make sure Jayden was healthy enough for anesthesia. At ten pounds fifteen ounces, she looked like the picture of health to anyone who didn't know better. She suggested I call the pediatric endocrinologist myself so I could hear directly from Dr. Sinclair how to inject Jayden's insulin before the procedures.

Debbie, one of Dr. Earles's staff members, walked me through instructions for Jayden's preparation and gave me directions to the hospital's outpatient clinic. At this point, we knew this office of angels well. Each nurse and staff member had a word for her on the way in and the way out. Small gestures that meant more than they knew.

A long chat with Stacy from Dr. Sinclair's office prepared me for what to expect with Jayden's insulin regimen the next day. She wished us well and asked that we send the diagnostic reports to their office, too.

Jayden kept them searching, always a step beyond the answers, inviting them deeper without saying a word. Something in her drew them all in.

The test would tell us if the initial dose of antibiotics in the NICU had cleared the syphilis. We might also learn something about the reasons behind her poor growth. I was eager. But mostly, I was afraid. Afraid of what they'd find. Afraid of what they wouldn't. Afraid of what I already knew deep down.

What would the MRI and the lumbar puncture reveal

about Jayden's future? Would they uncover the root of her struggles? Was Jayden still dying? Or were we on the brink of understanding how to help her live?

That week, Miss Pam came a day earlier than usual and picked up right where she left off before the holidays, encouraging Jayden to stack rings on the post. She could see my anxiety about the procedure the next day and decided to stay a little longer. It meant more than I could say.

After checking Jayden's glucometer reading, Miss Pam rocked her and fed her a bottle. We went over the plan for tomorrow: the procedure, the tests, what the doctors would be looking for. When Jayden drifted off, Miss Pam let her sleep on her chest while I began packing the diaper bag with a book and a few extra snacks for myself.

I prepared the diluted insulin we needed at the outpatient clinic, placing it in a small iced cooler, then storing it in the fridge so it would be ready to grab at 6:00 a.m. when I left for the hospital. No diluted insulin at the hospital would match Jayden's needs. If something happened to my supply, the entire procedure would need to be rescheduled.

I packed a clean sleeper to dress her in afterward, several diapers, and her favorite fuzzy blanket.

Jayden still ate every two hours through the night, but tonight would be different. She could have one last feeding at 2:00 a.m., a small exception to the usual midnight cutoff because breast milk digested so easily. Even so, she would miss at least two feedings before we left.

Miss Pam helped me problem solve. She suggested digging out a few old pacifiers Jayden hadn't used for months. I'd stopped giving them to her after realizing the sucking wore her out. In my mind, if she had the strength or desire to suck, she should be getting something with calories. But tonight, a pacifier might offer her just enough comfort to fall back asleep without food.

I sat across from Miss Pam in the matching rocker. I watched as she held Jayden close, the little girl sleeping peacefully against her chest. This little girl already touched so many lives, leaving a kind of quiet grace in each one. Maybe tomorrow would give us the answers we needed to help her live.

*Dear Lord,*
*Please help our little girl through these next hours.*

JOHN HAD another trip and would be leaving at the same time I needed to get Jayden to the hospital. I didn't think it would be a big deal. All I needed to do was drive Jayden to the outpatient entrance, bring her to the room designated by the nursing staff, give her the recommended dose of insulin, then turn her over to the nurses.

Whether John was with me or not, the hardest part would be walking away from my girl. I knew there might be obstacles. Would they struggle to get the IV placed for her fluids and medications? How long would they let her scream before offering her a break?

Amazingly, Jayden did well through the night. Better than I did. I rocked her through what would've been her 4:00 a.m. feeding and kept her close until we left for the hospital just before 6:00 a.m. I placed her in her car seat for the fifteen minutes it took to throw on my clothes and brush my teeth, and she just sat there, watching me, smiling. She wasn't a fussy baby, except when needles were involved. Otherwise, she was easygoing, especially when we were together at home.

John kissed and hugged us both, then started my car so it would be warm. He was on his way to Mexico. It was just Jayden and me, driving through the cold darkness to the hospital.

We arrived early. I walked her around the waiting area in our baby sling, hoping she might drift back to sleep, but she was much too interested in the lights and the people moving through the halls. Soon, we were escorted to her private room. I unsnapped her terry cloth sleeper, removed it, then dressed her in the miniature hospital gown given to us.

When the young anesthesiologist entered the room, he looked momentarily stunned by Jayden. She was the size of a newborn with the activity level of an eight-month-old. I recognized the expression. I'd seen it on professionals before.

I explained that I had followed orders and given her the reduced dose of insulin before we left, and she hadn't eaten since 2:00 a.m. I told him about her corn syrup allergy and asked if he would be using dextrose as part of her IV. He assured me it would be minimal and unlikely to affect her, but he understood the need to manage her blood sugar through the IV.

I told him about Jayden's past experiences, how miserable she'd been during previous procedures. He listened carefully. With compassion, he promised to keep her fully sedated for the entire duration. I watched him take Jayden's hand as he spoke to her.

"I'll be right here for you the whole time."

That small act of kindness reassured me. He saw her as a person. She would be cared for.

A moment later, another doctor entered to review the

orders: a lumbar puncture to check for syphilis, a hearing test, and an MRI to evaluate her pituitary gland and pancreas. Then the nurse came in. She reached for Jayden, who was warm in my arms, tucked into her fuzzy blanket. With tears in my eyes, I kissed her forehead and gave her a squeeze. She looked up at me, wide-eyed and searching, as this stranger carried her away toward faraway places she'd never been.

As she disappeared around the corner, I swallowed my tears and walked toward the waiting area, heart hollow, clinging to hope. Left with nothing but time and the incredible weight of waiting for the two and a half hours the procedures were scheduled to take.

I SETTLED into the most comfortable chair I could find and pulled my novel from Jayden's diaper bag. An hour passed, and it still lay unopened on my lap. I just sat in silence, lost in thought, my mind opening to all the possibilities I'd been trying not to imagine. Without Jayden on my lap to distract me, I had nothing left but anxiety.

What would these tests discover? And more importantly, what would they mean for Jayden? Would there be any way to give her a healthy life? And under it all, the same fear: could I handle what was ahead?

Around me, the waiting room filled with people trying to hold onto a sense of normalcy, even as anxiety flickered behind their eyes. I whispered a prayer of gratitude, humbled by how seldom I'd been asked to endure rooms like this.

Families clustered together, young and old, sharing snacks and soft conversations. I had family too, on speed dial, but all of them at least a day's drive away. It hadn't even occurred to me to ask someone to sit with me. I didn't yet understand the heightened anxiety and the gnawing fear that this kind of waiting really meant. Live and learn.

After two hours, the audiologist came and sat beside me. She explained she was able to perform the hearing test while Jayden was sedated. Her voice was warm, reassuring. Jayden's hearing was perfect. I already knew she could hear well after these past few months, but the confirmation still brought a small wave of relief.

I thanked her, and she added that the rest of the procedures were taking longer than expected. Jayden had begun to come out of sedation before the doctors were finished so they had to re-sedate her. That added more time, but it shouldn't be much longer.

I reached for a magazine and flipped through it without seeing anything. The family around me munched on their snacks, whispered, waited. An older man kindly offered me the leftover donut his children had abandoned.

Maybe it was my inexperience that saved me from falling apart. Five hours in the same chair. Afraid to move, afraid to miss the moment someone said my name.

When the nurse finally called my name, I leapt from my chair and I nearly ran to the room where the recovery nurses were fussing over Jayden. Her eyes scanned the room with desperation, until she heard my voice. Then her eyes locked onto me and didn't waver. I lifted her from the nurse's arms and held her close. Another nurse guided me to a rocking chair so I could feed my Deedle girl and help her ease out of the anesthesia. She drank a full four-ounce bottle. Then I dressed her, complete with hair ribbons. Everyone in the recovery room made a fuss over her.

Jayden was doing well as the anesthesia wore off, and

we left the hospital an hour later. Jayden, with a full belly. Me, with a stomach full of new anxiety. The procedures were over, but answers would take a few days. With Jayden nestled into her car seat, just enough anesthesia left in her system to keep her sleeping during our car ride home, I pulled through a drive-thru restaurant and eagerly opened the bag, grabbing the fries while they were hot. The salty crunch paired perfectly with the ice-cold soda. The burger could wait.

Once home, we slipped easily back into our familiar rhythm. Jayden drained another bottle and drifted into a deep sleep as she melted into my chest with each pat I gave her bottom. I followed her cue, reclining my seat just enough to rest. It had been a long time since sleep felt like a friend. But we'd made it through the last twenty-four hours, and for now, rest came easier.

I WAS JOLTED AWAKE NOT long after by Jayden crying. This was strange. She was not one to cry. My mind scrambled for reasons, grasping first at the memory of her being left alone in the procedure room, the start of the IV sedation, the moment they rolled her away. Maybe that fear was lingering.

I patted her bottom to soothe her, and she soon drifted into a deep sleep, seemingly comforted. I reclined again, trying to calm myself enough to follow her lead. But less than twenty minutes later, she was crying again, a high, thin scream. I thought about everything she'd been through in the last ten hours: the hospital, the procedures, the anesthesia. Maybe she just needed time to believe it was over. That we were back in the safety of our routine. There were no obvious signs of physical pain I could see.

It had to be emotional. She just needed reassurance that the procedures were over, the separation was over, the needles were over, and we were home.

I kept encouraging her to eat and sleep, hoping it would help her delicate body recover from the day's invasions. But the more I tried to help her escape it all, the more desperate her crying became.

Just then, my friend Linda called to check in. As we spoke, Jayden's cries rang out so sharply that Linda stopped mid-sentence. I excused myself to tend to Jayden, and minutes later, Linda was at my front door. She was worried. This wasn't like Jayden at all.

She took her turn walking the floor with Jayden bundled in her fuzzy blanket, whispering to her. But nothing worked. Jayden didn't respond to either of us. Her eyes wouldn't even focus on us. She was unreachable, curled deep within herself. We couldn't give her the relief she needed.

The hospital had discharged us with an emergency hotline number. Linda held Jayden in the other room while I called, explained the day's events, and asked what we could do to help her. Was she in pain from any of the procedures? Could she have the spinal headache that others had warned us sometimes followed a lumbar puncture? What were we supposed to do?

The voice on the other end advised us to take Jayden to the emergency room for evaluation. We moved quickly. Linda and I grabbed bottles and stuffed them into the already bulging diaper bag, still sitting by the kitchen door from when we got home hours earlier. I strapped Jayden into her car seat while Linda climbed into the back seat beside her.

I pulled out of the driveway as Linda called ahead to the ER, warning them that a medically fragile, insulin-dependent, eight-month-old was on the way who was fresh from procedures done at their own hospital. They needed to be ready. She also left a message on John's cellphone, telling him where we'd be so he would know what was happening as soon as his plane landed.

We made it to the emergency room quickly, thanks to a stretch of green lights and my not-so-light foot on the gas pedal. At check-in, I gave the necessary information, and we were ushered straight to an exam room. Linda and I were terrified.

The ER nurse entered the room and, unhurried, took Jayden's vitals. No fever. Blood pressure, though difficult to obtain, seemed normal. No signs of vomiting, diarrhea, or nasal drainage. She was eating, her diaper output was fine, and her glucometer readings were within range. The nurse charted everything and promised a resident would be in shortly.

Twenty more minutes of nonstop screaming passed before the resident entered. Linda and I repeated everything we'd already told the nurse. He did a brief exam, said nothing of substance, and left the room without offering so much as a guess.

Jayden kept crying. The only thing I noticed was that lying her down made her scream harder. Was lying flat painful for her? Or did the pain simply make her want to be held? I didn't know. I'd never seen her like this. I didn't know how to decode this kind of distress. I was grasping for answers. I was hoping the ER would give us some.

We had been in the ER for ninety minutes when John arrived to find us worn thin. He could see we were shaken, but gently urged patience. Jayden's case was unusual and complex. We agreed to trust the process.

The resident returned with an intern and a tall attending physician whose coat bore years of wear. I recounted the history: the congenital syphilis, the lumbar puncture that morning, the failure to thrive. I told them we were looking for a pituitary or pancreatic deficiency.

I explained that the MRI had been extended so they could get a clearer look at her pancreas. She'd needed a second round of sedation because the imaging wasn't complete the first time. Long enough to make me wonder whether there was anything to find.

They all laughed. All three of them. Each one a little louder than the last. The attending physician spoke first. "Of course she has a pancreas. She's alive, isn't she?"

*Just barely,* I thought.

Then they asked who had ordered the tests.

I answered proudly, "Dr. Earles."

Their expressions shifted. No one said a word. Their eyes said enough.

I was stunned. Offended. They had just mocked one of the few doctors who had listened. Someone who looked at Jayden as a whole child and not just a set of symptoms. I was angry, and more determined than ever to stand by Dr. Earles.

The attending physician asked to examine Jayden, and as I laid her back onto the crinkly exam table, she let out a shrill scream and reached for me. She was in pain. The three doctors leisurely examined her from head to toe while she wailed. I stood there, resisting the pull of her desperate outstretched arms. A chest X-ray was ordered to rule out any bronchial issues. The three physicians left the room, leaving us to "wait and see" what it might show.

I just needed this night to end so I could get her to Dr. Earles in the morning. The only question was, could we make it until then?

Before the room filled with more equipment for the X-ray, and now that John was with me, Linda excused herself. She was still very concerned but knew she couldn't help us any further. She drove John's car back to our house, then got into her own car to make it home in time for some sleep before work the next morning.

The chest X-ray showed Jayden's lungs were clear. The resident stepped out to call our pediatric office's on-call associate, and relayed his findings, recommending Jayden be discharged from the Emergency Room. But the on-call pediatrician knew of Jayden's case and had heard enough from the dismissive ER physician. She asked to speak with me directly.

The resident returned and told me to follow him. I passed Jayden to Papa John and walked with the resident to the white phone on the wall at the nurse's station. Dr. Raymond's voice came through calm and assured. "How's Jayden doing right now?" she asked.

As I began to answer, my eyes drifted to the large whiteboard directly in front of me. Jayden's name was there. Next to it, in bold black marker, someone had written: "FUSSY BABY."

I felt my throat tighten. I turned away quickly and tried to stay focused on Dr. Raymond's question.

"She's in complete distress," I told her. "She hasn't stopped crying since a few hours after we got home from the procedures. But apparently, nothing's wrong with her, at least according to the ER doctors."

Dr. Raymond asked if I'd be willing to give her Tylenol until she could be seen in the morning. I said I would, except Jayden was allergic to corn syrup and I was pretty sure the liquid form had a large concentration of it. She agreed and offered an alternative: a Tylenol suppository.

"Yes," I said. "That should work."

Dr. Raymond relayed her opinion to the resident,

who instructed the nurse to administer the correct dosage, only half of the suppository. We waited. After thirty minutes, Jayden began to settle. The resident wrote a prescription for additional suppositories and told us about two nearby 24-hour pharmacies. We were discharged at 12:30 a.m.

Our first stop after leaving the hospital was the local pharmacy to fill the prescription for Tylenol suppositories. Jayden could finally sleep, either from the suppository's pain relief or sheer exhaustion, and we knew we'd need more relief for her within the next four to six hours.

Thankfully, the 24-hour pharmacy had a well-lit parking lot. Jayden and I waited in the locked car, on alert, while John went inside. He passed the handwritten prescription to the older, white-haired pharmacist, only to be told they were completely out of Tylenol suppositories. It was January, prime flu season, and their stock was gone. A new shipment might come in the next few days, but for now, we were out of luck.

John asked where we might find the medication for our little girl at this ungodly hour. The pharmacist kindly called around to the few pharmacies still open, but none had any in stock. Within minutes, it was clear: we had no options.

John returned to the car empty-handed. He explained the dilemma. There were no available pharmacies with suppositories, and I quickly blurted, "Except one." I called the hospital ER, explained our situation, and made a desperate plea for help. Could they fill the prescription at the hospital pharmacy?

I was put on hold. It was 1:15 a.m. We waited. Finally, the answer came through the speaker. Yes.

They would allow us two suppositories, just enough to get us through the night until we could track down some more. John ran into the ER to collect the medicine. Then we went home.

I had powered through the day with less than two hours of sleep and a few French fries. John had started his morning in Mexico, flown home, and been launched straight into this crisis. We had no idea what the night would hold, only that we hoped for some measure of peace, and maybe some sleep.

Jayden lost precious calories from crying for six hours straight.

*Don't let her cry.* It was the quiet rule we lived by. She burned too much energy that way, and she had no reserves to spare. Tonight she had been too upset to eat a thing. Only two bottles since 2:00 a.m. We'd have to make up for what her body had lost in the days ahead. But not tonight. Tonight, we were too exhausted.

---

THE NEXT MORNING, I called Debbie at Dr. Earles's office bright and early to ask when we could bring Jayden in. Debbie had heard from Dr. Raymond about our long night in the ER and asked how Jayden was doing. She said everyone at the office had been worried. She scheduled us for an 11:30 a.m. appointment with Dr. Earles.

After giving Jayden her morning insulin injection, I quickly bathed her. Her glucometer readings were elevated again, likely from the previous day's stress, poor feeding, and dextrose used in sedation. She still wasn't feeling well, though the suppositories had helped her sleep most of the night, with only a few brief cries.

I grabbed the diaper bag, tossed out the clutter from yesterday's nineteen-hour ordeal, tried to make sense of the chaos, then repacked it for today. We left early, hoping to check with Dr. Earles about giving Jayden more Tylenol before her scheduled appointment, but there was no time. Dr. Earles met us at the door and waved us straight back.

She led us to the exam room, explaining she'd read the ER report, but that only told part of the story. Not what we'd lived. She wanted to hear the complete details from us. There was a big difference between the ER physicians' notes and our account.

The first thing she noticed was that Jayden had lost pigmentation around her eyes again. That familiar masked look had returned, the same one we'd seen in her first months, tied to her corn syrup allergy.

Within minutes, Dr. Earles announced, "She has a sinus infection. Likely brought on by the dextrose IV yesterday."

I was stunned. We had spent hours in the emergency room with three physicians and a chest X-ray, leaving with nothing more than "fussy baby" and two Tylenol suppositories. But in the calm, measured space of the pediatrician's office, the real answer surfaced almost immediately. I didn't know what to do with that.

Dr. Earles applied pressure around Jayden's sinuses, just above her eyes. Jayden immediately began to scream. When the pressure stopped, she settled. Then Dr. Earles touched under her eyes. Again, Jayden cried. That was it. A sinus infection.

But what kind of treatment could she have without corn syrup? Most liquid antibiotics would be sweetened, and sweeteners meant risk.

Dr. Earles didn't hesitate. "A Bicillin injection," she said.

Of course, even that had its challenges. The closest pharmacy that stocked the injectable antibiotic was at a nearby hospital. The problem? Medicaid wouldn't cover it. John spoke up immediately: we'd pay out of pocket. Dr. Earles warned us it could be $100. John didn't blink. If it meant Jayden would be more comfortable, we would do whatever it took.

The plan was simple: drive to the hospital pharmacy, buy the Bicillin, and return to the pediatric clinic where Dr. Earles would administer the injection. As we waited in the hospital pharmacy, I made the required call to Nicole, telling her about the emergency room visit the night before. I updated her on the antibiotic injection soon and that we expected MRI results tomorrow. We had already scheduled a follow-up appointment and we'd be seeing Dr. Earles for a third time this week.

Nicole took notes as I spoke, clearly concerned. Over those monthly in-home visits, she'd grown to adore Jayden, always lingering an extra minute to play or stroke her tiny hand. She asked me to give Jayden a kiss from her and requested we call with updates when we could. I promised to email her after tomorrow's appointment with a full recap. She appreciated my detailed emails, usually with photos, and used them to process any necessary paperwork.

John paid for the antibiotic and a box of Tylenol suppositories he'd found at the hospital pharmacy. I lifted Jayden from the baby sling and settled her into her car seat. With Bicillin in hand, we returned to Dr. Earles's office. This time, the path forward felt solid.

Once there, Dr. Earles took us straight to an exam room and gave Jayden the injection. We were to continue using the suppositories and wait for the antibiotic to take effect.

"It won't take long," she assured us. She expected to see improvement by tomorrow. The antibiotic would remain active for the next twenty-one days. With her now-familiar pat on the back, she sent us off... to rest, I hoped.

Nurse Kay came to our home in the afternoon to perform reiki on Jayden. The little one had continued her painful cries until Kay's gentle hands worked their magic. Within moments, Jayden relaxed under her touch. At last, she was able to rest for the remainder of the day and, hopefully, to begin healing.

# January 2010 —
# Part Two

J ayden's court date was scheduled for the following day. The same day as we were scheduled to receive the results from her MRI. John had a decision to make: attend the court hearing, as we had always promised to do for the children in our care, or come with me to the pediatrician's office to hear the results.

He chose wisely. He stayed with me.

I called Nicole to explain the situation. She immediately agreed. The MRI results were the priority, and we both needed to be there. Nothing significant was expected in court anyway. It was a routine review, and nothing had changed since the last hearing. Nicole's only update would be to renew the request that Jayden not be placed in a permanent home until she was stable enough to transition without physical or emotional distress.

With that reassurance, we let go of the court hearing and turned our full attention to what lay ahead. The results were coming. We braced ourselves.

At 10:00 a.m., John carried Jayden into Dr. Earles's office. I followed with the diaper bag, watching him parade her through the waiting room we'd always avoided before, his whole face lit with pride. Papa John had loved every baby who came to our home. But Jayden wrapped herself around his heart and stayed.

Before we could sit down, we noticed the whole staff giggling. Were they celebrating? Huge smiles stretched across every face. Nurse Melissa led us back to the exam room, balancing Jayden's ever-growing chart, now as thick as an encyclopedia. She told us Dr. Earles would be right in. No need to undress or weigh Jayden. It was unusual, but it was our third visit that week, so we shrugged and waited, trying to balance the fear and hope.

Dr. Earles danced into the room, spinning and sliding, light on her feet like a ballerina in a lab coat. Her face was radiant. She looked straight at us and reached for Jayden. Cradling her in her arms, she practically sang the news.

"The MRI technician had trouble finding Jayden's pancreas, so the radiologist spent twice as long as expected reviewing the images. After several passes, he came to a startling realization: there was no pancreas to assess."

She paused, then repeated it.

"There. Was. No. Pancreas."

"Let me say this again." She took a deep breath and a smile overtook her face as she exhaled. "The MRI shows she was born without a pancreas. None at all. Not even a damaged one. Just... none."

Shock and relief shared the same breath.

Dr. Earles beamed. "Now that we know what we're dealing with, we can do our best to figure out how to help her survive."

My mind couldn't catch up, as though I'd fallen through the floor. Like every answer I thought I wanted had arrived, but in the wrong language: unreadable, inescapable, unbearable. It took me several minutes to understand what she was saying.

"The pancreas is what makes insulin," she said, "and it also releases enzymes that let us digest food. Without it, the body can't regulate sugar or break down what we eat."

"In an adult, losing a pancreas is rare and life-changing, even when it's planned. For a newborn, being born without one, that's almost unheard of."

This wasn't just diabetes; it was a body trying to live without an organ that made survival possible.

Finally, I managed one question. "If the NICU had done extensive testing during Jayden's first two months, how did they miss this?"

Dr. Earles explained, "The initial MRI was inconclusive because Jayden's stomach was so distended from gas, it obscured the image. Fewer than one in a million babies is born without a pancreas. Most don't survive. It's so rare, the radiologist likely didn't consider the possibility. Why would they?"

She added, "That distention was likely caused by her intolerance to the high corn-syrup content in the formula they were giving her. It's also highly unlikely the attending physicians involved with Jayden's case had experienced caring for a baby born with congenital syphilis. The doctors simply didn't know what to look for."

My thoughts were spiraling. Still, a few more questions surfaced. "If all of this was caused by congenital syphilis, is that also why Jayden was blind and deaf at birth? She recovered from those. Could her pancreas heal too?"

Dr. Earles placed her hand on mine. "I don't believe she was born blind and deaf," she said. "Her body was shutting down. In crisis, the body sacrifices the nonessential functions first. She was so close to death that her system couldn't manage even the basics, vision, hearing, not because she lacked them, but because her energy was being rerouted just to breathe and keep her heart beating."

"She was dying in your arms."

Her words took the breath out of my body. The lump rose in my throat. Thick. Unrelenting.

She continued, her voice calm but heavy. "Jayden has healed remarkably from her initial diagnoses. But this is different. I believe the congenital syphilis actually destroyed her pancreas during fetal development. Feeding her those formulas was slowly killing her. Every bottle was a sugar bomb her body couldn't process. And because no one thought a baby could survive being born with congenital syphilis, they discharged her without even realizing their role in her decline."

It was all beginning to make sense. I was numb. Questions swirled, half-formed. John stood beside me, silent. Stunned. Then Dr. Earles said something that stopped the spiral. Something that stopped the world.

"Judy, you saved her life by suggesting breast milk."

Everything stilled. My body went cold. Then hot. Then I broke. I wasn't ready. I was just trying to keep her alive one day at a time. I knew how close to death Jayden had been. I remembered the weight of her frail body, the lifelessness in her limbs, the slow fading in her first weeks. I felt the urgency. *Do something. Anything.*

But this? This changed everything.

I remembered the trembling weight of her body on my chest that first week. The shallow rise and fall of breath, the way her skin clung to mine, the way she clung to life.

If Jayden had no pancreas, was she still doomed?

Three doctors from the ER had laughed out loud at

the idea of living without a pancreas. Had I only delayed the inevitable? Was she just living on borrowed time?

I could tell the staff at the pediatrician's office were in awe of the latest discovery. Finally, an answer. The mystery solved. They had a name for the problem, and now they could build a plan for Jayden. For them, it was a break-through, a celebration.

Was there any protocol for caring for a baby born without a pancreas? These questions swirled through my head even as the office staff celebrated. John and I fed into their relief, wore the smiles they expected. No words escaped my tightened jaw. This was Jayden's medical team. The people who had searched for months to understand what was wrong. If they were celebrating, shouldn't we trust their reaction? Shouldn't we join in?

We scheduled the next round of appointments, thanked everyone for the good news, and stepped into the sunlit parking lot.

The mystery was solved. Somehow, we felt more lost than ever. We'd waited so long for answers. Fought for them. Prayed for them. But now that they were here, we weren't ready. We buckled Jayden into her car seat and climbed in.

Then everything fell apart.

---

ONCE THE DOORS clicked shut and locked, the illusion cracked. In that familiar cocoon of safety, the smiles slipped away. Silence settled between us, thick and heavy. I was afraid to speak the words echoing in my mind. All I could hear were the voices of the three ER doctors from two nights earlier. They laughed when I explained Jayden needed an MRI to see if she had a pancreas.

*"Of course she has a pancreas,"* one scoffed. *"She's alive, isn't she?"*

What did it mean? Had we been fighting to save a child whose body was already destined to fail? Had we misunderstood her chances from the beginning? If that was true, why had Dr. Earles been smiling? Dancing through the office? Did she not know?

Or worse, did she know, and we were the only ones who didn't?

John kept glancing at me in the rearview mirror, eyes flicking between the road and my face. He was unusually quiet, jaw clenched. I sat beside our baby girl, holding her tiny hand in mine. I kept thinking back to the NICU: the first moment I laid eyes on her, the way the nurse handed her to me like a formality.

*Had we saved her only to watch her fade in slow motion?*

I saw John's reflection, tears slipping down his face. We cried the entire way home. John lifted Jayden from the car. I followed them inside, lowering the garage door behind us. No interruptions. Not now.

I dropped everything and collapsed into John's arms. We stood in the kitchen, weeping, our precious little girl between us. For a moment, time stood still. The house was silent except for our sobs. The only stability in that moment was John's arms around Jayden and me. He held me up when everything inside me was falling. I couldn't imagine a future that didn't hurt.

*How could this be happening? What were we supposed to believe?*

Eventually, I pulled away and laid Jayden down for a blood sugar check. The numbers swam on the screen; I couldn't see them through the tears. I steadied my hands.

Jayden needed care, not collapse. Whatever this meant, she was still here. Still mine.

I remembered the celebration at the pediatrician's office. They wouldn't have been rejoicing if there were no hope, right? They loved Jayden. Not like we did, but still, they cared. If this was a death sentence, surely they wouldn't have been smiling. Maybe there was more to this than we could understand yet.

After all, it was Dr. Earles who caught the sinus infection the ER missed. The emergency room doctors had brushed off Jayden's distress as fussiness. Was it possible that Dr. Earles knew something they didn't?

Jayden was waking from her nap when Miss Pam stepped in. She immediately sensed something was off. Maybe she felt it in the air, saw it in our swollen eyes.

She froze by the changing table, her eyes reading ours. She knew today was the court hearing and the MRI results were due. She didn't know which of these events had put that aching in my eyes.

I broke the silence. "The MRI confirms it. Jayden was born without a pancreas." I took Jayden's burp cloth to wipe my eyes, as if they might actually stop. "That's why she was diagnosed with diabetes so early in life. It wasn't a damaged pancreas that might recover. There's just no pancreas at all."

Miss Pam's eyes filled. Her questions came one after another, careful and kind. I had nothing to give her. Not yet. Miss Pam might have kept asking questions, but Jayden had other ideas. As soon as she spotted Miss Pam's quilted blue bag, she bounced. She was ready to play. Miss Pam sat on the floor, her eyes still glistening, and let Jayden lead the way. There were no expectations, no goals, only joy.

I sat quietly, watching this woman who had given

Jayden so much patience, strength, and love. I saw it in the way her face changed, hope slipping through the cracks in her worry. That was Jayden's magic, she softened people, changed them, and sparked hope beneath fear.

Miss Pam's laughter mingled with Jayden's squeals on the living room floor as they stacked and toppled bright plastic rings. Whatever this news meant, it wasn't only ours to carry. Jayden had already left her mark.

# January 2010 — Part Three

John did his best to take care of Jayden and me, like bringing home my favorite takeout dinners and holding Jayden near the living room window so she could watch the neighbor kids sledding through the fresh snow. He needed to do something. We all did.

The week had been relentless. Jayden had lost weight after the MRI prep and sinus infection. She had cried more during that ER visit than she did in all the months before it. For hours, there was nothing I could do to settle her. All I could do was hold her.

We kept up the cadence of care. Miss Pam, Miss Marsha, Nicole, and Nurse Kay came to us for appointments. The only outing was to Dr. Nancy's. Even that drive felt long.

The news that she'd been born without a pancreas settled on us, heavy and unmoving. John and I were both shaken, but I was the one struggling to hold my footing. I moved through each day in a fog of timers and numbers. I forced myself to maintain the routines I built for Jayden's care, but beneath the surface, I was splintering.

I wanted to crawl inside a cave and not come out. But Jayden needed me present. Attentive. Predictable. So I showed up. Again and again. Even when it felt impossible.

John was set to leave on Friday for a two-week trip to Europe. It would be his last trip with the company. Their jets had recently been sold. We had no idea what came next. There was no way to turn down what might be his last work for a long while.

January settled in bitter and gray, the kind of cold that seeps into your bones. With John gone, I planned to keep everything simple. Jayden needed calm and stability. No errands, no extra anything.

I called Cressie and Terri. They each came by on different days while John was away. They played with Jayden as I caught up on dishes, laundry, and the small domestic threads that had unraveled. It was more comforting than I expected. Just having another person in the room. Someone who cared.

Other days, I found a flicker of connection in the quick drop-ins from the Pumpin' Mamas. Small talk, kind eyes, cold bags of breast milk. I handled each bag carefully.

I didn't take Jayden anywhere. The world outside felt too sharp. Too cold.

When John got back home, there were no more flights on the schedule. That part was over. He would miss flying, a hollow ache under everything. But some-how, the timing felt right. He would be here for whatever came next. He would be home with us. Our home. Her home.

My mom called nearly every day to be sure we were okay. My sisters checked in often with calls, emails, and little notes to remind me we were never far from their thoughts. My aunt called in tears when she heard the latest report. They'd been with us from the beginning.

It lifted my spirits to find a funny email from one of them when I finally had a moment to sit at my computer. No matter the distance, they were with us every step of the way. I often found myself depending on their sanity just to hold onto mine.

THE WINTER SUN flared off the snow as we drove. Bright, merciless. I rode in back with Jayden, her hand in mine. Steam from John's coffee drifted between the seats, and the familiar smell of vanilla creamer steadied me.

We took Jayden to see Dr. Sinclair, eager to hear his take on the MRI findings. He came into the exam room, sat at his desk, and opened a manila folder. Page by page, he read, and after each one, he paused to watch Jayden.

She wasn't used to seeing him this solemn. Each time he looked up, she answered with a grin, like it was peek-a-boo. Soon she was clapping pat-a-cake whenever their eyes met. He chuckled, returned to the file, then glanced up again, only to find a new performance waiting. She loved his attention.

He asked a few questions, and John and I answered as best we could. He went quiet. So quiet we could almost hear him thinking. He asked to examine her. I slipped off her clothes and set her on the table. He began at the crown of her head, touch feather-soft, and moved methodically through the exam. Then he checked her chart again and said her weight out loud: "Eleven pounds one ounce."

Only two ounces gained in two weeks.

He opened his arms and Jayden launched herself into

them. He bounced her as he moved slowly along the wall from picture to picture, breathing in her lavender-gelled hair, rubbing the dry skin on her back, and singing under his breath with the music playing softly in the background.

John and I watched as he took her in, as he took it all in. Then, without a word, he tipped her back toward me, and she settled against my chest. He returned to the chair and stared at the chart again.

Dr. Sinclair opened his mouth and John tensed. But instead of speaking, he looked away, out the window. My stomach dropped. I sat hard in the molded chair beside John. He took Jayden from me and began pacing the length of the room. He couldn't sit. I couldn't stand.

Then Dr. Sinclair turned back and looked straight at me and asked if we would be willing to have Jayden hospitalized so an entire team of specialists could work on her rare, complicated case. We would need the state of Michigan to approve the stay, but under the circumstances he expected they would.

He wanted to consult with Dr. Earles and align on next steps. We agreed to wait for his call, and we started the process of asking the state for approval.

---

JOHN HAD BEEN RESEARCHING since the day we got the diagnosis. Late at night, he sat at the computer, typing with his two index fingers: "pancreatic agenesis."

Different sites reported different statistics, but the gist of it was this condition was extremely rare. Only a handful of cases had ever been recorded. The prognosis was devastating. Many didn't survive the first weeks. Most didn't make it past the early months.

It was a hard truth for John to face about our Deedle. I didn't feel it yet. I was still reading, waiting for them to change. We talked. We cried. We cried some more.

Maybe there was a reason we weren't meant to understand. Her tiny body had defied every expectation. The statistics said we should have lost her. But she was alive, laughing, and impossibly present. Maybe survival itself was the message.

No wonder Dr. Sinclair stared at her chart so long, caught between what he read and what she was: bouncing, radiant, undeniable. It made no sense on paper.

At nine months old, barely eleven pounds, she was doing what no one believed possible. Nicole secured approval for Jayden's hospital stay almost immediately. I hung up the phone and didn't move, letting the reality of it settle in. Approval wasn't the hard part. It was the surrender, fear, and uncertainty that came next.

This was happening. No more guessing. No more waiting. We had to be ready. And we would be ready. We'd show up.

There was a lot to prepare. With this new diagnosis, Jayden had no choice but to start enzymes. They'd been prescribed before, but her body had reacted violently. Now we understood she would have to take them, or she would die.

Jayden couldn't tolerate most formulations, which sharply limited our options, so Dr. Nancy took the lead in choosing the few enzymes her body had a chance of accepting. She worked with Jayden nearly every day, introducing them one at a time, easing her system toward what it had once rejected.

Nurse Kay also made space for John and me in her life and in her home. She welcomed us to her farmhouse, where two exam tables were waiting in the living room.

She gave us each a full session, and when it was over, we walked out feeling like we could do this.

The county dietitian, Ms. Chase, admitted she hadn't even heard of a baby without a pancreas before, but promised to dive into the research. She began crafting a new plan to help Jayden gain weight.

And Miss Pam squeezed in a few extra therapy sessions, showing up with new tools and a quiet joy. She brought a beach ball to help Jayden practice balance. Jayden didn't seem quite ready for it, but that didn't matter. She would be in the hospital bed soon. For now, all that mattered was presence.

During her monthly visit, Nicole shared the latest court update. The case was no longer being reviewed by the judge as he had terminated Jayden's biological parents' rights. The January session was being overseen by a referee, who reviewed everything that had happened in the last three months.

Then she reminded the team of the judge's earlier ruling. She pulled out her reading glasses and read aloud, "Although this baby was legally available for adoption, an adoptive family was not to be pursued until there was a ruling stating she was physically and emotionally healthy enough for the inevitable transfer."

Jayden's health was a priority. Everyone nodded in agreement.

Nicole and Jeannette had also filed the paperwork stating John and I would not be adopting her. It was just a formality. Before leaving, Nicole made sure I had her private cell number in preparation for the upcoming hospital stay. She urged me to call her anytime with updates or concerns.

Nicole had our back. Not just in words, but in action, in follow-through. Even Jayden's rare and complicated needs didn't slow her down. Her competence steadied me. She was a gift.

---

THE DAY before we entered the hospital, John and I took Jayden to church. We hadn't brought her before, not to our 2,500-member congregation. She was too fragile for that. Crowds weren't safe, and I knew the moment we walked in, people would want to meet her. We couldn't sneak in even if we tried.

I remembered trying to get from the parking garage to a doctor's office and being stopped by complete strangers. Sure enough, the moment we took off her winter jacket in the vestibule, we were surrounded. People gushed over how adorable she was.

*This couldn't be worse than the hospital's germs and hands, right?*

Sharing Jayden never got old. And that morning, the service filled us with strength. I knew it would carry me through the week ahead.

When the message was nearing its end, Jayden started squirming. She'd had enough of sitting still. It was a solemn moment, and I didn't want her to cause a distraction. I slipped out to the vestibule, where I could still watch the service on the TV monitor mounted high on the wall.

As I stood there holding Jayden, a man in a yellow church security shirt approached us. His name tag read Daniel. He started with the usual questions: "Who's this beautiful girl?" "How old is she?"

But then, he said he'd already heard of Jayden through Maggie and the prayer team. Apparently, some of our

Pumpin' Mamas had been spreading the word, asking for prayers on our behalf.

I shared that we were heading to the hospital so a team of specialists could build a long-term care plan. He listened closely as I explained what little we understood about the path ahead.

Then Daniel did something that caught me off guard. He placed a warm hand on my shoulder and asked, "How are *you* doing with all of this?"

I cracked, right there in the vestibule. For months now, I had been fixated on Jayden. Sleep, comfort, anything resembling normal life had been eclipsed by the work of keeping her alive. But in that moment, with Daniel's hand on my shoulder, I felt seen. The tenderness of his voice, the sincerity in his question. It cracked something open.

I whispered through my tears, "We need your prayers."

He promised them. Every day.

Daniel's hand was warm, reassuring, like an answer that arrived before I knew how to ask for it. I closed my eyes, holding Jayden tighter.

John found me as the auditorium emptied. As we walked out, Jayden burst into a sharp, joyful squeal. I had no idea why. She was usually so quiet, still finding her voice. But she was happy that day. The squeal delighted us and everyone around us.

The family walking just ahead of us turned at the sound. The mother smiled immediately, spotting the source. She began asking the usual questions. "How old is she?" "How much does she weigh?" "What's her name?"

I answered each one, and when I said, "My husband calls her his Deedle girl, but her name is Jayden," this woman gasped, her hand snapping over her mouth. I expected something typical. Maybe she had a niece named Jayden. Instead, the room seemed to close in around us.

"For the past few months," she said softly, "I've been pumping breast milk for a little girl named Jayden." Her friend Courtenay had asked her to help a sick baby who couldn't tolerate formula and needed nourishment to survive.

We stepped away from the crowd and found a quiet corner. She asked if she could hold Jayden. "Of course," I said, handing her over without hesitation. She gathered Jayden into her arms and told her family this was the baby she'd been trying to help. Tears pooled in her eyes. She traced Jayden's cheeks with her thumb and whispered, "I made these cheeks."

Her husband watched the baby they'd been praying for. His eyes filled. His smile, unguarded.

Her name was Carrie Leigh. We hugged, traded numbers, and kept talking all the way to the parking lot. That afternoon, they brought a box of baby clothes. Their kids ran through the house, Dudley chasing behind, giggles spilling from room to room.

Meeting another one of Jayden's milk donors was a gift. Carrie Leigh had seen a single photo of Jayden and heard bits of her story, but it had been enough for her to start pumping milk. She was kind. Committed. Generous. From that moment on, she was a friend.

We still hadn't figured out what to do with Dudley while we were in the hospital. He was never far from us, but he couldn't come to the hospital. Watching him play so easily with Carrie Leigh's kids, I asked if she knew anyone who might take him for a few days.

She didn't hesitate. "We'll take him." Then, like it was the most ordinary thing in the world, she asked, "Should we take him now?"

I laughed, because she meant it. We didn't know exactly when Jayden's hospital stay would begin, or how long we'd be there. John asked if we could call as soon as we had details. She nodded, already committed. They backed out of the driveway, buzzing with plans for Dudley.

A few hours later, the phone rang. The hospital was ready. And somehow, so were we.

# January 2010 —
## Part Four

Sunday night, Dr. Earles called. Everything was in place.

Jayden's hospital stay would include a full team of specialists. We were to come to her office first thing in the morning: bags packed, insulin ready, a cooler of frozen breast milk. We'd head straight to the hospital from the office for a ten- to fourteen-day stay. Dr. Earles had arranged a private room to minimize Jayden's exposure to germs. I would have my own bed. A real bed with no real rest.

I was jittery with adrenaline. My hands didn't stop. I called Nicole to update her and Miss Pam to cancel Early Intervention appointments. I asked my sister Doreen to be our family's point person. Then I started packing. Two suitcases. Jayden's clothes barely filled a corner. Syringes, bottles, toys, blankets, diapers. It piled up fast. She got the larger one. Mine was easy: three shirts, three pants, pajamas, a toothbrush.

I left dog food and Dudley's toys by the door for Carrie Leigh. John filled the tank and returned with

Mexican salads from the diner. Lime, salt, cold plastic forks, it was the best food we had in weeks, but the nerves stole our appetite.

Tomorrow, a new chapter would begin. Tests. Questions. And only one thing mattered:

Keep this baby alive.

---

WE LOADED the car and drove to Dr. Earles's office. I packed Jayden's toys and asked John to rotate them when he brought breast milk up each day. That was his job now: managing the cooler at home and the PICU freezer.

This was our first time back at Dr. Earles's office since the MRI report. The smiles continued, almost too much. I didn't know how they could smile. I was sure our baby was dying.

John met my eyes. A quiet plea: go with it.

*How? Why?* My stomach turned.

Dr. Earles was radiant. She'd refused to let Jayden be dismissed, pulling a full team into place for a case that didn't come with a script. Jayden wasn't going to the hospital for treatment. She was going for answers. The diagnosis, pancreatic agenesis, was astonishingly rare. We needed a plan. A way to keep her alive.

"She looks good," she said, almost smiling. "Healthy. Strong."

I almost laughed when Dr. Earles called her healthy. Healthy, aside from the absent pancreas.

But she beamed. "We'll keep her safe," she said.

I smiled back. Let them celebrate. Jayden needed us to focus.

I gathered her bag, steadied my hands, and prayed.

Not for answers. Not even for healing. Just for strength. Enough to carry her through whatever came next.

---

WE ARRIVED on the pediatric floor of the hospital around noon. I braced myself for scrutiny. A team of strangers with clipboards and questions. Seven specialists. One afternoon.

They expected a case study. A tragedy. What they got was a little dumpling who knew how to work a crowd. Jayden, normally shy, scanned the room and looked at me. I smiled, nodded. She understood. No one was here to hurt her. Then she bounced. Giggled. Played pat-a-cake. Squealed.

The team cheered her on as she continued to put on a show. Nurses from other floors stopped in to see the baby who wasn't supposed to be alive. Jayden loved the attention, as long as she was in my arms.

John delivered the breast milk to the nurses' station down the hall. They labeled it and slid it into the PICU freezer. I lined up the bottles, grateful to find a fridge right in our room. It felt like a hotel room from another life. This one came with nurses and needles. While I unpacked our supplies and tried to make it feel like home, John walked his Deedle in the hallway.

Reality arrived. The hospital insisted on using their own lancet system for Jayden's glucometer readings, adult-sized and connected to their network. It left deep cuts in her heels. I asked the nurse to call Dr. Earles to approve our thinner lancet and let me log her readings myself.

Dr. Earles didn't blink. "There's no reason to change what's been working."

I exhaled. We kept our routine. The one that had kept her alive for nine months. Diaper. Reading. Injection. Feeding. Every two hours.

My next question was simple: "Do you have size 2 diapers?"

"No. Babies grow out of them too fast."

Jayden had been in size 2 for four months.

Private room or not, there was no privacy. Staff came and went, day and night. Jayden greeted each one with a smile. It didn't matter if she'd been asleep for two hours or two minutes. I tried to follow her lead.

THE NEXT MORNING, I woke up for her two-hour glucose check and found Jayden's crib empty. I froze.

By the time I reached the door, it opened. The day nurse entered, carrying Jayden. Puffy-eyed. Sniffling.

Bloodwork. Multiple failed sticks. A scalp draw, finally.

She'd been strapped to a baby board the whole time. Rigid, helpless, velcro straps where my hands should've been. I was quietly livid. If I was awake, I could've helped. I knew her veins. But I wasn't given the chance.

I watched her chart Jayden's "SCALP DRAW ONLY" directive. Not a suggestion. More of a Mama Bear boundary. I gathered her back to me and rocked until her body loosened. I patted her bottom, our familiar metronome. Her breathing settled. Sleep came.

After that, I kept the TV's music channel low. Jayden needed sleep, and the sound helped soften the constant interruptions.

Day two: seven uncoordinated visits. Care kept coming. Well-meaning. Unending.

When the pediatric GI arrived, I handed her the enzyme plan from our naturopath, Dr. Nancy. The enzymes had been prescribed. Dr. Nancy helped us figure out which ones Jayden could tolerate, and in what order. I wanted the GI to see where we'd started. What we tried. How carefully we'd gotten Jayden this far.

The GI prescribed pancrelipase capsules to be opened and sprinkled onto Jayden's tongue. Then she recommended starting baby food immediately. I explained Jayden's past reactions. The doctor waved me off. "The enzymes will help."

Soon the OT arrived with strained peas. "If we don't introduce solids, she'll risk oral aversion later."

I said nothing.

One bite. Six hours of crying. No bottles.

Her skin broke down again, red and raw.

And it repeated for ten more days.

The math didn't work.

I started questioning the whole concept of *oral aversion*. Would withholding solids cause it? Or would forcing food that hurt her teach her that eating was pain?

The specialist's answer: "Jayden needs to eat. Period."

It felt like a slap. No room for discussion. Just prescriptions: Prevacid, vitamins with iron.

All meds were kept under lock, dispensed by the nurse on duty. Every two hours, I had to hunt one down before I could feed her. Day and night. Same with insulin. When Jayden's blood sugar spiked after each stressful event, I had to wait for approval.

Wait. And listen for footsteps outside our door. We'd been managing her care for nine months. Now the protocol was in charge. We practiced patience. Again.

DR. EARLES WAS A REGULAR PRESENCE. Scrubs rumpled, clipboard tucked under one arm. She carried authority like armor. When she appeared in khaki pants and a bold red leather jacket, unannounced one Sunday afternoon, she caught me off guard.

I looked up from the jumble of toys in Jayden's crib, expecting a nurse or a tech. But it was Dr. Earles. I hardly recognized her. She scanned my handwritten logs, quietly impressed. Then she asked how I felt.

I told her the truth: everyone had an opinion. I was the one holding it.

She listened. "None of them have a map," she said. "There's no protocol for Jayden. They're doing their best. In their own way."

She closed the notebook and looked at me. She saw it. Not just the charts. The mother behind the numbers. And for a few minutes, I didn't feel so alone.

---

WE ADAPTED. Our room had a rocking chair, a private bath. Snow drifting outside the window. Jayden's crib was raised. Perfect height for John to play peek-a-boo. His duck quacks brought giggles that echoed down the hall. John managed the milk supply meticulously. Morning and night. It became a rhythm. His way of caring.

Visitors lifted our spirits. Terri knew what we needed most; desserts, magazines, and the kind of laughter only another foster mother could bring. She and her husband joined us for Friday night pizza, letting a cafeteria slice stand in for our takeout tradition.

John's friend Bob surprised us one day with a big container of homemade chili. Carrie Leigh arrived with more clothes for Jayden and pictures of Dudley playing with her kids, easing the worry I carried for him.

Miss Pam came often, her calm presence filling the room as she read to Jayden or strolled the hallway with her, giving me a few precious minutes to breathe.

It was grace disguised as chili, desserts, and one shared story at a time.

For a few days, we had found a rhythm. Then came a call from Nicole. The state was refusing our daily reimbursement. Four nights out of the home, and the stipend stopped. Eighteen dollars a day. Not much, but it was never about the money.

She was furious. "You haven't left her side," she said.

John found Dorothy, the head nurse. The same nurse from our earlier labs who performed the scalp draws, put her card in my hand, and insisted we call her directly if we needed help. When John explained the situation, she shook her head in disbelief. She drafted a letter confirming my presence was medically necessary and faxed it to Nicole.

---

CARRIE ANN, the organizer in Ann Arbor, asked to meet Jayden. She wasn't a Pumpin' Mama herself, but for the past five months, she'd been quietly delivering breast milk to our home once a week.

She was soft-spoken, with an unmistakable joy about her. She sat cross-legged on the quilt spread across the tile floor and began singing with fingerplay. Jayden leaned in, swaying to the song. When Carrie Ann sang *"Twinkle, Twinkle,"* Jayden joined with her hands making a shaky "diamond in the sky." Carrie Ann's eyes welled with tears. She asked for a photo to share with the other Pumpin'

Mamas. We said yes. And for that one sweet moment, it felt like the whole world had leaned in.

***

Dr. Sinclair, who usually visited in the mornings, surprised us when he popped in that afternoon. He wanted to revisit an idea: feeding Jayden every four hours. He suggested this would allow for a fasting window between checks.

I burst into tears. I didn't mean to. It just happened. The frustration, exhaustion, worry... all the months of vigilance all collided in that moment. She was surviving on breast milk. And now we were rationing it?

I sobbed. Harder than I had in years. My heart hurt. These doctors were trying. I knew that. But I couldn't bear the thought of unraveling everything we'd done to protect her just to satisfy some chart.

Dr. Sinclair didn't argue. He didn't speak. He lifted Jayden into his arms, danced around the room with her, whispered into her ear. Then he handed her back to me.

"Keep up the good work," he said simply. "I'll see you tomorrow."

He left, and the air felt different. I wasn't sure if it was respect, or fear that I might melt down again, but the mood changed. The nurses rallied around us. Three of them came in that afternoon and insisted we take a short break.

I hesitated until I saw the look in John's eyes. Maybe he needed me to step out, for him. Maybe I owed him that. So I agreed. I handed Jayden's bottle to Nurse Sandra, who headed off to the locked med room for her enzymes. I prepped Jayden's glucometer while the other two nurses settled in, ready to help however we needed.

Jayden was in good hands. I knew that.

We took the elevator down, bought two iced teas, and sat near a pianist playing Broadway tunes. We held hands, sipping quietly. It felt good. Strange. And good.

Still, I couldn't shake the tug in my gut. Jayden needed me. John saw it on my face before I said a word. "Twenty-five minutes," he smiled. "That's enough for a first time."

I smiled back at the man who knew me better than anyone else. He loved me anyway. We hurried back to the elevator. As we rose to the third floor, my chest tightened. As soon as the doors opened, we heard her. Jayden was crying. Not fussy or cranky. A desperate, gasping wail that cut down the hallway.

Nurse Sandra stood bouncing Jayden, her face tight with concern. "She hasn't wanted to eat," she said. "She's been crying since you left."

Something in me went cold. They had meant well, but they didn't understand. We weren't just bonded, we were one rhythm. She wasn't ready to let go. And neither was I.

I scooped her up, rocking until her cries softened. Then I laid her in the crib for a glucometer reading.

**438.**

*That's what separation did to her.*

I felt it in my body before my brain caught up. I asked for the fast-acting insulin. When it arrived, I injected it into her thigh, whispering as I did: "I won't leave you again. Not until you're ready." I meant it with everything in me.

ON THURSDAY AFTERNOON, after a twelve-day stay, Jayden was discharged. She had gained a pound. Twelve pounds two ounces. It was hard-won.

Each specialist gave us detailed follow-up plans for home. Jayden tolerated several new medications well in the hospital. We left with a handful of prescriptions and a hospital bag packed with carefully labeled supplies.

John made the rounds through the pediatric floor, carrying his Deedle in his arms, saying goodbye to every nurse, doctor, and technician who had become part of our days. They had been kind. Some had gone above and beyond. But nothing matched the relief of coming home.

He loaded up a rolling cart with our belongings, and pushed it to the parking garage. I carried Jayden to the elevator and met him at the car. The air was warming. Less than a mile up the road, he pulled into our favorite burger joint on Woodward Avenue. We devoured a bag of greasy sliders, like we hadn't eaten in days. They tasted like freedom.

And then, finally, he turned onto our street. The garage door creaked open. Tires crunched into place. Engine off. Silence. Home.

The smell of our house hit me first. I held Jayden close as we crossed the threshold, grateful. No monitors, no shoes squeaking in the hallway. We dropped our bags by the door and didn't unpack a thing.

That chapter we feared? We lived it. And now, under our own roof, we could exhale.

Jayden curled against me as if she knew. We didn't need words. It didn't need to be grand. It was ours. Hers. And it was enough.

# February 2010

January had drained us. A swing between hope and fear, hospital and home. Saturday morning, we eased back into routine. I didn't have to wake Jayden every two hours. I let her sleep until she stirred.

Three hours between feedings felt like mercy. I had always heard the hospital was no place for sleep. Two weeks under fluorescent lights and relentless stress confirmed it. We had three days to breathe before the next set of visits. We planned to rest. Real rest, the kind that comes with silence.

Then the mail arrived. The agency letterhead. The new adoption supervisor wrote to schedule a meeting with a potential adoptive family, offering two dates and a reminder we could choose "only because of Jayden's appointments."

The family had been chosen for their experience with medically fragile children. They were already caring for eleven. Eleven schedules. Eleven alarms. Comfort was a task. Care was constant. Grief, too. A house built around survival, not belonging.

The supervisor sounded excited that they might take Jayden. The meeting was for them to meet her and decide. "We are fortunate to have this option available," the supervisor wrote.

I thought I was going to throw up. I might have, if I'd had the strength to move. I just sat there. Empty. Like an answer to a question I wouldn't let myself ask.

Two weeks earlier, Nicole sat in our living room and explained the judge's orders: Jayden wasn't to be moved until she was stable. We just received a rare, life-threatening diagnosis. She was ten months old, twelve pounds. Dependent on breast milk. Still unable to digest solid foods.

In that house, who would have time to hold her? How could she survive another separation when even twenty-five minutes in the hospital nearly undid her? The system was ready to move her anyway.

I wasn't sure I could move at all.

Jayden stirred on my chest. I tightened my hold.

---

AT CHURCH THE NEXT MORNING, Maggie and the prayer team met us at the door. We told them about the hospital and the letter. Maggie didn't ask for details. She just reached for us, placing one hand on Jayden and the other on me. John stood behind me, steady at my back. He knew I was barely upright.

Maggie prayed, soft but firm. She asked God to go first. To shield us and give us strength to protect Jayden. Something in me settled.

From the beginning, people asked if Jayden was

adoptable. We always answered honestly. Legally, she was available. Physically, she wasn't. Not yet. The state was waiting for her to stabilize. That answer held. It gave us time.

Now it seemed like our time was up. We needed to find a family for Jayden, and church felt like the only place where someone might say yes. They'd seen Jayden's face. Her light.

That afternoon, I sat alone and prayed for guidance. How could we keep her from being placed in a house built for medically fragile children? Could we find someone else willing to say yes, knowing the diagnosis?

Monday morning, I called Nicole and told her about the letter. She promised to check with the adoption department and get back to us. She scheduled a home visit for Friday. We'd sit down and make a plan.

I just needed to stay upright until then.

---

Tuesday, Miss Pam arrived. A welcome distraction. She was delighted to see Jayden at home. Jayden was thrilled, too. She had something to show her. After two weeks cooped up in a hospital bed, she was overjoyed to be back on the floor.

When Miss Pam sat down in her usual spot, Jayden took off rolling the full length of the family room. Miss Pam squealed, hands to her cheeks. Jayden couldn't have offered a better surprise. She'd finally learned to roll over.

When "teacher time" ended, it became "friend time." Lately, Miss Pam was both. I told her about the letter. Her face changed. She could already see what came next. She knew what separation does to a body that small.

I STALLED. I couldn't make myself call the adoption supervisor. Jeannette, the adoption worker who'd been with Jayden's case from the beginning, was away at training for most of the month. That explained the supervisor's involvement, but not why she'd sidestepped the court order.

I sent daily emails, copying everyone from the agency. Questions and pleas. Everything in writing. I asked if they'd wait until Jayden had some reserves.

The only reply: a reminder about the meeting. Maybe they thought I was too attached. I was attached. I felt closer to Jayden than any baby I had ever cared for. And I'd seen her glucometer readings after even brief separations. I knew what it did to her and to me.

But more than that, I worried about what she would go through. If she was okay, I was okay. I also knew she deserved a family of her own that would love her in every way that mattered. This wasn't about me. I was terrified she might lose the few things keeping her stable. She had almost died in my arms. No pancreas. No margin.

Now the system was funneling her toward a bed reserved for babies who weren't expected to live. On paper, she fit that description. In person, she was different. Her diagnosis hadn't changed, but she was making progress. Breast milk. The pancreas discovery. There was hope. But that home wasn't built for hope.

John kept reminding me we had to fight for humanity in the process. He tried to hold me together.

NICOLE WAS FRUSTRATED when she arrived Friday. Adoption wasn't her department. She hadn't seen it coming either. She sat down, exhaled, and added the next piece. Jayden's birth mother was pregnant again. Given her history, no one expected her to carry to term. If she did, the baby would likely enter foster care.

The news landed heavily. We set it down, not because it didn't matter, but because something else was already crushing us. What consumed us was the placement decision. It overshadowed everything.

I was still drowning in a relentless cycle. Diaper. Reading. Injection. Feeding. Even when Jayden slept for two hours, I didn't. I watched for symptoms and wrote down every number in my spiral notebook. I sent updates to Nicole and our support team. Appointments filled the day, one after another, as if the calendar couldn't see what we were holding.

John carried the rest: laundry, groceries, meals, the whole house. He also held Jayden when I needed a minute to fall apart. We spent the weekend sitting with the placement decision. We knew Jayden better than anyone else and yet no one asked us if she was ready.

I kept hearing the words from the letter: *We are fortunate to have this option available.* Maybe that was the crack in the door. Maybe it meant the agency wasn't sure they could find anyone else.

Would anyone say yes to a baby with no pancreas?

And beneath it all, how long did she have?

WE WALKED into church on Sunday and overheard a young man announce, "Jayden has entered the building!"

John and I chuckled. Jayden was becoming a bit of a celebrity. That was good. This campus drew nearly 2,500 people each week, and it was only one of five campuses. In a crowd that big, there had to be one family who'd feel called to adopt Jayden.

So we made it our mission. We talked to church leaders, asking them to help spread the word. They'd seen Jayden's glow. They didn't know what it took to keep her stable, but I did. I believed the right person could do it. John and I agreed. If the agency needed options, we'd offer them.

As we carried Jayden into the auditorium, we saw Carrie Leigh and her family. Of course, they needed a little squeeze from Miss Jayden. Carrie Leigh sat cross-legged on the floor, holding her while the kids gathered close. We asked her to help spread the word. Jayden was available for adoption. Then we slipped inside as the band opened the service.

That afternoon, Carrie Leigh and her husband Jason stopped by. They asked if they could be the ones to adopt Jayden. They said they already loved her.

I didn't know if this was the right home. They were struggling financially, raising four little ones. But I didn't turn away. We told them what the agency had planned: placement in *that* house. We shared our concerns. As I spoke, it hit me. If Jayden went into that house, her needs wouldn't just change, she'd be surrounded by sorrow.

Jayden might be delayed in motor skills, but she was sharp in other ways. She was sensitive to her surroundings. Her glucometer readings proved it. This placement might not just alter her life. It might end it. My voice cracked as I tried to explain that to Carrie Leigh and Jason. John heard it too.

Carrie Leigh offered to call the agency the next

morning to ask how they might be considered. What could it hurt? Carrie Leigh wasn't pushing for placement. She was weighing what it would require, and whether they could sustain it.

Carrie Leigh's breast milk ran through Jayden. That felt like a kind of covenant. One that couldn't be undone.

MONDAY MORNING, while I expected Carrie Leigh to call, I emailed. Again.

I asked about other potential adoptive families. I raised the state's preference for keeping siblings together, just in case. I urged them to postpone the meeting until we knew more about Jayden's condition. Could we at least wait until after the court hearing on April 8?

That email went unanswered.

John and I started calling attorneys. One of our Pumpin' Mamas was a lawyer. Another, a "friend-of-a-friend" had inquired about adopting Jayden in January, before she was legally available. Both women offered counsel over the phone, free of charge. That felt like a small mercy.

OUR CALENDAR FILLED AGAIN. Clipboards. Waiting rooms. Parking garages.

Dr. Nancy, our naturopath, worked to balance Jayden's new medications. Ms. Chase, the county dietitian, suggested textured foods. The ophthalmologist said her eyes were responding well to the tiny pink glasses. The geneticists ordered more labs.

We struggled to get her prescriptions filled. It was hard

to keep up with her needs while trying to stop an adoption already in motion.

A welcome distraction arrived in a note attached to a breast milk delivery. One of the Pumpin' Mamas we hadn't met wrote that a friend, a children's photographer, wanted to gift Jayden a session. Free. With her first birthday less than two months away, the timing felt perfect.

I called Karla, the photographer. Her voice was small, like her. She could schedule a two-hour session for March 3. The day after the agency meeting with the prospective home. I hesitated, only for a moment. It would give me something else to focus on. Something beautiful. I said yes.

Jayden saw Dr. Earles and Dr. Sinclair for follow-up after the hospital. John and I told them about the potential adoption. Both looked concerned. They already knew how thin the margin was. Jayden still weighed less than thirteen pounds. She had no reserves for a stressful transition. I asked if they could write a letter to the adoption supervisor, something official, stating what they'd just told us. They agreed.

Since the agency was responsible for a baby this fragile, why weren't they talking to her doctors about timing, and what a permanent home would require? We'd chosen this agency for its Christian ethics. This wasn't what we expected. Not from them.

THAT AFTERNOON, Miss Pam managed to get Jayden to sit up for several seconds without help. Despite the turmoil, Jayden was still making progress. Not leaps and bounds, but real and worth waiting for. She was happy. Everyone noticed. Jayden didn't know our home was at risk. Her home. All she knew was that she was loved.

She hadn't tolerated her new meds. At discharge, we'd started Prevacid tablets and digestive enzymes. Her intake dropped to twenty-two ounces a day, down from her usual thirty-four to thirty-six. Her glucometer readings spiked. I followed the hospital instructions to the letter. The only change was the new meds.

I suspected the artificial sweetener in the tablets. So I stopped both medications and went back to breast milk and insulin only. Within hours, Jayden was calm, drinking again, and her blood sugar stable.

Dr. Earles called with a new plan: she'd phoned in a diluted liquid version of Prevacid to the specialty pharmacy. We'd go slow now.

Dr. Sinclair followed up the next morning. He agreed. But he had another reason for calling. The GI specialist in his office said she would no longer see Jayden. In her view, there was no point if Dr. Earles wasn't following her instructions.

By the time the call ended, I already felt like I was catching the consequences before I understood why. Jayden slept through it, warm against my chest. I left Nicole a message.

Jayden's case was unique. This was the only pediatric GI group in the complex. Once one refused, the others wouldn't touch her case. There were fewer places to turn.

Nicole called back within the hour. She asked me to call our agency president, Mr. Ennis. I wanted to lead with the letter, the court order, and the meeting. But the GI refusal was already hurting Jayden. So I started there. He said he'd follow up and call me back. He gave me his personal number. I kept my voice steady and thanked him.

Then the mail brought another letter. The paper shook in my hands. I read it twice. The case conference: Tuesday, March 2, at 1:00 p.m.

JAYDEN WAS HERSELF AGAIN. Just breast milk and insulin. The diluted Prevacid arrived that day. Knowing how sensitive her system was, I decided to restart slowly.

In the hospital, there had been such a rush to fix her. Every specialist was eager to see improvement. Eventually, it took a toll and aggravated her digestion. Now, with no GI specialist to call, we could at least take our time at home. I planned to begin with a quarter-dose of each medication, gradually increasing over a week until we reached the recommended dose. We didn't see her doctors again for another week. For once, time seemed on our side.

TECHNICALLY, it was March. Emotionally, I wasn't ready to admit it. John and I took Jayden to Dr. Earles for a weight check. Jayden weighed twelve pounds fifteen ounces.

I didn't know how much she lost during her refusal to eat, but now she was nearly thirteen pounds. Dr. Earles told us she faxed her letter, warning the agency not to place Jayden in a home already caring for medically fragile children. She also faxed Jayden's readings to Dr. Sinclair. He was relieved to see they were stable.

We made it through another day, but morning was waiting. The meeting. Their decision.

# March 2010

Tuesday, March 2. I woke before the alarm, already aware of what the day would ask of me. Jayden lay in her crib. For a moment, I stayed still, watching her breathe, trying to hold the morning in place before it moved.

People often asked the same question when they learned we fostered. "Don't you get attached?"

Yes. And the day we don't, we'll stop fostering. Every child needed someone to love them long enough to make it stick. We believed that if a baby could attach, she could carry that bond forward into whatever family came next. Without it, trust could break before it ever formed.

We couldn't control where they would go. But for a time, under our roof, they would know they belonged.

That morning, I finally said the part I'd been avoiding.

*Dear Lord,*
*May Your will be done. If this is her family, let it be*
*     clear.*
*Give me grace to accept it.*

The words lodged in my chest. I had to push them out, one by one. For us, faith wasn't a feeling. It was showing up anyway.

I drew a deep breath and gathered myself for the day. The only way out of bed was to pretend it was a normal morning appointment. The clothes on the dresser felt too casual, so I chose something nicer from the closet. I showered and dressed before Jayden stirred.

Her routine steadied me. Diaper. Reading. Injection. Feeding. The breast milk, warm and familiar, the one thing that never asked anything of her. I added Prevacid, sprinkled two digestive enzymes on her tongue, and logged it in the spiral notebook.

The phone rang while I was snapping the cap on my pen. "This is the genetics office," a woman said. "I'm calling with Jayden's results."

I closed my eyes.

"She tested negative for the GATA6 mutation, the only known genetic explanation for a missing pancreas."

"So, then what?" I asked.

"Sometimes there isn't a clear answer," she said. "It just means we keep looking, if you'd like to."

No tidy reason. No sentence that made the story easier to tell.

I thanked her and hung up.

I wrote "GATA6: negative" in the margin of the spiral notebook. I stared at all my careful entries: times, doses, numbers. Everything that could be measured lined up neatly on the page. The answer didn't.

After feeding came her bath. She still fit in the baby tub on the kitchen counter, splashing as I lathered her curls. Wrapped in her ducky towel, she smelled of lavender. I styled what little hair she had, dressed her in a cute outfit with a matching bow and ruffled socks. I didn't know where the day would lead. But I knew this part.

Before leaving, I emailed the caseworkers, asking again to delay the process until Jayden was healthier. Jeannette called back, requesting we come thirty minutes early to discuss it. I agreed.

On the floor, Jayden clapped and mimicked my fingerplay songs, beaming. She had no idea her future was being decided. When we sang *"You Are My Sunshine,"* my chest tightened at the quiet plea... *don't take her from me.*

Was this the day she began to leave us?

John and I couldn't stomach lunch. We packed her bottles, insulin, syringes, then the diaper bag. After her feeding and a big burp, John carried her car seat to the car.

The twenty-minute drive was filled with *"The Wheels on the Bus,"* her CD gift from Miss Pam. John kept his eyes on the road. I watched the trees blur past the window. The song played round and round.

By the time we reached the agency, Jayden was asleep. John lifted the car seat, draped her pink blanket, and together we put on brave faces as we walked inside.

Jeannette greeted us and led us to a conference room. I set the diaper bag beside me. Jayden slept at John's feet, her pink blanket tucked close. We didn't want her on display.

The adoption supervisor opened the meeting with our concerns, then moved past them. Sibling placement? No issue, she said. If a sibling ever entered the picture, they would go to a different home so Jayden's medical needs wouldn't be "distracted."

We nodded. My jaw tightened.

She reminded us Jayden had been legally free for adoption since November. Finding a family for a child with Jayden's needs would be difficult, she said.

I interrupted, "What about the family who called asking to adopt her? Why weren't they considered?"

"They were never called back," the supervisor said flatly. "Jayden's family has already been chosen."

Minutes later, that family walked in. The Garretts.

They introduced themselves with a long list of children in their care: children missing parts of their brains, others who were blind, some terminal. Eleven in all. Phones rang through their introductions. Mrs. Garrett excused herself. Mr. Garrett filled the silence, then he repeated himself, stopping mid-sentence.

"Oh, we forgot about Jesse." One of eleven.

When they referred to Jayden by her birth last name, I corrected, "You can just call her Jayden."

Mr. Garrett nodded. "We had a Jayden until Christmas, when he died."

Jayden stirred. John handed her to me. She blinked at the new faces and settled against my chest. She smiled at Jeannette and Nicole, then tucked her head against my cheek, a tiny arm around my face. The table sighed.

"She is showing affection!" the adoption supervisor gasped, surprised. She'd only read reports. Jayden was born without a pancreas. We had no idea what that meant for her life. But in that room, she was bright, present, alive.

The Garretts asked to hold her. I placed Jayden in Mrs. Garrett's lap, giving her hands a gentle squeeze. She studied the stranger's face, then turned to me and began to cry.

I sang her favorite song, guided her hands through "*Itsy Bitsy Spider*." Slowly, her body softened. She even smiled, though she leaned toward me, arms outstretched.

The meeting wrapped after an hour. We thanked the Garretts for their work. Their home was a blessing to children whose care never let up, sustained hour by hour through medical intervention.

As John buckled Jayden back into her car seat and we walked into the parking lot, my stomach twisted. I bent over the bumper, retching.

Nicole's hand rested on my back. "I didn't think you were doing very well."

She was right.

JOHN AND I WERE WRECKED. For months the agency had asked us to keep Jayden because she was unstable. Now they insisted she needed a "special placement."

The diagnosis of pancreatic agenesis explained so much. With careful management, she could live. But that didn't mean she was stable enough for a sudden transition.

The court had acknowledged any move would have to be slow and gentle. A new family would need time to learn her care, time to read her symptoms. Not just an open bed. Where would we find such a family? And how would we convince the agency to consider them when forms had already been signed?

That evening we gave up on cooking and ordered pizza. The girl at the counter greeted John by name. Jayden lit up when the bright yellow box came through the door. She ignored strained peas but adored gnawing on the garlicky crust. We smiled at her delight.

THE NEXT AFTERNOON was Jayden's one-year photo shoot. Karla, a photographer and friend of one of our

Pumpin' Mamas, welcomed us into her studio. She offered outfits and props, her walls lined with striking portraits. Karla told us Pumpin' Mama Jackie's hospital department had covered the prints, an unexpected kindness.

Jayden wouldn't cooperate. Karla coaxed, posed, snapped. Each frame caught only the moment before or after tears.

I tried new outfits, including a pink tutu cinched with chip clips. Nothing worked. Then Karla suggested a family portrait. She had John and me dress in black so Jayden would shine.

At first, Jayden sat on the floor, tears running silently down her cheeks. I scooped her up. The moment she realized I was holding her, not only posing her, she squealed. Her smile burst wide, contagious.

Karla's camera clicked fast. Jayden didn't need a pose. She needed us.

BY SUNDAY, we craved church. Erin, the campus director, greeted us warmly and made her usual fuss over Jayden's outfit. She led us to meet the music team, singers from across the church. Jayden charmed them with her wide eyes and tiny waves.

Callie, Pastor Mark's wife and one of the singers, shared a story about her newly adopted daughter, who had recently insisted, "I'm not black, I'm brown!" The group chuckled. Even Jayden giggled, as if she was in on the joke. Hands reached for her everywhere. People touched her fingers, waiting for her smile, unaware of what they were witnessing.

The prayer team promised to keep praying for her. I let myself breathe.

We spent some time with our friends Penny and Sam, longtime church members who had adopted a baby boy, Hayden, the summer before. They hadn't met Jayden yet. They'd heard whispers about her.

When they finally met Jayden, they fell in love. Hayden was two months younger, but his growth was on track, making Jayden seem much younger. Penny, special education teacher, and Sam, who worked at Children's Village helping kids in crisis, already had experience navigating adoption and developmental needs. Their home hummed with love and understanding.

We invited them for a play date, planning to see how the kids interacted. What started as an afternoon of introductions turned into hours of family fun. They asked careful questions. They didn't flinch. They were a real possibility.

WE EASED BACK INTO A RHYTHM.

Miss Pam suggested Jayden might be ready for the activity center in the basement. I paused, then carried it upstairs and scrubbed it clean.

Jayden lit up the moment she saw it. We tucked blankets around her until she sat snugly. Her face bright, she struck the lion and it played music. Her feet dangled until Miss Pam slid a box of books beneath them. Jayden planted both feet and began to bounce.

We looked at each other, grinning.

She grabbed. Laughed. Played.

It was a big day.

The next morning a text came from a number I didn't

recognize. Usually it was one of the Pumpin' Mamas. But this message asked about visiting Jayden. It was Callie from the music team at church. She said she hadn't been able to stop thinking about Jayden since meeting her at church. Would it be okay to come by and pray with us?

John and I held Mark and Callie in high regard. They had been part of the church since the beginning. Mark directed the music program and wove rock songs into his sermons. Callie's voice carried across thousands at countless services. Now they were asking to sit in our living room. I panicked about the messy floors, then quickly texted back. Yes, Wednesday evening would work.

That night, John picked up pastries. I tried to time Jayden's nap. We ate a quick dinner, loaded the dishwasher, and the doorbell rang. Mark, Callie, and their teenage daughter, Lyndi, stepped inside. Their eyes went straight to Jayden.

We settled in the family room. Jayden perched on my lap, studying them. Callie asked about her progress and listened, eyes on Jayden as she flipped through a cardboard picture book, pointing at shapes.

Soon, I carried Jayden over and eased her into Callie's lap. She leaned against her, resting a small hand on Callie's arm. Her eyes stayed on me. No tears. John served pastries. Callie didn't look up. She was smitten with Jayden. After a while, Mark asked if they could pray.

Then he told us their story. How they adopted a daughter named Hope, abandoned at age five. He was hesitant at first, already stretched thin with four kids. "But then I saw her eyes," he said. "Just look at her eyes." He showed us a photo of that first meeting.

Before leaving, they asked for a picture with Jayden. Something to pin to their fridge, they said, so they would remember to pray. I lifted my phone.

Callie kissed Jayden's forehead, handed her back to me, and said, "Goodnight, Jayden."

Jayden settled against my chest, warm and heavy. Her name had been spoken, carried by voices beyond our own. I held her close until my breathing slowed. The house went quiet again. The spiral notebook was waiting.

# April 2010
## — Part One

Court was coming fast. Our attorney advised us to speak for Jayden ourselves. We would need to write a letter to document the facts of her life, facts that had nearly taken her, and facts that kept her alive.

She nearly died at three months. In the middle of everything else, we found the missing piece: Jayden had been born without a pancreas. Some doctors spoke as though her life were an exception that wouldn't last. Others offered what they could: seven specialists, a twelve-day hospital stay, and ways to try to keep her here.

We needed them to understand. Jayden fought to be here. Brave. Bright. Alive. We believed her strength wasn't only hers. It lived in the bond between us. Jayden stayed against me every minute of every day. Most often, she rested against my chest, skin to skin. When she couldn't be there, she was held by warm hands and gentle arms. We set her down only when we had to. Then we lifted her again.

Holding her had been our priority since the two-week

stretch before her NICU discharge. Since the phone call. Since they asked us to do just that. We were there every day. She deserved a home that would protect that bond. If they moved her into a medically fragile home, we didn't know if she'd survive it. Her doctors had put it in writing.

I asked Miss Pam to babysit Jayden so John and I could both attend the morning hearing. Dudley saw her in the rocker and made a beeline. The rocker meant snuggles. Miss Pam chuckled as he wormed his way onto her lap beside his little girl.

As we drove away, our hearts raced. We were fighting for Jayden to be seen, not as a label, but as the child she was. I knew John would have to speak. He could keep his voice firm. I couldn't. My voice cracked too easily.

He knew our letter by heart. Every phrase we'd chosen. We wanted *consideration* for the *fragility of the child* and the *problems with transition*. And above all: *no rush*. The judge himself had said it.

They were proposing a home with eleven medically fragile children. We feared the stress would undo everything Jayden had fought for. Stress spiked Jayden's glucose. We'd seen it happen in the hospital.

The room was crowded with caseworkers: DHS, Ennis Center, adoption, and, for the first time, the director of adoptions. Someone mentioned the weather. No one was listening.

After minutes that stretched thin, the clerk called us in. The referee greeted us and reviewed the last hearing's notes. We went around the table introducing ourselves.

An attorney sat at the end of the table. The GAL, Guardian ad Litem. John met Jayden's previous GAL in the NICU ten months earlier. We hadn't seen a GAL since then.

How could anyone know what a child needs without

seeing them? So we stayed involved. We showed up and spoke up.

When it was our turn, we rose from the chairs along the wall. John smiled and introduced us as Jayden's foster parents. The referee welcomed us and thanked us for caring for her.

Then the updates began. One by one, each worker read their report. DHS covered the legal pieces. Parental rights terminated. Jayden was legally available for adoption.

Nicole spoke next: weight, height, development, how Jayden could sit up now, how she was learning to belly crawl. Nicole named the diagnosis we'd received the same day as the last hearing, no pancreas. She listed each specialist.

Then Jeannette presented the adoption plan. The referee's eyes stayed on her. The director of adoptions sat beside Jeannette, but Jeannette was assigned to the case, so she did the talking. She described the "perfect" family they'd contacted for Jayden's placement. We knew she'd been away at training when the decision was made. She sounded like a messenger.

"The chosen family has nurses in their home," Jeannette said. "They've met Jayden. They're ready to take her."

John and I held our breath. I grabbed his hand. Mine wouldn't stop shaking. He unfolded our letter, ready to speak for Jayden while she couldn't. We didn't have the chance.

The referee cut in, eyes fixed on Jeannette. "What were you thinking?" Each word came measured, clear. "This baby would never survive in a family of eleven medically fragile children. There is no rush to place her. She is doing well where she is. Leave her there." Then she added, "You may look for a family before the next review in three months. But do not rush her placement."

I don't usually cry in public. That day I couldn't stop. When the room settled, the referee turned to us. Were we in agreement? We nodded, and John said quietly, "Thank you."

She set the next court date, July 15, and dismissed everyone. Then she asked John and me to stay behind.

Up close, her expression softened. She grinned as she told us about her grandson, just two weeks older than Jayden. We asked to see pictures, then shared a few of Jayden. She flipped through them, then passed them to her clerk. They both teared up.

"She's a miracle," the clerk said.

The referee nodded. "Yes, she is."

It felt like mercy. We left the courthouse before noon. The rain disguised our tears.

Jayden was here. We were watching it happen. We prayed a forever family would find her. The Garretts weren't the right fit, but someone out there might be. Jayden needed to be embraced. Her needs were intense. Still, help kept arriving. Hands. Calls. Coolers. Enough light to take the next step.

Today, the court had protected her. Maybe one day, when she was stronger, I could loosen my grip. I didn't know when. Only that, for now, she still needed me right here.

---

JAYDEN's first birthday party was one week away. We had a full week of appointments, so prep time was limited. Prep meant one thing: cleaning.

Over the past year, I couldn't get used to the stream

of people through our house. Everyone who came through knew I was caring for a fragile baby on little sleep. I felt their kindness as they passed by my messy kitchen.

For a party, I wanted the house to look like we lived here on purpose. John and I started cleaning, then surrendered and bought decorations. Jayden curled comfortably in the ring sling, watching us fill the cart. We printed professional photos of her and picked frames to go with them. Jayden reached for anything I held, delighted by her own mischief. We placed the photos, her story beaming from the walls.

I made a photo collage online: one picture from each month of Jayden's time with us. The early photos showed a baby barely clinging to life. Then came breast milk. The transformation was startling. Most of our guests lived those stages with us.

We had invited everyone who had been part of her journey. The invitations asked for memory letters for Jayden's book. Some arrived early. My mom and kids mailed stories from afar. Envelopes came with pictures of donor babies whose milk helped Jayden thrive. Her book was filling up.

My sister Doreen and her friend Laurie arrived from Pennsylvania Friday night. Dudley raced in circles when he saw Aunt Doreen. Jayden, in a pastel sleeper, offered her shy dimpled smile and a finger in her mouth.

Then came a knock. John expected a neighbor. I opened the door and froze. Aunt Ethel. She tagged along to surprise me. I hadn't seen my sister or aunt since Jayden arrived. They had driven six hours after work just to be here.

John carried their bags. Dudley zoomed upstairs, unsure whose bed he'd claim. As John handed out fresh towels, I wondered, did he know Aunt Ethel was coming? I couldn't stop smiling.

---

JAYDEN WOKE the next morning smiling at the sound of voices down the hall, her hands opening and closing. People gathered, and she watched and reached.

She seemed at ease with our guests, as long as she stayed in my arms. She played pat-a-cake with Aunt Ethel. With Aunt Doreen, she tapped her thanks and sang her little star song, all oohs and aahs and smiles. John praised her every action with a proud smile and the softest, "Deedle, Deedle girl."

Jayden weighed fourteen pounds and measured twenty-six inches. She looked like a baby now... soft skin, plump cheeks. She could sit up on her own and was learning to belly crawl.

Sometimes she said, "ma-ma-ma." But she didn't babble. And she didn't eat. She tolerated only breast milk with added coconut oil. We tried solids, but after a few tries, she refused. Usually after a night of stomach trouble.

Miss Pam helped me frame the delays. Jayden was born eight weeks early and failed to thrive for three months. She had been blind and deaf at first. No wonder her speech was slow. I tried not to worry. I was grateful she had survived. Talking could wait.

That morning she clung to me. She tolerated familiar guests, but only in my arms. She didn't want to be held by anyone else. We learned each other through long nights and small changes, especially after the hospital stay.

She depended on me to read her symptoms. She didn't cry or shake when glucose was high. Her distress was quiet.

I was the one who felt it first. I could trace the spike. A blood draw. A separation. A moment of fear. Her numbers would soar. I had learned to prevent what I could.

Jayden stayed close during the morning of her birthday. Others wanted snuggles, but she chose me. Dudley handled guest entertainment. He made the rounds with his squeaky toy until Aunt Doreen tossed it for him. Jackpot.

April 17. One year.

The kitchen quickly filled with food, laughter, and love. Cressie and her daughter Stephanie arrived early with home-baked goods. John and Laurie set up tables while Aunt Ethel prepped fruit. Doreen arranged the memory table. Doreen got to walk Jayden around the house while I showered. Then she and Aunt Ethel left for balloons. John picked up the cakes.

After her uninterrupted nap, I dressed Jayden in a white ruffled dress, size 3 months, with matching socks, patent shoes, and a feathered headband. My heart fluttered as we opened the bedroom door.

Green and pink balloons floated above the table and the cakes. Fruit overflowed in color. Linda and her husband were already there. She hadn't seen Jayden since the ER. She was stunned.

I checked Jayden's glucose. All was well. I sat in my rocker with her. Doreen brought me iced tea. Aunt Ethel leaned close, asking, "Where are your toofies?" Jayden smiled wide, showing all four. When Jayden finally reached for her, Aunt Ethel whispered, "That made it worth the trip."

Soon, the house was full. Friends, donors, providers, supporters. Some had provided breast milk. Others had brought meals or sat with me during the hard days. Now, the Pumpin' Mamas posed with their babies and Jayden. Milk siblings.

Doreen greeted guests and handed out photos of Jayden in her pink ruffles. Laurie guided people into the family room. Cressie and John kept the food and drinks flowing. Jayden stayed on my lap. Her choice. We kept her calm, as if that could keep everything else from unraveling.

Then Callie arrived with her adopted daughter, Hope. They knelt to Jayden's level and offered soft birthday wishes. Jayden looked up, curious. Callie moved beside us, hands open. I placed Jayden in her arms, not because I needed a break, but because something in me said it was time. Jayden was comfortable in Callie's arms. So was I.

Callie moved to a seat by the fireplace, lifted a familiar toy, and offered it gently. Jayden stayed quiet. Settled. I stood for the first time in hours, stretching my legs. Karla caught my eye, and we talked about the photo she'd taken, the one we were handing out. The one people kept tucking into their pockets.

Penny arrived next with her daughter. She had left Hayden at home for his nap. She slid into the seat beside Callie and reached toward Jayden. Jayden didn't make eye contact, but let Penny join in for a moment. Both women were praying about adopting Jayden.

Two days earlier, Callie had written to say she and Mark were seeking clarity. She wasn't sure, but she felt pulled to open her arms, open their home. That very morning, Penny had called. She, too, wanted to move forward.

These women felt like a possible answer. We'd had others express interest over the past few months, but none had followed through. I didn't know how likely either of these might be, but here they were. Side by side. Neither aware of the other's hopes. Either could be her mama. Her forever family. That decision wasn't mine. I could only keep showing up.

All around us, the house buzzed with laughter and movement. Jayden stayed close to Callie. When Callie and Hope said their goodbyes, Jayden turned back toward me. She climbed into my lap, quiet. Holding a book. Watching.

She stayed with me, love gathering like light. Warm and heavy in my arms. Unhurried. I lingered with her in that moment, somehow just outside the party's noise... tender, still, full. Then the door opened again.

Murielle and her husband came in, Elias racing between them, already looking for Dudley. Jayden brightened and reached for them, familiar faces, woven into her days since she'd come home. Murielle once talked about adoption too. These glimpses helped me imagine Jayden's possible futures. I needed that.

When most of the guests had gone, Doreen counted sixty-five. Many left memory pages and stories. Each child got a balloon. The kitchen was clean. John folded tables and stored them in the garage.

Jayden's glucose read 347. The highest in weeks. The cost of a beautiful day. A number written in the spiral notebook. Our Deedle girl. I reached for the insulin and gave the injection. Then we rocked. She drank her bottle and napped on my chest. We exhaled. We dimmed the lights and let the house go quiet.

We sat around the family room and read letters. One man, adopted himself, said he hoped, someday, Jayden would find a way to forgive her birth mother. Photos slipped from envelopes. Babies we never met. Names we knew by heart.

John's friend reached into a paper bag and pulled out

a small puppet. His mother had made them for children in hospitals. This was the last one she'd finished before she passed. He placed it in Jayden's lap. No one spoke.

Cressie and Stephanie lingered at the counter. Miss Pam and her husband stayed, talking low. No one in a hurry to leave.

Jayden sat on my lap. Studied faces. Leaned in. Stayed. I watched her. How easily she belonged.

The house settled around us. Not silent. Just enough.

# April 2010 —
## Part Two

Two weeks after the birthday party, stories and cards kept coming. I placed them in the basket where Jayden's memory book would begin.

Spring had arrived, but nothing felt settled. I slipped Jayden into her spring jacket, grabbed the mail, and settled her in the stroller. As we turned the corner, we saw our neighbor Denise walking her yellow lab, Charlie. Jayden immediately reached to pet her new friend.

Denise waved. "Well hey there, little one," she said, bending toward Jayden. "You look stronger than I've ever seen you."

I had called Denise soon after Jayden's placement. She lived just a few doors down, a retired NICU nurse, calm and unflappable. She was also a Type 1 diabetic. She understood the highs and lows in her own body.

As she fell into step beside us, she asked, "How's she tolerating the enzymes now?"

I filled her in, the way I did with Dr. Earles. After a while, Denise glanced over. "You know, Judy, I'll admit something. When you first called me... I thought you were in over your head. This case is more complicated than anything I ever saw in the NICU."

I nodded. "I needed to know someone nearby understood what we were up against," I said. "Knowing you were down the street made it possible. It kept me going."

She gave me a small nod and reached down to scratch Charlie's ear. "Well, she's lucky to have you."

I said goodbye and continued our walk. Jayden studied the flowers in bloom and listened to the neighborhood dogs. These were things I hadn't expected for her. Now, she was happy.

---

WE WERE STILL WAITING for the agency to choose.

We opened our home to the families considering adoption. Most came cautiously, drawn to Jayden, but afraid of attaching. Afraid of falling in love only to be told no. It asked something of them. Time. Heart. Hope without promise.

I urged them to spend time with Jayden anyway. As much as they could stand. To be part of her life, not as applicants, but as people who cared. It wasn't theirs to win. Only theirs to give. This was an investment in her future, a way to write themselves into her story.

Each family agreed and gave presence, patience, and prayer. I took pictures of everyone with Jayden so she would see herself with them early on.

Even so, my stomach ached when I imagined her looking back on photos with her new family. That grief was easier to face than the thought of holding her while she slipped away.

She looked healthy, happy, rarely cried, quick to learn. But what if she stopped gaining weight? What if breast milk stopped being enough? She refused solids, except for the pizza crust she liked to gum.

Jayden's digestion faltered again. Her latest blood-work showed low iron. Supplements were recommended, but they upset her stomach. Her appetite dropped to less than half her normal intake.

During therapy, she cried while Miss Pam held up the laminated picture cards. She searched for the matching toy and couldn't settle. This wasn't her.

My skin went cold. I couldn't bear the idea of losing her now, not after all the work it took to keep her here. And I couldn't imagine the other life either. The one where she survived and I held all of it for as long as it lasted. I didn't trust my strength the way everyone else seemed to.

Not when everything still felt this fragile.

I told Dr. Earles. She discontinued the iron supplement.

I hated knowing Jayden needed what her body rejected.

I asked Dr. Nancy to help with supplemental iron. She'd guided her through enzymes, one careful step at a time. If anyone could ease this transition, it was her.

For now, it was enough.

JOHN and I had to let go. The adoption process was not ours to manage. The referee ruled. She gave us time for Jayden to be with us. Our work was clear: feed her, love her, and get her ready to go. Penny and Sam wrote their letter first. They had prayed over the decision and now waited with quiet hope. Callie and Mark sent theirs soon after. They loved Jayden from the moment they met her at church. Their letter held longing. Both families knew her. Both had held her in their arms. It was out of our hands. We had done what we could.

Back home, the rocker creaked as I shifted her weight to my chest. Her breath warmed my neck. Familiar.

The phone rang. We weren't ready.

# May 2010 —
## Part One

Before that phone rang, it had been quiet for a while. We had just begun to breathe again, long enough to notice it.

Jayden was healthier than she had ever been. John and I were loosening our grip on fear. Her belly crawl grew into hands and knees, and she carried herself across the room. She loved the activity center, turning it into a trampoline. When she wanted to play pat-a-cake, she'd take my hands and clap them herself. All I had to do was meet her eyes. She trusted me to understand.

Callie and Mark decided to pursue adoption. They had four children by birth and one by adoption, Hope. Their birth children were grown, or nearly so: one was married, one away at college, one graduating that spring, and the youngest in middle school. A full house. Still, something was missing.

Callie said she hadn't stopped seeing Jayden's face since March. In dreams. In the quiet moments between things. She believed Jayden had been placed in their path, not promised, just set there to be noticed. She asked if they could visit again.

That evening, they returned. Hope raced straight for Dudley. Mark asked questions about Jayden's care, and I answered as honestly as I could. Jayden stayed relaxed in Callie's lap, her hands exploring their faces, her body loose, her breathing even.

She performed *"Itsy Bitsy Spider"* and *"Twinkle, Twinkle."* Mark and Callie, both musicians, watched her, their faces softening as she sang.

I told them they were welcome any time. It mattered that they come to know Jayden, but more than that, it mattered that Jayden come to know them. Callie said she'd visit often. She was eager. Careful, too. The agency had other families under consideration. Nothing was guaranteed. I reminded her that showing up meant something. Being present in Jayden's life was its own gift. That time in the room mattered.

A few days later, Penny and Sam visited again. They, too, had been thinking seriously about adoption. Penny brought Hayden, and after that we got together for a few playdates. She said her older kids were ready to help. Grandma lived nearby, close enough to count on.

Penny and I had talked about the way adoption time-lines usually unfolded. The waiting. The long middle. When love is allowed to grow before it's asked to let go. Before anyone knows how it will end. We stayed there in the calm, not knowing what was coming.

I began sending emails to both families with photos and small stories from the day. They knew the other was interested. They trusted God to lead. They offered help when I'd allow it. They were falling in love with a child they might not get to keep. I recognized it. I knew what it meant to surrender. I'd done it before. There was peace in letting go. And an ache in wanting to help anyway.

I made space for them.

---

WHEN JEANNETTE CAME for her monthly placement review, she told us the other approved families had backed out. Only two remained: Mark and Callie, and Penny and Sam. Both from our church. Both experienced with adoption. All they needed was updated home studies.

*Thank you for answering our prayers.*

Miss Pam's next visit brought puzzles and coordination practice. As usual, she ended with reading and music.

"Ready to sing?" she asked.

Jayden raised her arms overhead, fingers splayed.

"Out came the sun," Miss Pam said, translating.

She smiled and began *"Itsy Bitsy Spider."* Jayden watched her hands and joined in, moving with her, already knowing what came next.

Miss Pam's eyes met mine. We both understood at the same time. Jayden had just asked for a song and been understood.

Her sign language had taken off. She could sign "more" and "eat." And now, songs. Her words were still delayed. Her mind was not.

Near the end of Miss Pam's session on May 10, the phone rang. The caller ID read Ennis Center for Children.

---

I ASKED Miss Pam to stay with Jayden while I answered. I expected paperwork updates. Or information about

Jayden's adoption. Instead, it was a placement worker. Her voice was practiced.

Jayden's birth mother had given birth to a baby boy on April 30. He arrived five weeks early. He tested positive for cocaine, marijuana, and alcohol. Medically he was stable, aside from the withdrawal symptoms. They weren't offering placement. They were notifying us. They planned to place him elsewhere. They said no family could handle both.

John and I had an agreement about these calls. I handled them. Usually, I accepted without pause. But they'd already decided. We wouldn't be asked. Still, I hesitated.

*Should they be separated? Should we take him?*

Jayden required around-the-clock care. Her medical routine was intense. I didn't know how I'd manage a newborn on top of that. But... could we not?

I asked the worker to wait before pursuing a different foster family. I needed to call John.

Miss Pam overheard the call. Her eyes grew wide. Panic. She gently asked the obvious: "How would you juggle both?"

I looked back at her, puzzled. I heard myself answer.

"How could we not?"

John felt strongly that siblings should stay together. He reminded me his work slowed down. The plane he usually flew had been sold. Now he flew occasional charters.

"If we say yes," he said, "I'll take the new baby when I'm home. You won't be alone with both of them."

He was ready. I wasn't sure I was. Still, I called back and asked them to place Jayden's baby brother with us. It would be short-term, I told myself. We could do anything short-term.

THE NEXT DAY, John brought the matching bucket car seat from the basement. I found a newborn outfit and packed the diaper bags. We loaded Jayden into the car. We decided to bring her to see her NICU nurses. It was like returning to the beginning. John would take her inside while I received discharge instructions and dressed the baby boy.

John couldn't wait to show off his Deedle. He also couldn't wait to bring home a baby boy. We had already chosen a name: Joey. Back then, we watched *Friends*. Joey was the loyal one. The one who showed up. No questions. I wanted Jayden's brother to grow into that kind of love.

And the names fit. Jayden and Joey. A team. Together.

At the hospital, DHS and Ennis Center staff met us in the lobby. They made a fuss over Jayden. They hadn't seen her since last summer, when they sent her home with only one instruction.

*Just hold her.*

I slipped into the NICU alone. Joey lay curled in his isolette, swaddled tight. His head was full of dark curls. Long lashes framed deep, watchful eyes. He scanned the room. He was beautiful.

I picked him up and whispered, "Welcome, little one."

The nurse returned. No discharge today. They needed the birth mother's consent for a few procedures, and they couldn't reach her. So I took my place in the rocker beside his bed. I cradled him close, tucked the miniature bottle into his waiting lips, and held my breath. Joey drank. Two ounces gone within minutes. Then he slept.

From the rocker, I overheard the nurse on the phone

explaining the need to get consent for circumcision and newborn shots. The birth mother immediately approved the circumcision, but hesitated over the vaccines. Would they hurt him?

She said she planned to do things differently. She wanted to parent her son. I heard this before.

When the NICU nurse hung up, she met my eyes and shook her head, half-smiling. She joked about pain and permission in the same breath.

I laid Joey back into the isolette and whispered that we'd come back tomorrow. His sister was waiting.

MAY 12.

Joey was five pounds fourteen ounces. A different kind of beginning than Jayden's. I sat beside them in the back seat and told Joey about Jayden. I made up a rhyming song using both names. Jayden giggled.

At home, we unpacked. Dudley greeted the new arrival with his usual enthusiasm. John looked around and smiled. "Let the games begin."

We rocked in tandem. Each of us with a bottle, a baby, a rocker, and fast food on the side tables. Later, we laid both babies on a blanket on the floor. Jayden reached for Joey's hair, fingers careful. Then, without prompting, she leaned in and kissed his forehead. As if welcoming him. Or maybe blessing him.

John and I squeezed hands. Something had already begun.

THAT NIGHT, we settled both babies.

Jayden's numbers were stable. She took her insulin, fed well, and snuggled to sleep in her too-big bed.

Joey screamed. And didn't stop.

Swaddling helped. The baby swing, set on high, helped for a few minutes. But mostly, he was inconsolable. I remembered his nurse telling me: *He just wants to be held.*

Joey didn't even seem comforted by that. His cries were relentless. My heart ached. This baby had no choice. His withdrawal wasn't fair. Babies don't just cry during withdrawal. They shriek. They flail in pain.

It was time to call for help. I told Penny of Joey's birth first. She went quiet. Shocked. She said her husband would be overwhelmed. But if they were chosen for Jayden, they would take Joey, too.

"Siblings belong together," she said.

Then I called Callie. She was stunned. Silent for a moment, as if catching her breath. Then she asked questions. About his size. His cry. When could she see him? She wanted to meet him.

That evening, Mark and Callie came alone. Joey screamed. Jayden studied him, curious but unafraid. Callie smiled. Mark stared, still. I took a picture of them holding both babies. They didn't say much about what the future might hold. But they each held a child like they already knew how. Like their bodies remembered.

It was just a visit. Still, something in the way they moved through the room while juggling both babies told me they were already imagining more. They were patient. They stayed, unhurried.

JOEY'S first pediatric visit brought good news. He was gaining weight. But also, a rash and blood in his stool. Clear signs of formula intolerance. A different formula recommended.

Two days later, Jayden's checkup showed progress, too: over fifteen pounds now. But she still gagged on solids. Dr. Earles adjusted her Prevacid and referred us for more OT.

We looked at both babies. One with a pancreas. One without. Both struggling to eat. Siblings.

---

A WEEK LATER, the agency interviewed both potential adoptive families. Now it wasn't just Jayden. It was Jayden and Joey. Joey carried unknowns. Exposure. Withdrawal. No one could predict the long-term effects.

Callie rode with me for Joey's infectious disease follow-up. One baby for each of us. She fed Joey. Burped him. Wiped his mouth with the corner of the burp cloth. She showed up.

The doctor explained that Joey was treated prophylactically with antibiotics for syphilis, given the family history. Labs ten days later would tell us for sure.

On the drive home, Callie held a bottle, juggled a burp cloth, and answered a call. I tried not to listen. Then I was crying.

Jeannette, the adoption worker, had called. Penny and Sam had withdrawn. With Hayden, Jayden, and Joey all so young, it was more than they could manage.

If Callie and Mark agreed, Jayden and Joey would be placed together with them. Callie's hands were shaking. Tears slid down her cheeks as she spoke softly to Jayden and Joey.

"I'm going to be your forever mama."

I bit my lip, trying to still the tremble. The handoff had begun. The paperwork was moving. Like a metronome, it kept time without asking if we were ready.

At home, we fed the babies side by side. When they fell asleep and were tucked in, Callie walked to the door. We hugged.

"See you soon, Mama Callie."

I closed the door and held the knob one beat too long, before my tears could decide what they meant.

# May 2010 — Part Two

One morning, after John's coffee, I drew him a sleep chart. Jayden up top. Joey beneath. The bottom row showed when I could lie down. Not sleep, just close my eyes. It wasn't pretty. I was barely functioning. Each day, less so.

I considered separating them. One baby in each room, two doors shut, two sound machines hissing. They might've slept better. I wouldn't have. I couldn't imagine rocking and feeding one baby while listening to the other baby cry down the hall, counting seconds, bracing for the moment it turned into an alarm. I needed John beside me, close, awake, ready when I couldn't be.

He was already helping during the day. Joey napped against John's chest, his bottom patted in the one rhythm that worked. When that wasn't enough, John took a slow lap through the house. Joey draped over his shoulder until he settled.

I usually did whatever it took. Whatever they needed. But I was too tired to pace the halls. I couldn't carry both babies through the night.

So we made a plan. I'd take Jayden. John still wasn't confident using her glucometer or syringes. I'd take care of Joey until 4:00 a.m. After that, John would take him to the guest room so I could rest. It gave John a block of uninterrupted sleep. It gave me a few hours.

The plan worked. For about a week. Then I begged John to take over full nights with Joey. I couldn't string together a sentence. At appointments, I stammered through the basics.

We set up a room for Papa John and Joey with a rocker, crib, and dim lamp. I set the rules. Lights low. No talking. The more time they spent together, the more John fell for him. Somewhere in there, Joey became Buster.

John had said we needed to be a team to do this. I think he pictured his role as comic relief and pizza runs. But he kept showing up.

<hr>

I STARTED SENDING regular updates to Callie. She deserved to know the truth of our days. Every detail. She would be their mother.

Callie and Mark agreed to adopt both babies. Joey's birth mother still had rights, and she wanted to parent. Court wasn't until August. We didn't say that part out loud.

Callie wrote back with warmth and encouragement. She offered to run errands, pick up diapers, even cook dinner. Generous. Dependable. She made help feel normal, like it belonged here.

One night, she brought dinner to our house. Mark came too. We put Jayden in the highchair and buckled her in snug, straps clicking. Jayden could pick up puffs with her index finger and thumb. She preferred her fist. She was working on it.

Callie brought homemade applesauce. She filled the spoon and passed it to me. Jayden reached for it. A small victory.

Callie beamed. "She's got that down!"

Mark leaned in, smiling. "You gonna share that with me?"

Jayden blinked, then looked down.

"She's watching you," I said.

"She's pretending not to," Mark grinned. "But I'm irresistible."

Jayden glanced again, then away. That was her tell. She was thinking.

"She looks away to decide if it's safe," I said. "It's how she warms up."

"She's smart," Mark said.

Joey squawked. John stood up and took him into the living room, bouncing him on his shoulder. Callie followed. She rocked Joey. She didn't ask what he needed. She read him. She patted his freshly diapered bottom in a familiar rhythm. He sighed.

Later, after we'd eaten and were lingering at the table, Callie asked if she could give Joey his bath. I was surprised. "Sure," I said. "He likes the water."

She stood at the kitchen counter beside the baby tub and eased him into the water. His shoulders dropped. His fists uncurled. She reached for the washcloth. Joey kept his eyes on her, as if he already knew.

After she dried him and zipped him into his sleeper, she looked to me. "I think he's relaxed." I nodded, and she carried him to the rocker for his bottle.

After they left, John and I sat quietly. The kitchen still smelled like garlic and apples.

"She's getting attached," I said.

He nodded. "So are we."

---

THAT SUNDAY, we strapped the babies into their slings. Joey against John's chest, Jayden facing outward from mine. We walked the path from the driveway to Mark and Callie's front door. Their screen door clicked behind us. Rock music drifted from the stereo. Cupcakes lined the counter.

Someone called out, "Hi!" from the kitchen. The table was already set when we arrived. Grandparents from both sides gathered in.

Hope met us at the threshold with a card she'd made for Jayden. Jayden looked once, then pressed her face into my chest. "You're okay," I whispered. When she peeked back out, it was only her eyes.

Callie's daughter Jordin pressed a small stuffed lion into Joey's hands. He flinched, then let it rest against his chest.

Mark came in from the backyard, laughing. "Well, look at this crew," he said. "You brought the party with you."

We wished him happy birthday. Jayden leaned back into me, her body stiff as she stared at him. "She remembers you," I said.

"I'll take that as a compliment." He smiled. "She looks like she's thinking hard."

"She does that," I said. "She watches first."

"She's allowed," Mark said, voice warm and soft. "The best kind of brave is slow."

He didn't reach for her. He just stayed nearby.

Callie scooped up Joey and rubbed his back. He

melted into her shoulder like he'd been there forever.

Their oldest daughter brought out bubbles and waved the wand. Hope chased them barefoot, squealing with laughter. Jayden lifted her fingers toward the bubbles, braver than she'd been a moment ago.

Before gifts, Mark asked quietly, "How do you really feel about transitioning foster children to adoptive parents?"

He wasn't making conversation. He was asking because he cared. When others asked, I had my script. "It's not about us. It's what's best for the child." Sometimes I joked, because it was easier than telling the truth. I told them the words mattered: a baby *gets* to go to a family, never *has* to go.

But this was different. I couldn't pretend. All I managed was, "This one will be hard." I choked up. John stepped in with the familiar words, his hand on my shoulder. "It isn't about us..."

A few months earlier, I found their big family intimidating. That night felt natural. We stayed for nearly two hours. Every child in that house found a way to welcome us. There was no performance. Just ordinary delight. Cupcakes and coloring pages. A borrowed bouncer in the corner. Joey slept on Callie's chest while Jayden sat in Mark's lap, rigid at first, then slowly settled.

Mark opened the video camera his daughter and son-in-law had given him, meant to capture life once the babies were home. Our gift, a framed eight-by-ten of Jayden from her first birthday photo shoot, went straight to the mantel. No hesitation. John and I had loved being with Mark and Callie's family, but Callie had seen it: how exhausted we were, how hollow I felt. She offered to come overnight to help with Joey. Her work schedule made Sunday and Thursday nights easiest, but she said she'd come even on work nights if we needed her.

As we were saying our goodbyes, Hope came close, looked into Jayden's eyes and whispered, "She's pretty."

"She thinks you are, too," I said.

On the drive home, we didn't talk for a long time.

Then I said it out loud. "That felt like a visit with family, not just friends."

John nodded. "It did."

Still, it felt like practice for goodbye. The transition had started. That visit was the babies' first time inside the home that would one day be theirs. *Their home.* Brother and sister together.

CALLIE CARED for Joey the next night, working to keep him rested and content. In the morning, she gave a full report: ounces, sleep, diapers. She had held him most of the night. She wanted to do it right. She did. She didn't just want to help. She was already in love. It was a comfort. A grief. A beginning.

Now, we were working to ease the shift. We adjusted names first. I stayed Mama Judy. She became Mama Callie. We needed Jayden to learn there could be more than one safe mama. To let Callie's touch feel like home, too. We let her take it slowly. Over time, I'd fade from Mama Judy to Judy. Callie would move in the other direction.

We agreed to co-parent. Not just in title. In action. We went to appointments together. I showed her how to measure Jayden's insulin, how to hold her nebulizer. Callie learned quickly. Jayden watched her. Each time I handed her the glucometer or guided her fingers on the syringe, it felt like a quiet tear in the seam that held Jayden to me. Stitch by stitch. An invisible goodbye.

I wanted this. I wanted Jayden to be safe, cherished. But I was scared of disappearing from her story. Of not being there when she needed me. Terrified of what came next. Of what life might be like when she wasn't here.

There was a pause ahead. Mark and Callie had a two-week trip planned to Europe for their 25th anniversary. We agreed not to start anything major until they returned. The legal steps still needed time. We were looking at the end of summer for any official transition.

For now, we'd keep moving slowly. New names. More visits. Gentle shifts in routines. Jayden needed to see Mama Callie as someone she could trust. Someone who could feed her, soothe her. Hold her. Joey, we agreed, would be easier. Still so young.

But Jayden had only ever known one mother. Me. She had no memory of life before that. We'd been through it all: surgeries, diagnoses, therapies, midnight checks, milestones. I was her constant.

I had asked for the right family, and we found them. I hadn't asked to be replaced. I hadn't prayed to let her go. But I knew it came with a cost. So this transition would need to be slow. Intentional.

She wasn't ready yet. And neither was I.

---

A FEW DAYS LATER, Jayden got sick. A low-grade fever and bronchial congestion. It started in the middle of the night.

Thank goodness John was already up with Joey. I spent the whole night in the rocker with Jayden. I could hear the wheeze in her chest, so I gave her a nebulizer treatment with the medication we kept for nights like this. It helped. Her breathing calmed, and she smiled like she was fine. But I knew better.

Joey had an eye appointment that morning. I couldn't risk leaving Jayden at home when her breathing sounded like that. John was preparing for a rare opportunity to fly, and Callie had to work. Miss Pam offered to come while John finished getting ready.

Jayden seemed content between coughing fits, so we decided to go. Miss Pam would stay with her in the gift shop while I took Joey for his exam.

From the ophthalmologist's waiting room, I called Dr. Earles's office. Her team said we could stop by after Joey's appointment. They'd work Jayden in.

Joey cried constantly, loud enough to turn heads. I bounced him and swaddled him. I tried everything, but nothing worked. The eye exam was short, and thankfully normal.

Jayden stayed calm the whole time, bright-eyed between coughing fits. The contrast was striking. I felt like I was on autopilot. One baby in distress, the other quietly struggling, and me just trying to get through the morning without falling apart. Miss Pam never wavered. Her presence gave me just enough air to keep moving.

On the drive to Dr. Earles's office with Jayden reclining in her car seat, her breathing worsened. Just before we arrived, she gagged on her congestion and vomited all over herself. She'd been trying to warn us. We thought she just wanted to be held. Miss Pam caught what she could with a blanket, and we kept going. Five minutes away. Stuck in traffic.

The diagnosis was Respiratory Syncytial Virus (RSV). Common in preemies. Dangerous enough to make my stomach drop. She'd been getting monthly preventive injections, so her case was milder than most.

Nurse Melissa gave her a nebulizer treatment right there. I watched Jayden's chest rise and fall, slower now. We were sent home with instructions to repeat the treatments every four hours.

She hadn't gained any weight that week. The iron supplements upset her tummy. Getting sick wouldn't help. But we were grateful. We'd gotten a same-day visit. We caught it early.

Miss Pam had taken Joey outside during Jayden's appointment. He cried the entire way home. We pulled into the driveway, both babies finally quiet. Joey spit up. Just formula, thank goodness. But it felt like a full stop at the end of a very long morning.

Miss Pam had been remarkable. Calm through RSV. Through vomit. Through backseat acrobatics and waiting-room meltdowns. I wasn't sure she knew what she was saying yes to. I only knew I couldn't have done it without her.

I learned to read Jayden's needs. But that day, she'd been the one reading me. Quietly holding on until I could catch up.

Jayden's RSV could've been worse. Joey's eyes were healthy.

We made it through, even as I felt myself slipping. But this life didn't come with breaks. Not yet.

---

THAT NIGHT, I called Callie to ask if she might want to come spend the night. She said yes without hesitation. She just needed to wait until Hope was asleep. Callie was being careful. She didn't want Hope to feel replaced by the two babies who would soon be sharing her parents. That mattered to Callie.

She planned to arrive around 9:30 p.m. and stay until 7:00 a.m., in time to wake Hope for school. Her house was only fifteen minutes away. That helped. She'd be with her little boy all night. That helped, too.

John would get a full night's sleep before his flight the next day. He loved his Buster, especially in the daylight hours. Nights were harder.

We offered a bed, but Joey slept best curled up on someone's chest. She opted for the "mama rocker." The same one I'd used with Jayden. I showed her the ropes and promised to keep my phone nearby. If she called, I'd be there in seconds.

Over the next week, Callie cared for Joey nearly every day: overnights, nap shifts, errands with him tucked into the sling. I watched her fall in love with him. We were trying. Trading sleep like currency. Building a bridge of care between families, one night at a time. All of us holding. All of us held.

Sometimes I almost laughed at how many arms it took to comfort two babies. But it wasn't a punchline. It was our life.

# June 2010

D r. Earles's office was able to see both babies the next week, a small mercy in a calendar that never let up. Jayden for an RSV recheck. Joey for a formula follow-up.

I introduced Callie as Jayden's identified adoptive mother. The staff greeted her warmly. Dr. Earles examined Jayden. A week after her RSV diagnosis, her lungs were clear again.

Joey still struggled. He squirmed with pain after every feed, spitting up and fussy. Dr. Earles adjusted his formula, adding reflux meds and then antacids. Later, we tried gripe water. Nothing helped for long. He drank forty-four to forty-six ounces a day. At $57 a can, the only silver lining was that when he was drinking, he wasn't crying.

Callie continued to take overnight shifts at least once a week. John looked forward to those nights most of all. When she wasn't with us, I still tried to give John a break by taking a few of Joey's feedings myself.

I would go upstairs with Jayden at her bedtime. John

would stay up as late as he could, with Joey on his chest. After midnight, he'd sneak into our bedroom and lay Joey in the bassinet. I had Joey's care from then until late morning, when John woke. It worked. But we were tired.

The doctor visits and therapy appointments kept coming. Some were spaced out more now that we had two babies. Jayden's team felt comfortable with her progress and trusted that I'd call if something changed. That was a relief.

Callie still came weekly to play. Jayden leaned toward her, arms lifting, a small sound in her throat. They sang songs and read books while I slipped away to wash a sink full of bottles. Callie held Joey while Jayden bounced in the activity center. Then she'd settle Joey across her lap and help Jayden crawl after a ball across the floor.

Jayden no longer kept her eyes fixed on me. She was watching Mama Callie now. That was progress. Slow and sacred.

---

JOHN and I brought Jayden with us to a nurse-only appointment for Joey at the GI clinic. His stomach pain hadn't let up, even with all the changes. Dr. Earles worried something more serious might be going on, possibly an obstruction.

There were no GI doctor openings for a month, so we took the earliest available visit with one of the GI nurses. I hoped it would be enough.

The nurse examined Joey thoroughly and asked thoughtful questions. She talked about the effects of prenatal cocaine exposure and suspected he might be over-responding to sensory input. But after she observed him post-feeding and felt his distended belly, she changed course.

She suspected colon spasms and called the doctor in to confirm. The doctor agreed with her diagnosis and approved drops to give before each feeding, up to five times a day.

They worked. For thirty minutes after each meal, Joey relaxed. Then the crying would begin again. But those thirty minutes? They felt like air. He'd lie in the bouncer and smile while I sat beside him on the floor.

And for a few precious minutes, I felt like I could breathe too.

JOHN and I were invited to Mark and Callie's oldest son's graduation party. On the way there, I noticed Joey working through a difficult diaper. These episodes were still hard on him.

We walked into the party and Callie took Joey upstairs to change him. Holding Jayden close, I edged toward the kitchen. People were everywhere: extended family, neighbors, old friends.

It was an opportunity for Mark and Callie to introduce the babies as theirs, and for Jayden, who was extremely cautious around people, it was a test. Her birthday had ended in a blood sugar spike. Maybe it had been a fluke.

At first, she seemed okay, even curious. She glanced around from my arms, her hand warm against my neck.

In the kitchen, Callie's dad was waiting. He held out his arms for Jayden, smiling. She hesitated. I encouraged her gently. She let him hold her for a minute or two, then turned back toward me, fear in her eyes.

Still, those few moments were a good start.

I found a quiet corner and spread a blanket, a small safe place where Jayden could play. People could visit her there, but I didn't want her passed from lap to lap. Not yet.

Callie floated through the room with Joey, radiant and proud. He soaked up the attention, arms draped over her shoulder, peaceful.

About an hour later, I checked Jayden's blood sugar.

The glucometer read 416.

It wasn't a fluke. Her birthday party hadn't been a one-off. Jayden really did struggle with stress, especially in crowds. And this family was large.

I swallowed the worry. I prayed love would outshine overwhelm, that gatherings would soon feel familiar, that what felt like a crowd would start to feel like home.

But a small voice inside me asked:

What if it doesn't? What if she's not ready? What if I'm not?

As evening came, the back patio turned into a stage. Mark and Callie's children performed songs. Guests gathered under the canopy like an audience at a summer concert.

I stood beside Callie, who held Joey fast asleep on her shoulder. I shifted Jayden, secure in her sling, and looked out over the crowd, watching them cheer as the graduate sang a duet with his sister.

These babies, our babies, would be surrounded by some of the kindest, warmest people I had ever met.

This was already theirs.

---

MARK AND CALLIE left for their anniversary trip soon after the graduation party. They'd be gone for two weeks, home again by June 29. John was the saddest to see them go. With Callie gone, night duty was his.

Some mornings, I'd come downstairs early with Jayden, ready to check her blood sugar and prepare her insulin only to find Papa John asleep in the recliner, Buster straddling his chest. Both of them snoring.

They didn't stir while Jayden and I moved around the room.

Later that morning, I'd hear the full report: how many laps John walked before Joey gave in, how long he slept before it started again. And every few days, he'd say the same thing: "I have a whole new respect for what you've done. All the twins. All those nights. I get it now. No wonder you were cranky sometimes."

Jayden had another appointment with Dr. Earles on June 29. She was fourteen and a half months old, and still weighed fifteen pounds three ounces. Not an ounce gained since May 20.

She was doing better with solids, but gagged on certain textures. Dr. Earles increased her Prevacid again and reordered feeding therapy.

We tried spicy foods like the occupational therapist suggested. Jayden loved them. She could devour half a sloppy joe in one sitting. But each time, she was up with stomach cramps. For days afterward, she'd stop eating, barely touching her bottle.

I wanted so badly for her to be thriving by the time she was placed with Mark and Callie. But her stomach still wasn't stable. And I didn't know what to do about it.

The Pumpin' Mamas were amazing. Donations still arrived daily. Just when we thought the flow would dry up, another gift landed in the cooler.

At home, John and I kept caring for Deedle and Buster, as they were more often called now that John was in the trenches with me.

Dinner was pizza at least two or three nights a week. It gave John an excuse to get out of the house, to breathe fresh air, to drive, to carry their names into the world. A hot meal with no cooking and no dishes. One less decision.

I spent most of my days in the rocker, often with both babies in my lap. They were nearly the same weight now. Except for Jayden's head start on motor skills, most people thought they were twins.

I'd feed them both. Burp them both. Rock them both. Sometimes I'd fall asleep with one on each shoulder. When Buster needed another nap, he'd sleep on John's chest. And John would fall asleep, too.

It was a wild, exhausting, sacred time.

We stayed focused on the goal. These babies belonged together. They were going to be adopted together. We prayed for this. We begged the agency for this outcome. And now we were living inside that answer.

No matter how hard it got, we would see it through.

---

THAT NIGHT, we did what we always did: rocked the babies, cleaned bottles, folded laundry. The house felt still, but it wasn't settled. John said he didn't feel well. His voice sounded tight, like he was trying not to make it a thing.

I heard that voice before.

He had a long history of asthma. Three years earlier, he'd been hospitalized and intubated during a sudden attack while out of state. Our whole family gathered in Lexington, Kentucky, and stayed a week.

So when he started wheezing that night, he knew what to do. He took his medications and used his inhalers. He tried to stay calm. He was sure he'd feel better with time.

Around 5:30 a.m., he came upstairs and woke me. He whispered, "I'm not doing well. You might need to take care of Buster soon. But I'm okay for now."

Then he disappeared back down the hall.

I thought I'd be ready. It took a minute for his words to sink in. If he stopped breathing, I wouldn't know unless I was downstairs.

I forced myself out of bed and turned on the baby monitor so I could hear Jayden when she woke. When I reached the family room, I froze.

John was sitting on the floor with Buster over his shoulder.

He couldn't walk. He could barely breathe. But he didn't want Joey to cry alone in his swing. So he sat on the carpet, swaying back and forth to keep his little Buster calm.

It was the most precious and terrifying thing I'd ever seen.

I took Joey from John's chest and started asking questions: What have you taken? How long has it been this bad? Can you get a full breath?

John was pale. Shaking. His breath came in gasps. He tried to respond, but his voice cracked. Finally, he mouthed the words: "Nine. One. One."

I ran for the phone and dialed 911.

The dispatcher's questions came fast. I answered in clipped pieces, trying to sound calm.

I explained the urgency, then laid the now-sleeping

Joey in his swing. I opened the front door, turned the porch light on, following every instruction the dispatcher gave. I cleared the living room floor: tossed the bouncy seat and activity center onto the couch so the paramedics would have space. Then I ran upstairs for Jayden.

By the time they arrived, John's chest was barely rising. His eyes locked on mine. He mouthed, "Not much left."

I told the EMTs about the last asthma emergency, that this was the same. We were running out of time. They got to work immediately. Oxygen mask, vitals, gurney.

I stood in the corner, unable to move. Joey slept in his swing, undisturbed. Jayden clung to me as I followed the paramedics outside. I told my sweet husband I'd meet him at the hospital. That he was in good hands. I'd be there soon.

He motioned for his wallet. I promised to bring it.

The siren wailed and the lights flashed. The ambulance pulled away.

And suddenly, I was alone.

The commotion woke our neighbor, Kate, who ran toward our house in a bathrobe. She found me standing barefoot on the porch, holding Jayden. Her hand met my elbow and guided us back inside. I hadn't realized how much I was shaking until her touch steadied me.

"Do you have a plan?" she asked. "How can I help?"

I nodded toward Joey, still asleep in the swing, then handed Jayden to her and ran upstairs for my cellphone. I called Miss Pam. I hoped she'd be free since it was summer. No school. She promised she'd be on her way in minutes.

Then I hesitated.

Callie and Mark had just returned from Europe the

night before. Jet lag. Their kids would be home. It was early. Everyone might be asleep.

But this was an emergency.

I called. Apologized. Explained.

Callie put me on speaker so Mark could listen. Her voice stayed calm. "We're on our way," she said.

Before Miss Pam and Callie arrived, I had checked Jayden's blood sugar and packed bottles for the entire day. Jayden had clung to Kate as they stood in the kitchen watching me. Soon, each baby had a labeled cooler. Diapers. Outfits. Medications. Car seats. Diaper bags. It was instinct now.

Joey started to stir, and I panicked.

Mama Callie arrived in time to lift him from the swing. Miss Pam took Jayden from Kate's arms and dressed her. Kate filled my to-go cup with iced tea. I ran upstairs to get dressed and brush my teeth.

Callie stayed with Joey and told me to call with any news.

Kate packed the stroller and the rest of the day's supplies into the car.

Forty minutes had passed since the ambulance left.

Miss Pam insisted on driving. I was barely function-ing. She dropped Jayden and me at the ER while she parked, then brought in the rest of the gear.

The stroller became Jayden's mobile command center. Bottles, diapers, toys tucked into every pocket. I reclined the seat to use it for diaper changes.

It worked. We were ready. We were doing what we always did: Adjusting. Managing. Showing up with what we had.

I ASKED to see John the minute I arrived at the ER. They told me he wasn't ready. The doctor was still with him, working to stabilize things. I took that as a good sign. We hadn't taken too long to get there. But each time I checked, the answer stayed the same.

An hour passed. Then two.

My chest tightened. The unknown was louder than the beeping machines around us.

Miss Pam stayed with Jayden in the waiting area while I paced, prayed, and waited. After nearly three hours, a young intern appeared and asked me to follow him. I shot Miss Pam a look. She nodded, pulling Jayden close.

The curtain peeled back.

John lay motionless. Sedated.

The doctor stood beside him, still watching his vitals. He confirmed I was John's wife before he began to speak. He told me John had stopped breathing on the way to the hospital. The ambulance had to pull over just three miles from our house so the paramedic could intubate him. That intervention had saved his life.

By the time they arrived at the ER, his lung had collapsed. The team had inserted a chest tube to inflate it.

In the midst of it all, they believed John may have suffered a heart attack. They wouldn't know for certain until more tests came back, but the signs were there. It had taken them these past few hours to get John stabilized.

He was now on life support. I stepped closer.

This was worse than Lexington. Worse than before. Collapsed lung. Possible heart attack. Sedated, intubated, barely stable.

I stood there, holding the railing of his bed with shaking hands, nodding slowly as the doctor explained the rest. I don't know how long I stayed. John's team continued to buzz around his bed. Eventually, I turned and walked back to the waiting room, unsteady.

I paused by the nurse's station, gripping the counter to steady myself. Miss Pam saw my face before I said a word. Her eyes widened. She guided me to a chair beside her.

I told her what the doctor said. The words came in pieces. Tears threatened to spill.

I took a breath and asked if she was okay to stay with Jayden a little longer. Then I stepped outside and made the hardest calls of the day.

I called all four of our kids, then John's sister and brother, everyone out of state. I explained what happened, what the doctors said, what might come next.

I called John's best friend, Wagner. They were both named John, both "JW." My husband started using his last name, and it stuck.

He arrived within the hour with a box of donuts. He went back to the ER to see John, then returned to sit beside me and steadied my shaking hands. He didn't ask what I needed. He just stayed until we knew more.

Miss Pam kept Jayden occupied in the waiting area while I slipped back to my husband's bedside. I still had to leave every few hours for Jayden's glucometer check and insulin dose. No one else could do it yet.

Wagner sat with John while I cared for her. It helped to know someone I trusted was at his side. When the ER doctor confirmed John would be admitted to the ICU, Wagner and Miss Pam made sure I ate something.

Miss Pam offered to cancel her plans to go to her daughter's soccer game. I insisted she go. She left her car at our house, so Wagner offered to drive her back and then return. I told them I'd be okay. Jayden could come with me behind the curtain now. I could hold her and sit with John at the same time.

Our son Andy called. He was driving in from Milwaukee with Emily, Kelly, and her husband, Adam. Casey was on her way from New York with a friend. John's sister would fly in from Virginia the next afternoon. If Wagner could help me get through the next few hours, we'd make it.

When John was admitted to the ICU, he was stable but still sedated and surrounded by machines, tubes, and beeping. All constant reminders that his life was still hanging in the balance. I held his hand and whispered to him often. I wasn't sure he knew I was there.

I drove home with Jayden around 9:30 p.m. Wagner stayed behind with John, waiting for the kids to arrive. They were expected by 11:00 p.m. I had to get back to Joey. Bedtime was calling. I had nothing left. Callie offered to stay with Joey that night. I felt the relief before I answered yes. We'd made it through the day with the help of wonderful friends.

Once home, I called the kids and told them where to find their dad. I had asked the ICU staff to make an exception and allow them to visit, even if they arrived after hours.

I told them to come in through the garage when they got to the house, the keypad still worked. I asked that they enter quietly. Joey would be in the family room with Callie. Everyone else could head to their usual rooms upstairs.

I wanted to be awake to hug them. But if not, I'd see them in the morning.

OVER THE NEXT WEEK, Callie cared for Joey every single day. Between her and Miss Pam, the babies remained blissfully unaware of the chaos swirling around them. Their days were filled with stroller walks around the hospital lobby, visits with new faces, take-out lunches, books, toys, and a rotation of doting hands. They must've thought they were on vacation.

At the hospital, I was joined by my children and John's sister, Linda. While we hovered near John's bedside, the babies became beloved regulars in the ICU waiting areas. Nurses and doctors constantly commented on how beautiful and well-dressed they were. One nurse even said, "You all make this floor brighter."

After days of waiting and watching, the nurses began easing his sedation, bringing him back to me. Once his eyes found mine, tears flowed... first his, then mine. After a moment of unspoken love, he tried to speak. His throat, tender from the intrusion of intubation, made it a struggle. He didn't seem to notice the roomful of love waiting for him, not yet.

The first thing he said was: "Where's Buster?" He needed to see his boy.

The staff granted us permission to bring the babies to see him. That decision came not from protocol, but from compassion. They understood. It was their gift to him.

---

ONE AFTERNOON, Linda and I sat in the waiting area, counting down the minutes until another brief ICU visit. Jayden grew restless in my arms, tugging at her diaper. I laid her on a changing pad across an empty chair beside Linda and reached for a fresh diaper. As I unfastened the tape on the old one, it exploded. Apparently, it had reached capacity.

Linda burst into hysterics, laughing until tears rolled down her cheeks. Her laughter cut through my fog, and I started laughing too. I didn't even remember the last time I'd changed Jayden. My head just wasn't in it. But in that moment, laughter was more healing than guilt.

Eventually, John was well enough to be moved to the step-down unit. With the Fourth of July approaching and all of our kids home, we asked the nurses if we could celebrate together. We proposed a small picnic in one of the nearby conference rooms. To our surprise, they said yes.

Andy grilled ribs and chicken on the charcoal grill. Kelly and Casey made baked beans and macaroni salad. Emily bought balloons, a party hat, a goofy patriotic bow tie, and little gifts for her dad to unwrap. She even found a red, white, and blue T-shirt in his size.

The hospital conference room was transformed. Balloons and streamers hung from the ceiling tiles. Ribbons curled around the chairs. Emily, a nurse herself, helped get her dad settled into a wheelchair, oxygen tank attached, legs tucked under a blanket.

She wheeled him down the hallway, slow and deliberate.

We were all waiting in the decorated room when he arrived. The babies were dressed in red, white, and blue. When they saw Papa John, they both reached for him. Andy presented his barbecue. Adam fixed a plate of everything for the guest of honor. Kelly, Casey, and Emily danced around John singing a silly made-up song in celebration.

It only lasted twenty minutes. But for those twenty minutes, we weren't in a hospital. We were just a family. All of us together for the first time since Christmas.

John had survived another sudden-onset fatal asthma attack. We were celebrating the Fourth of July, but we were also celebrating something else entirely. My husband, the man who held my life together, was still here.

Later, when the babies were once again being entertained by our children and his room emptied, John turned to me and whispered, "I didn't think I'd live to see this."

His voice was thin, his body still fragile, but his eyes were clear. He had felt it too. That this might be one of the last moments he could hold... not just the babies, but all of us.

And though he didn't say it, I could see it written in every slow breath. His body was telling him what his brain already knew. We couldn't do this much longer.

I HAD SIGNED the paperwork back in November, stating that John and I would not adopt Jayden. We had prayed for the right forever family to be chosen for her. That prayer was answered.

Then came what Mama Callie affectionately called "the bonus baby." Joey's arrival was never expected, but it solidified the plan: these babies belonged together. And still, even with that clarity, some part of me struggled. I kept imagining scenarios where maybe, somehow, Jayden would need to stay with us.

Not in my head, but in my heart. After John's emergency, something shifted. I saw what it cost him to keep going. I saw the toll of sleepless nights, the weight of constant care. I saw his life and limits. And I knew. We could not keep our Deedle girl.

I needed to begin the slow work of accepting what I already knew. Jayden was not ours to keep. My heart wasn't there yet. I pictured her crib empty, mornings without our songs, quiet already gathering in the corners of our home.

So I prayed. Not for the outcome to change, but for the strength to release her as she deserved.

*Please, Lord.*
*Teach my heart what my hands already know:*
*how to hold her gently and let her go.*
*She's still my baby.*
*She always will be.*
*Like a breath I once held and must now release...*
*She is not mine to keep.*

# July 2010

John came home from the hospital feeling better than he had in weeks, but he still lacked his usual strength. Dudley had more energy than John could manage. He zoomed through the house, then jumped into John's lap.

John's body had been through a lot, so we tried to keep our expectations realistic. The babies couldn't. They were thrilled to have Papa John back, and they missed the extra attention from our older kids and John's sister Linda.

The babies expected him to carry them from room to room, pointing at the pictures and telling the story behind each one. Jayden expected him to place his yellow baseball cap perfectly on her head as he sang his *"Time to get the mail"* melody.

I suggested that his time with the babies could be quieter: sitting with them and reading. Afterward, he'd start the finger games, *"This Little Piggy,"* again and again.

Jeannette, the placement caseworker from Ennis

Center, needed to visit. We didn't know why. When she came, John lay in his recliner under a blanket. She sat on the sofa across from us and explained that she needed to *"write us up"* because we hadn't contacted the agency within twenty-four hours of John's emergency hospital admission. I called a day later, when I was rescheduling Jayden's appointments. But it wasn't soon enough.

It was agency policy, she said, to know of any changes in the foster home within twenty-four hours. I was stunned. We hadn't asked for respite care. We hadn't left the babies with anyone other than Mama Callie. I kept them fed, clean, rested, and safe. And yet, we were written up.

She apologized. We accepted our write-up. What else could we do? It sat in my chest all afternoon.

---

ON JULY 8 at Dr. Sinclair's office, Mark and Callie joined us so Dr. Sinclair could walk them through Jayden's case. John and I arrived first, Jayden in the ring sling, Joey on John's hip. When Mark and Callie arrived, Callie reached for Joey and held Jayden's hand in greeting.

I handed Callie a matching ring sling. She slipped it on, nestled Joey inside, and paced the room until he settled, snug and still. When Jayden's name was called, four adults and two babies in ring slings walked back to the exam room.

Dr. Sinclair entered. I reintroduced Mark and Callie as the identified adoptive parents. He greeted them warmly and commented on Jayden's progress while he washed his hands. Mark and Callie sat quietly as Dr. Sinclair and I went through our usual exchange. By now, I knew the question. I kept my answers simple, trying not to overwhelm them.

Mark asked if there was a training course they could take. Dr. Sinclair handed them some printed materials and nodded toward me. "Start with her. She knows this child." He reminded them that I'd been there since the beginning. If they learned from me, they'd be in good hands.

Then he asked me what I thought the next insulin step should be. He wasn't testing me. He was confirming. I told him what I expected we'd see if he increased her fast-acting insulin. He nodded and raised her morning dose to 20 units. He reminded me to fax her weekly documentation.

At the end of the visit, he did what he always did. He picked up Jayden, held her close, and waltzed with her while humming a soft tune.

***

JAYDEN'S next court review was scheduled for July 15. We invited Callie to come. There was no requirement, just a chance for her to see how the system worked. We brought both babies. I wanted the referee who had once fought to give Jayden a chance at family to see that family taking shape.

After the caseworkers updated the referee on Jayden's progress, John, Callie, and I brought the babies forward. The referee was surprised to see Jayden's baby brother. Her expression softened. She said the reports didn't do Jayden justice.

John thanked her personally for the ruling that gave Jayden this family. It only felt right. That day in court marked a shift, from hope to something you could almost reach out and touch. Painfully. Beautifully.

* * *

THE VISIT with the GI specialist was a follow-up for Jayden.

I was glad Callie was with me. In the waiting room, we talked more about co-parenting. It made us laugh. I had the diapers, the bottles, and the sleepless nights. I bathed them and dressed them. Then she showed up to help carry the babies and sat beside me for the appointment.

"You have the better part," I joked.

She said she wanted to keep working as long as she could, so that once the babies were placed, she could be home full-time. I understood completely. And selfishly, I wasn't ready to pass them on just yet. Then they called us back.

The GI doctor asked her questions. I gave the best answers I could. Concerned about Jayden's weight, she suggested a high-calorie supplement. I reminded her that Jayden was allergic to corn syrup. Of course, I knew better. I should have said intolerant instead of "allergy," but it slipped out. She corrected me immediately. She wasn't interested in my shorthand. To me, either word meant the same thing: Jayden couldn't have it.

Then she suggested switching to formula. I gently reminded her that Jayden couldn't tolerate milk or corn syrup. Then came cereal. I told her I tried every baby cereal on the market. Each one left Jayden's bottom raw. The doctor insisted that with enzymes and Prevacid, Jayden *should* be able to tolerate these things.

Then she said it.

"Failure to thrive."

It landed hard.

She said she'd speak with the nutritionist and follow up with a plan.

---

She called two days later. The plan: two scoops of formula in each six-ounce bottle of breast milk for two weeks. I asked her which formula she recommended.

"Any milk-based formula will be fine," she said, as if she hadn't heard me.

I hung up and called Callie. When I told her, she was upset, but not surprised. She had watched the doctor's face during the appointment.

"She wasn't listening."

Callie believed me, and that made all the difference. We decided to find a new GI specialist. Maybe co-parenting wasn't so bad.

---

Mark and Callie met me at the next visit with Dr. Earles. I started talking about the GI specialist: the dismissal, the contradiction, the plan. Dr. Earles listened, then said she'd be removing the GI specialist from her referral list.

"You know what we call kids like Jayden?" She grinned.

"PITA cases," she said.

We looked at her.

"Pain in the ass."

We all burst out laughing. Jayden defied every text-book. One of a kind. She was fifteen months old and weighed only sixteen pounds. But she looked great. She was alert. She was hitting milestones. Six teeth in. Molars pushing through. Dr. Earles wasn't worried. Neither did we.

———

THEN IT WAS Joey's turn. He was nearly twelve pounds and eating constantly. Still, he was on four medications to manage his discomfort. Dr. Earles reviewed his prescriptions. One of the meds used to soothe colon spasms was 5% alcohol, part of the formulation. We all stared at her. He wasn't even three months old. Born to a mother who had used alcohol and drugs. And now he was being prescribed alcohol?

I asked if we could try donor breast milk for him too.

Dr. Earles blinked. "I don't know why it took you so long to ask," she said. She wrote a letter for state approval, listing every failed formula and recommending donor milk.

Nicole did what she always did. We got the green light.

———

WITHIN DAYS, Joey changed. He was calm. Comfortable. Present. I had assumed Jayden needed breast milk because she didn't have a pancreas. Joey did have one. I thought he'd adjust to the formula eventually. But it wasn't about my theories. It was about what worked.

Jayden and Joey were being sustained by the milk of women, most they would never meet, some who traveled just to feed them. Women who said yes to life, yes to the pump, yes to the stranger. They held us.

---

CALLIE'S CHILDREN were giving her a baby shower. It had been thirteen years since a baby joined their family. Now Callie needed everything twice over. A few weeks before the shower, they came to our house for the invitation photo. Callie had asked for a photo that captured all of them together. Something that would announce this as a new chapter for their family.

After church, the whole family packed into our living room. I had the babies dressed in adorable outfits that Callie requested. Curtis, Callie's son-in-law, set up his tripod. Mark and Callie sat in the center of the couch. The kids arranged themselves. Curtis adjusted the timer and jumped in next to his wife. Mark had Joey on his lap. Callie reached for Jayden.

The babies were too distracted to look at the camera. I stood behind the tripod, clapping, calling, playing peek-a-boo. We finally got a few pictures. The invitation photo turned out beautifully, so much so that Mark had it printed and framed above their mantel.

This was real. They were becoming a family. And soon, the whole community would gather to celebrate them.

---

ON THE DAY of the shower, Miss Pam came over to help prepare the babies. It wasn't just ribbons and bows. They needed to be fed, bathed, and rested. Calm. This was their big debut.

Hope picked out a ballerina dress for Jayden, complete with a lacy hair band. In the basement bins, I found a plaid outfit for Joey and pink ballet slippers for Jayden. They looked just right.

After bottles and baths, Miss Pam rubbed Jayden's feet with lotion, slipped on the ruffled socks and ballet slippers, then held her hands above her head. She helped Jayden dance a little ballet across the family room. Jayden was delighted. We laughed. She soaked up our laughter.

Miss Pam couldn't come with me to the baby shower. Her daughter had a ballet recital. Murielle and Elias joined me instead. Murielle had received an invitation and was happy to help. She helped me with the car seats while I packed the bottles, insulin, and my ring sling.

Joey fell asleep in the car. We carried the babies in. Callie greeted them warmly, kissed Jayden, reached for Joey, and led us to a quiet space, where Jayden could be seen but not overstimulated. She already knew our rhythms and theirs.

---

THE HOUSE WAS WARM, voices layered with laughter. I saw the community Jayden and Joey would grow up in. Callie began opening the stack of gifts: clothes, gear, supplies. Enough to care for two babies for a long time.

As bedtime neared, I whispered to Callie that we'd be leaving soon. She nodded, then slipped away. She returned with a small wrapped gift. In front of everyone, she turned to them and began speaking. Her words blurred. I was already somewhere else, trying not to panic.

But I heard this: she thanked me. She said her babies had never known a day without a mother's love.

Then she handed me a gift. Inside was a silver necklace: one large heart wrapped around two smaller ones, each with a small gem. *How had she found something so perfect?* Tears flowed. Not from sadness, but because I felt seen. In her moment of joy, she turned toward me and gave thanks. I held the necklace in my palm. From deep inside, I whispered,

"Thank you."

# August & September
# 2010

Mark and Callie wanted to do everything they could to make the transition from our home to theirs comfortable. They asked John and me to meet with the psychologist who consulted with the church staff. We all needed a clearer understanding of attachment and what a handoff can do to a child.

John and I brought the babies to the church office. Callie greeted us at the door and introduced us to a few coworkers as we passed on our way to the therapy room. Mark joined us within minutes, offering the warm hug we had come to expect.

The psychologist came in with a practiced calm, the kind that doesn't rush you. He had adopted, too. The hour felt practical. He set a few goals, offered guidance, and invited honest conversation.

I said what I couldn't stop thinking, what happens when the only parent a child knows disappears? He looked at Mark and Callie and said that the sooner the babies could think of Mark and Callie as *their* parents, the better. He thought the love and care of Mama Callie and

Papa Mark would eventually meet the babies' need for Mama Judy and Papa John. I felt that truth settle in my chest like a held breath, tender and letting go.

What stayed with me was how eager they were for guidance. They were asking the hard questions. They wanted to do what was best for their soon-to-be children. I had such deep respect for them. They weren't trying to figure it out alone. They knew where to go for help, and they would build a strong circle around their family. That kind of wisdom matters. They were going to be okay. If they were okay, I could be okay.

Before we left the church, in the swirl of hugs and kisses, Jayden looked up and said, "bye-bye."

Her first words.

Mama Callie squealed with delight. I just stood there, tears rolling down my cheeks. Some part of Jayden already knew.

***

MISS PAM WAS THRILLED to hear that Jayden's first words were for Mama Callie. She kept working with Jayden even after the school year ended. Jayden's body was waking up that summer. She had been crawling for a month, but never left the family room. Even when I was in the kitchen, she'd sit at the step into the kitchen and watch me. But now, with Miss Pam's encouragement, Jayden was pulling herself up to stand. She was wobbly, unsure, waiting for permission. She'd only stand when Miss Pam coaxed her.

She looked so tiny beside the overstuffed sofa, and I felt my own hesitation again. I held back because she never seemed old enough. But she was sixteen months old. It was time for her to stand. It wasn't neglect. It was love.

Mistaking protection for patience. I promised Miss Pam I'd keep helping Jayden stand and build strength, even when she wasn't there.

---

BY THE END OF AUGUST, Dr. Earles found that Jayden's hemoglobin was 5.3 (normal is 11–16). She examined Jayden, watching her move, watching her eyes track me. Jayden did not manifest any symptoms. A count under 7 is considered life-threatening. Most doctors would order a transfusion on the spot. But here was Jayden at 5.3, acting completely normal.

Dr. Earles sent me to the natural food store in the same plaza where I bought coconut oil a year earlier. Jayden needed a gentle iron supplement since she hadn't tolerated the ones we tried in recent months.

Dr. Earles called hematology to get Jayden seen. She had to explain the unusual case, Jayden, born with no pancreas. Even after hearing her diagnosis, the first available appointment was September 22. I promised Dr. Earles I'd do everything I could to help Jayden tolerate the supplement.

The supplement upset Jayden's tummy, like the others. She stopped eating. It was heartbreaking to watch her fake the suck, bottle in her mouth, going through the motions, but not swallowing. She didn't want it in her tummy. It reminded me of the beginning, when she refused the high-calorie formula. I'd told myself it was developmental, that she couldn't suck. But what if she'd been refusing it all along, because her tummy hurt? Now she drank only sixteen ounces in twenty-four hours, and she barely slept.

I sent John back to the store for yet another iron

supplement. I started it drop by drop. Jayden did a little better. I kept it going, increasing the amount just slightly each day. I prayed under my breath between bottles.

---

ON SEPTEMBER 22, Callie and I took Jayden to the hematologist, Dr. Fitzgerald. We didn't have to explain. They already knew the headline.

In Jayden's presence, they looked at her like she mattered. But underneath the warmth was the same thing that always followed her into a room — concern, waiting, the sense that anything could change fast. They drew her blood first, a finger poke in the lab. Then they brought us into an exam room.

I fed Jayden her bottle. Callie fed Joey his bottle.

When Dr. Fitzgerald came in with the results, he said her hemoglobin was 5.0. After four weeks of iron supplements, she was worse. He sent us directly to the hospital. My head was spinning. *What do we do now? Do I have enough breast milk? Do I need state permission?* My brain leapt to logistics: who to call, and in what order. I stayed focused on Dr. Fitzgerald's instructions. He handed us the admission paperwork, the floor number, and the transfusion orders.

I watched Callie's face. I needed her to take it in and stay with me.

When the doctor left the room, I called John. Callie called Mark. I called the agency. There was no need for state permission since it was an emergency admission. We were allowed to do what the doctor recommended. No warnings this time. I asked if Joey could spend the night at Callie's. She was already cleared for unsupervised day visits. The agency gave permission to start overnights. They saw our friendship and they trusted us. Callie and I would make sure both babies were cared for. Callie rode in the back seat beside the two car seats while I drove.

When we got off the elevator at the third floor and entered the pediatric hall, we were greeted by the same wonderful nurses who cared for Jayden during January's visit there. They also loved our little Joey, amazed that Jayden had a baby brother. They gave Jayden a coloring book and some crayons, then showed us to her room. Jayden was older now and was suspicious of new faces.

ONCE WE WERE in Jayden's room, nurses buzzed around, quick and quiet. A few doors down, in the treatment room, I reminded them of Jayden's peripheral vascular disease and how hard her veins were to access. They remembered her. They worked for twenty-five minutes to place the IV.

I called for a break and lifted my screaming girl into my arms. The room was cold. I overheard them mention a "vein finder" they used in the NICU. I spun around.

"Why weren't you using that already?"

The vein finder came in on a cart. Infrared light mapped her delicate veins beneath her skin. Even with the vein finder, it took another twenty minutes to place the line. Twenty more minutes of screaming.

They drew blood to type and crossmatch. The arm board was secured, and the IV was taped to a rolling pole beside her. Saline dripped to keep the line open. Mama Callie stood in the doorway, watching all of it. She held Joey, asleep in the ring sling. Tears filled her eyes. Her sweetness didn't spare her. She knew Jayden hadn't asked for any of this. I shoved the thought aside. I didn't have space for anger.

Back in Jayden's room, I turned on the familiar music channel. I took the last bottle from the diaper bag and sank into the rocker with Jayden, still sobbing. She was completely worn out. She drank and fell asleep with the arm board resting on the rocker.

I was absorbed in Jayden's care when I looked over and saw Mama Callie and her little boy, settled into the rhythm they were building. She swayed to the music, Joey snuggling into her with his eyes half-closed. Two rockers. Two babies. The music holding us in place. For a moment, that was enough.

---

JOHN ARRIVED to find Mama Callie and me in rockers, each holding a sleeping baby. He had missed the worst of it, and walked into the day's most peaceful moment. He stocked the room's refrigerator with bottles and set Jayden's pajamas on the counter. He'd even brought food for Callie and me. Neither of us had thought about eating.

Mark was shuttling their kids to sports while we sat with IV tubing and lullabies.

Jayden's blood was typed, and the first unit was started. Protocol required two smaller units, each running three to three-and-a-half hours, with a one-hour pause between. Vitals were checked every fifteen minutes for the first hour. Two hours of monitoring after the second unit. If everything went well, Jayden would be discharged by 7:00 a.m.

Callie listened intently as the procedure was explained. Her heart ached for her little Jayden. I offered to take Joey for a walk so Mama Callie could have time with Jayden. Jayden would need to learn to depend on Mama Callie for this kind of care. They colored. They sang songs. I hoped this would be the memory. Not the pain or the IV. Just the music and her mama's voice.

When it was time, John took Joey home with Callie. The hallway swallowed them up, their footsteps fading toward the elevator. I stayed. I settled back into the rocker beside Jayden's bed and watched the line, the monitors, the slow drip of blood and time. Through the darkest part of the night, it was me and my girl.

The transfusion went smoothly. The nurses watched her closely, pausing between each unit, checking vitals, adjusting the IV. Jayden slept through most of it, exhausted but stable. As the hours passed, color returned to her cheeks. Her tiny hands looked less pale. Her breathing evened out. I stayed beside her, whispering prayers between lullabies, grateful for every beep that said she was still here.

A stranger's blood flowed through her. A gift never acknowledged. I tucked it deep in my heart.

---

MISS PAM WAS eager to see her little girl after being away. When she walked in, Jayden focused on the blue quilted bag and beamed, waiting for the magic. Miss Pam first looked at me, concerned. She heard about the transfusion. "What does this mean long-term?"

I reassured her. The transfusion had gone well. Jayden was recovering.

But we both knew there was no map. The few cases we could find had a framework: pancreatic agenesis, GATA6, an early diagnosis. We had none of that. Jayden had lived nine months without anyone realizing she didn't have a pancreas.

We looked everywhere. Case reports late at night. Forums. We couldn't find another baby who had lived that long without a diagnosis.

At least for now, this crisis had passed. Our Deedle girl was feeling better. By the time Miss Pam sat on the family room carpet, Jayden had pulled herself to standing by the sofa. Miss Pam grinned. "She already knows what's coming."

At that moment, Jayden took three tiny steps. Then she collapsed into Miss Pam. We held our breath, eyes wide. We didn't want our joy to startle her. Jayden was nearly seventeen months old and had just taken her first steps. The most beautiful part: she chose this moment with Miss Pam.

We ate cookies, whispered our cheers, and smiled until our cheeks hurt. I held Joey in my lap, angled just right so he could see his sister. Jayden managed to get in a few more steps with Miss Pam's guidance, then toppled to the floor. She gave herself applause. A small sound. A holy one.

JOEY'S COURT date came and went with little fanfare. John went alone to represent his little Buster. Joey's birth mother hadn't been heard from since the NICU, the day she gave permission for his circumcision and promised to do things differently.

It was a straightforward process. No birth father was named on his birth certificate, so there was no paternity test to slow things down before the judge terminated parental rights. The birth mother had already lost custody of three children. The older two boys had been adopted by her aunt and were now teenagers. That same seventy-six-year-old aunt had been offered custody of Jayden, but she declined once she learned of Jayden's medical needs.

Baby Joey was legally free for adoption. There was relief in the finality, but not without sorrow. He wouldn't remember. But I would for both of us. No one wins here. Not really.

MY NOTEBOOKS WERE FILLING FAST. I had started a second spiral notebook for Jayden's insulin. A red steno book held her daily data and appointments. A blue one tracked Joey's. Everything had to be documented and shared with the foster agency. I taped an envelope inside the back cover for the business cards: every doctor, every clinic. Caseworker numbers were on the first page.

I was communicating updates to the caseworkers and the adoptive family as they happened. John was helping as much as he could by washing bottles, doing laundry, and doing the quiet things that kept us going. Dudley had adjusted, too. He didn't steal baby toys anymore. He'd just lie nearby, watching. Not trying to claim what was never his.

The next step was inevitable. Our babies were going home. Their home. Could I do it? Not the schedule. Not the packing. The part with no instructions. The part where love stays behind.

# October 2010

John and I fostered forty-four placements in our home before the call. The one where the agency asked us the most devastating question I'd ever heard. I still feel it in my chest.

That meant forty-four goodbyes to children we had grown to love. Many returned home. Friends adopted some of the children in our care, and we still kept in touch. Adoptive parents came back to our home. We watched the transition. A child who had once been ours settling into their forever family.

Transition is a necessary heartbreak. The best way to begin is to loosen my grip. To stop making it about me. To stay with what the child needs. I had to say it out loud: they were not ours to keep. We were asked to hold them. To be a safe, loving home for a while. We couldn't keep them all.

Each transition depends on the child's needs, their age, what they understand, what they've been through, and where they're going. For older children, I developed a simple story to help them make sense of what was happening.

*Once upon a time, Mommy and Daddy were having some problems. They asked their caseworker for help so Mommy and Daddy could be better parents.*

*"I have a great idea!" their caseworker said. "You can go to Mama Judy's house where you will be safe while Mommy and Daddy get help."*

*So you came to Mama Judy's house to play and be safe.*

*Every Wednesday, Mama Judy will take you to the office to visit Mommy and Daddy. One day, when they're ready, you'll get to go home.*

Children ask for it again and again. After a few days, I'd hear them whisper it to themselves while they played or drifted off to sleep. The language gave them power. A way to tell their story. When it was time to go home, I'd adjust the story again.

*Yesterday your caseworker called to say Mommy and Daddy are doing better, and you get to go home and play with them.*

I'd ask what toys they wanted to bring. We'd pack together: blankets, books, clothes. Then I'd wonder with them what they'd do when they got there.

*You won't live at Mama Judy and Papa John's house anymore.*

*But Mommy will be there. What toy will you play with first?*

We'd pick out flowers or balloons for their mom. I wanted the child to feel like they were part of this moment. I wanted their mom to see what her child hoped for.

Many times, I brought a child to reunify with their parents, the struggle began the moment we walked in. Even after days of preparation, when the moment came, the child clung to me. They wrapped their arms around my neck and cried, "No, Mommy! Stay, Mama Judy!"

It. Is. Agony.

Many of these mothers weren't in a place to say thank you. In fact, only once did a birth mother thank me for loving her child when she wasn't there. She thanked me for giving her time to become the mother she needed to be. Some carried anger or shame. Often both. We were the ones who held their babies when they weren't there. We were the ones their children cried for. We saw their children's first steps. We heard their first words.

Still, I'd put on a smile and congratulate them. "You did everything the court asked. You should be proud." Sometimes they nodded. Sometimes they said nothing at all.

With adoption, there's more time. The state recognizes a child needs room to bond with their new family, and the handoff is more structured, less charged. These are the moments that steady me. Adoptive families often thank us with tears in their eyes. They've been waiting their whole lives for this child. And for a little while, I'm the one who gets to hold the space between waiting and home.

If we knew from the beginning which children would be adopted and which would return home, the job would be easier. But we don't.

So we grieve. Because that's the cost.

John and I have learned to move between two lives. One is quiet. Flowers on the coffee table. Music playing. Fresh wax on the kitchen floor, vacuum lines in the living room carpet. The other is full of toys and sticky end tables. Highchairs and bibs. Crumbs and car seats.

John couldn't come in the door yelling, "I'm home!" He tiptoed because I was rocking a baby who'd just fallen asleep. We knew our roles. When one life ended, the other began.

After a placement, we pulled into the garage and unloaded the car seats and blankets. The highchair went down to the basement. The coffee table came back up. The flower arrangement went back in its place.

John sank into his recliner and watched the news. I headed upstairs for a hot shower and a hard cry. I cried until the water ran cold. Then pizza on paper plates. Because pizza is for the in-between. It was the last time we'd have it for a while. Usually a few days. Sometimes weeks.

Until the next call.

It's our rhythm. And after ten years, it hasn't gotten any easier.

---

JOEY WOULD BE FINE. He had known Mama Callie his whole life. She had loved him since he was two weeks old. He knew he was loved. But Jayden... Jayden was another story.

She nearly died in my arms. She had no pancreas. No one expected her to survive. Her medical care was complex. Her spirit was tender. I was her constant for eighteen months. How do I transition a child who has only known me? I had to find a way. So I began training

Callie the way one mother trains another, one handoff at a time.

Every moment we were together, I handed Callie another piece of Jayden's care. How to read her blood sugars before the symptoms hit. How to give insulin when it was too high. How to get breast milk into her before she got too hungry. Before her blood sugar dropped.

Callie practiced using the glucometer. She learned the sliding scale from Dr. Sinclair. When she gave Jayden her first injection, she teared up and held her tight. I saw her love in the tremble of her lip, the pain in her eyes.

We worked as a team. When Callie arrived, I'd sing out, "Yay! Mama Callie is here to play with Jayden!" We made leaving a celebration, too. We'd blow kisses and say bye-bye. Consistency mattered.

By the time they were going out on little adventures and caseworkers were watching, Callie was managing Jayden's care even in crowds. Jayden learned it in her body. She could trust Mama Callie.

---

WE CONTINUED our regular playdates at Callie's home. Jayden chased the kitties, explored new toys, adored her big sister Hope. We considered a sleepover at our house, but I realized Jayden needed to learn Callie could care for her without me nearby. So we agreed. Jayden would spend her first overnight at their home.

Callie and Mark prepared: a rocker recliner, breast milk and meds stocked, two cribs assembled. They were ready. So was Jayden. She packed her favorite music box, her blanket, her smile. I used my happiest voice. "You get to sleep at Mama Callie's!"

I turned away to swallow my tears. Then faced her with a smile.

---

CALLIE AND MARK buckled the babies into their car seats. I tucked the blankets over their laps, just like always. I kissed Joey, whispered "night-night" to Jayden, and walked quickly back inside.

> *Dear Lord, please help her make it safely through*
> *this night.*

I watched their taillights disappear. Then I let the tears fall. Callie texted updates. She promised to call if Jayden needed me. I trusted her, but I still couldn't sleep. It was only one night. But it hurt like love with nowhere to go.

---

JAYDEN RETURNED THE NEXT MORNING, smiling. I forced my arms to hold still and waited for her to reach for me. But she didn't. She greeted Dudley. Grabbed her blanket. Found her toys. She was home. And so was I.

Joey stayed with Mark and Callie another night, so Jayden and I spent the day together. I didn't know who needed it more.

It was routine now. Callie drove to our home, hopped out of her car and into mine for each doctor visit. I was the chauffeur. She was the caregiver. She fed the babies, sang along with Miss Pam's CD, and smiled as Jayden answered with hand motions.

We talked about everything: my daughter's midwifery

school plans, Hope's delayed graduation, Jordin and Curtis hunting for a new apartment.

Jayden and Joey heard our laughter. They heard the ease in our voices. Children know when the people they love also love each other.

I couldn't stop thinking about it, so I just asked. Five kids. A full-time job. A ministry. Could Callie handle all of it and still hold Jayden? I offered help. I said John and I could be her backup for childcare when she needed it. Not to hold on to Jayden. To help her thrive. Staying present.

My arms were empty. There was nothing left to do but miss her.

# November 2010

Jayden's endoscopy was early Wednesday morning, November 3. Dr. Earles hoped it would explain why she still refused solid foods. Joey had spent the night at Mark and Callie's, so Mark kept him there that morning. Callie pulled into our driveway at 6:15 a.m., co-parenting already in motion. It would take all four of us to get through the day.

We handed Callie a coffee to-go, and she slid into the back seat beside her little girl. John drove. Callie and I escorted Jayden into the hospital's outpatient unit. John stayed in the waiting room, watching the morning news.

The hospital called me the Friday before with a list of pre-op questions to satisfy the insurance requirements. I used the chance to explain Jayden's peripheral vascular disease and the pain of IV placements. I requested the vein finder, a device that helped before. The nurse assured me it would be ready.

The nurses were warm, until the IV tray came out. I reminded them of our plan: the vein finder first. They looked straight through me and proceeded to poke her with the IV catheter. Jayden screamed, her legs kicking against the exam table. A nurse found a vein near her elbow, inserted the needle again — and got no return. She rotated it, searching. Jayden howled. Heat rose in my throat.

I asked again, firmly. The vein finder. Please.

One nurse held up a finger. "This is my vein finder."

Before I could snap, the anesthesiologist came back and calmly suggested we skip the IV. She would use a mask and oral meds first. Within minutes, Jayden went quiet. I held her while the tremor moved through her. Then the anesthesiologist carried her away.

CALLIE and I returned to the waiting room. We poured coffee, shared toddler stories, and caught up on our older kids. The TV murmured over our heads. Forty-five minutes passed. Then ninety minutes. Two hours. We watched the double doors; they kept opening for everyone but us.

After two and a half hours, a nurse appeared to escort us back to the patient room. Jayden was groggy. An IV in her wrist. Four bandages dotted her arms. They must have placed the IV after she was asleep.

"Her veins collapsed," the nurse said, like it was nothing.

Instinctively, I pulled her into my arms. I remembered: I wasn't going to be her mama. I turned to Callie. "Where would you like to sit?"

She sat in the corner, the hard plastic chair scraping against the linoleum. I placed Jayden in her arms and placed the bottle in her hand. Jayden tucked in, her cheek nestled against Callie's chest. The bottle moved in small pulls, then slowed to almost nothing. One sigh, then stillness.

A new nurse arrived to remove the IV and walk us through discharge. Once Jayden was awake and drinking again, we dressed her. We were ready to leave. The doctor met us in the hallway. No abnormalities. He'd send the report to Dr. Earles. We thanked him and left.

---

OUTSIDE, we let Jayden walk while John retrieved the car. She tottered on unsure legs, strangers pausing to marvel at the tiny girl. No one guessed she was almost eighteen months old.

We got back to the house and Callie went home to get Joey. They'd have the babies for the weekend, but Joey had to come back to our house that night. The paperwork didn't care what kind of day it had been. She brought him back after dinner. Jayden needed Mama Judy time.

We all needed rest.

---

BY FRIDAY, Jayden woke sick. No fever, but thick congestion. Clingy, too. Callie offered to take her if I thought she'd be okay. We brought both babies to her house. Jayden smiled when she saw Callie. Played with Hope. Ate well. It was only fifteen minutes away. The next morning, Callie texted: wheezing.

It was Saturday. Dr. Earles wasn't in the office. I gave Callie the name of an urgent care clinic and asked her to call ahead. Then John and I dropped the nebulizer on her porch. I texted, "POP 15." Put On Porch. Wait 15 minutes. Our new system. The wait spared Jayden the sight of our backs disappearing down the sidewalk. Spared us the ache of her hands pressed against the window. One less goodbye... for both of us.

Jayden made it through, wheezing but holding her own.

---

MONDAY, John kept Joey. Callie and I took Jayden to Dr. Earles. Coffee, iced tea, bottles. Jayden weighed eighteen pounds twelve ounces. Thirty inches tall. Nearly eighteen months old. She ran the halls like she owned them. Staff peeked out from behind desks.

"Is that the same baby?" someone asked, not sure they'd believe the answer.

Dr. Earles coaxed her into the exam room. "Come on, brave girl."

Everything looked fine until she listened to Jayden's upper left lung.

"Keep using the nebulizer," she said. She pulled a vial of antibiotics from the office cooler, a leftover from Jayden's January sinus infection, and injected it quickly.

Jayden's eyes widened. Silent tears. Dr. Earles held her. Jayden clutched the puppy cover on the stethoscope. After a minute, her breathing slowed, then her fingers still curled around the puppy cover.

Callie took Joey home. I kept Jayden. Co-parenting was working. Both houses started to feel safe. The babies adjusted faster than we did.

---

THE NEXT DAY, Miss Pam came with her quilted bag. She unwrapped a bed no bigger than the palm of Jayden's hand and a cradle that rocked with a fingertip. At last, toys scaled to her world. Jayden's face lit up.

While they played, I checked the garage freezer. John usually got the milk, but he was running errands. The freezer was almost empty. I called Courtenay. She was already on it. A group in Grand Rapids was hosting a "pumping convention" the next day. Flyers, pumps, bags, coolers. Jayden's story had reached them, three hours away.

Could they call me? Could they deliver Saturday? Yes and yes.

———

Saturday morning, Jayden and I went to her final baby sign language class. A gift from one of our Pumpin' Mamas, Lena. A way for Jayden to be heard. That afternoon, Amelia called from Grand Rapids. They had seven coolers of milk already. Did I have freezer space? Tears again.

"Yes, of course," I said. We did. Or we would. Our freezer. Callie's. Neighbors' spare freezer space.

When Amelia arrived, she brought her kids and a friend. They tumbled into our kitchen, eyes fixed on Jayden. She stood near Dudley, thumb grazing his fur, one sock sagging, unsure whether to run or stay.

Amelia's friend whispered, "She's smaller than I imagined."

But the room kept turning toward her.

Callie came to help store milk, and to meet the women who helped save her daughter. Another gift. Another circle of care.

———

TEN DAYS LATER, Jayden was sick again. She played, then napped early. Nurse Melissa checked her oxygen: 92%. After treatment: 97%. Lungs were clear. Likely viral. Dr. Earles renewed the nebulizer prescription.

I reminded Dr. Earles of the follow-up with Dr. Boyer, the GI specialist.

"You may not get answers," she said. "If she's not eating, there may be nothing new to see."

She was right. Callie and I met Dr. Boyer. No irritation. No signs of allergy. The next step was an allergist. Dr. Boyer would stay involved with her enzymes and meds.

"Callie," I said. "Go ahead and make that next appointment. She'll be yours by then."

MID-NOVEMBER BROUGHT COURT. Jeannette, our adoption supervisor, was ready. No surprises. Mark and Callie still needed PRIDE training (Parent Resources for Information, Development, and Education). John went alone. Callie and I stayed with the babies.

He came back with news. Progress. No GAL again. The court referee seemed pleased. If training wrapped up, permanent placement could come mid-December. John asked Jeannette if the babies could spend the holiday weekend with Mark and Callie while we traveled to Milwaukee for Thanksgiving. Jeannette approved. Four nights.

We wrote the request letter and packed their things. Most of their belongings were already at Callie's. Jayden helped me pack bottles and toys. I took the picture of Mark, Callie, Jayden, and Joey from the fridge. I sang the night-night song. I danced around the kitchen with her.

At Callie's, Jayden rang the doorbell. "Mama Callie, Jayden is here," I sang. Inside: chaos. Hope, Davey, Joey, and Jayden squealing. Jordin and Lyndi sat calm on the couch. One look from Callie, and the room settled.

We reviewed the meds. Jayden now weighed nineteen pounds twelve ounces. Morning insulin: 20 units. Evening insulin: 16 units. I logged it in the spiral notebook. I knew Callie knew. She let me say it anyway.

Jayden rolled a ball with Jordin. I didn't want it to stop. But I didn't sneak out. I kissed her, told her I was leaving — that I'd see her after "Friday, Saturday, SUNDAY!"

I handed her to Callie. They lifted her to the window so she could watch me as I wiggled and waved, a final bye-bye dance. Her smile caught the light and held it, like a flicker of stained glass.

<hr>

WE FINISHED PACKING. I wrapped the pies with foil, folded a towel around the roasting pan. I emailed Kelly the menu and stared at the blinking cursor. A meal we'd share without highchairs or insulin logs on the counter.

John loaded the car under a clear blue sky. Crisp autumn air. Pumpkin pies. Vanilla coffee creamer. I reached for his hand as we turned onto the highway. The road unspooled behind us, back toward Callie's home. Jayden's home. My tears came quietly, although not for long. Just enough.

# December 2010

When babies adjust to a new home, coming back to the old one can rattle them. I told myself to expect hesitation, to brace for it. But rehearsal isn't readiness. Hope and heartbreak were braided too tightly to untangle.

What if she didn't want to return? That would mean the transition was working. That was the hope. But it cast a shadow. I had to be ready for the grief.

Sometimes the in-between was harder than the goodbye. I could see it on the babies' faces, that flicker of confusion, the way they scanned the room, unsure where to land. A tug between homes they didn't choose. I tried to follow their lead, to be steady when they needed someone to belong to, even if it pulled at something in me. I would gladly be that someone if they let me.

MARK AND CALLIE brought the babies back. Papa John opened the door and scooped up his little Buster. Jayden clung to Callie's neck, her brow furrowed, her grip tight. I waited, holding still, trying not to reach too soon. Then she turned to me. She stared, long and unreadable. Then a smile spread across her face. She reached for me, arms outstretched, open. My heart skipped. She remembered.

I wrapped her in my arms, breathing in her hair, that soft lavender fragrance I knew by heart. The tension I didn't realize I was holding cracked open. Relief came quietly, like a whispered blessing, one I hadn't dared ask for.

Callie said Jayden did well. Mark said Jayden grabbed books and climbed into his lap. No distress. Just joy. That steadied me, but only just. Her joy with them didn't hurt. Not yet. It meant she was okay. And maybe I could be too.

Then Callie told us they planned to rename Joey. In their family, names came from relatives. Mark wanted to honor his youngest brother, Michael. John would still call him Buster, of course. He was so young, he'd adapt. I told myself it was okay. It still felt like something being taken back.

Most of their clothes were already at Mark and Callie's. All we passed back and forth now were medications and the spiral notebook. We dropped off diapers and wipes before Thanksgiving. The diaper bag, the one with the duck appliqué on the front, made the trip stuffed with clean clothes, bottles, and the glucometer.

Fridays through Mondays were theirs. Tuesdays through Thursdays, ours. Jayden still saw Miss Pam every Tuesday and Thursday. Mark and Callie had Friday and Monday off work together, and Callie had taken weekends off from singing at church to be with the babies.

It was hard for Mama Callie to leave. She lingered. Fastened a jacket that didn't need it. Kissed Michael twice.

I recognized the ache in her gestures, the same ache I carried for months. Watching her carry it now comforted me and undid me.

But she honored the slow transition Jayden needed. We stood at the door and waved until Mark beeped the horn twice and their car turned the corner. Theirs felt quieter. Ours felt fuller, for now.

Jayden seemed glad to be home. No pulling away. No hesitation. She clung, then laughed, making a bubbly, hiccuped sound that startled even her. That small, ordinary moment let me exhale. Not everything was gone. Not yet. She still belonged here. Even if only for now.

Questions lingered. Could she really transfer her attachment from one home to another?

WE DRESSED Jayden and Michael in Christmas best for the agency party. Red corduroy. Snowflakes. Pictures with Santa, who smelled faintly of cologne and candy canes. Gift bags with glittery bows. Caseworkers crouched down to baby-eye level. Flashbulbs popped.

By then, the back and forth had already begun. They moved between our house and Callie's with surprising ease. It was an adventure for them. For us, it became a weekend routine.

When they were with us, we gave them our full attention. Feedings. Notes. Snuggles. When they left, we switched it up. We vacuumed. Did laundry. I even started baking again. Grief tucked itself between mixing bowls and laundry baskets. It was a strange, sweet rhythm. The kind you only recognize when you know it's about to end.

JAYDEN KEPT PROGRESSING. Miss Pam taught her to jump, a little bounce that made her giggle. Her finger found the pictures in books. "Where's the kitty?" She pointed. This was new. This was everything. Miss Pam's voice caught, a joyful hitch, like wonder tripping over itself.

Jayden drank her bottles without a struggle. She nibbled on solids now and then, but always returned to breast milk. A rhythm that held. Callie saw it, too.

Co-parenting with Callie came easily. Handoffs were smooth. We texted updates and swapped supplies. We carried our babies into clinics wearing matching black slings, talking a mile a minute. She was trying. I was trusting. And between us, Jayden was thriving.

---

CHRISTMAS PREP KEPT ME MOVING. My mom and Doreen were coming. All four of our grown kids would be home. I hadn't deep-cleaned in eighteen months, only rearranged the clutter. But now I wanted everything just right. I wiped the baseboards and fluffed pillows with a vengeance.

My cookies were baked, bagged, and frozen. My menu was taped to the fridge. Lights twinkled. I wanted everything to be ready. If I kept moving, maybe my mind wouldn't notice the empty spaces where bottles used to be.

During Jeannette's December visit, she said the adoption paperwork had been mailed. She hoped the state would reply before Christmas. She visited both homes and was impressed. "No distress," she said. "They feel safe in both homes."

Tuesday morning, the phone rang. It was Nicole.

DHS approved permanent placement for both babies. She didn't come. She trusted us to handle the transition.

Joey... Michael, would be fine. He knew Callie's voice, her scent, from the start. Jayden was the question. I told Nicole she was doing well with the back-and-forth.

"It's a beautiful gift," I said.

I tried to set the phone down. Dropped it instead. The room tilted. The weight of it was heavier than I imagined. I couldn't hold it.

I stood there. Frozen. Staring. Empty.

The only sound was my heart. Pounding. Breaking.

Tears hit the floor one after another. Relentless.

"Stop," I whispered. *"Stop."*

But the tears didn't listen. Minutes passed. Or hours. I couldn't tell. Eventually I reached down. Picked up the phone. *Breathe. Please.*

Callie still had the babies. She was bringing them at 9:30 a.m. for Jayden's hematology appointment. I dialed.

"Happy gotcha day, Mama Callie," I said. I tried to make my voice smile.

"Would you like to take Jayden alone? I can keep Michael."

She said yes.

Callie arrived right on time. She handed me Michael.

"Bottle at eight. No dirty diaper yet." Her voice was soft. Familiar.

Jayden cried from her car seat. She knew where she was. Mama Callie climbed in and comforted her. A minute later, they pulled away. Michael napped in my arms. Callie texted, back in twenty minutes.

When she returned, Michael was dressed and ready. Jayden was sleeping. A soft handoff. Then gone.

THAT TUESDAY, December 21, they went to their home for good. Callie had promised a Christmas visit. She said Sunday morning worked best. I hadn't held her since Friday so waiting until Sunday felt like a thousand years.

I scrambled. Finalized milk drop-offs. Reconfirmed doctors. But some things I couldn't change. I never got her to the pediatric dentist. Her teeth were starting to worry me. Her conjoined toes, still unexamined. I had wanted every loose end tied before she left. She woke more at night. Hungry? Teething? Lonely? Unsure?

But it was time. Not because I was ready, but because the state decided she was. I had to trust someone else to finish what I started. To take her into the next chapter without the map I drew. The house echoed. Her absence filled it. I felt everything and nothing all at once.

But guests were coming. I moved on instinct. Highchairs to the basement. Changing table gone. Fireplace gate down. A tree stood where the diaper caddy had been. The house began to look like ours again. A house for grown kids and visiting family. Not a nursery. Not a medical ward.

I'd been moving non-stop all week. If I kept moving, maybe the grief wouldn't catch me.

CHRISTMAS EVE WAS BEAUTIFUL. John sat by the fire reading *'Twas the Night Before Christmas*. Our kids wore matching pajamas, laughing and interrupting with memories. Tradition. Our once little ones, now grown, filling the room with warmth.

Christmas morning, the Oak Ridge Boys played as we sipped coffee and tea with my homemade banana bread. We opened gifts from one another. Our girls harmonized on *Mary's Coming Home*, their voices dancing over each other, trying to out-sing and out-laugh one another.

My mom and sister Doreen arrived mid-song. More hugs. More tea. After dinner, the girls passed instruments back and forth. Piano, ukulele, harmonica. They touched shoulders. Held backs. Pressed knees. Their harmony stretched beyond music.

John and Andy disappeared for a conversation, coffee mugs in hand.

Friends arrived for dessert. Pumpkin pie. Chocolate fudge cake. Then a dance-off. Our children, scattered across states, had returned. For a few days, we were whole. It felt like grace — a borrowed stillness before the letting go. And still, I watched the calendar. One more sleep.

---

SUNDAY MORNING, I was up early. The babies were coming. They had grown. Doreen hadn't seen Jayden since her first birthday. My mom had never met them in person, though she spoke of them like they were hers.

When Mark and Callie arrived, it felt like family returning. Papa John reached for his Buster. Callie placed Jayden in my arms. She clung tight. The room was full of faces and noise. She tucked her head under my chin. I rocked us. She held on. So did I.

Then Callie handed me a gift. Wrapped in a gold ribbon.

"It's from Deedle and Buster," she said. "They insisted."

Jayden helped pull the ribbon. Inside were two picture frames. Recent photos. Joyful smiles. Beautiful babies.

The first read: **Michael John.**

I smiled. Fitting. Then I picked up the second frame.
**Jayden Wright.**

I read it once. A second time. Then again. It hit me like a wave. Slow, then all at once.

Callie saw it. "That's the look I was waiting for," she whispered, "the one with the pursed lips."

She had asked our girls how to honor us. "Jayden Judy" didn't sit right. But this? This was perfect.

I looked at John. His chin quivered. His eyes welled. I hugged Jayden to my chest. She would share our name. It wasn't a small gift. It was more than I knew how to hold.

---

MARK AND CALLIE STAYED. We sang. We laughed. Jayden danced with our girls, her little bottom wiggling to the beat.

Then it was time. Hugs. Kisses. Blown bye-byes. Just like we practiced.

Jayden Wright and Michael John were buckled into their car seats. Jayden looked back once. I smiled. I waved. She didn't cry. I whispered a prayer I couldn't finish. They went home. Their home.

# January 2011

Mark and Callie promised we'd stay in each other's lives. I believed them. Yet I could still see what was coming: two babies, one medically fragile, and a house suddenly full. Love is not always enough to stretch time.

The church counselor's words echoed: "The sooner you make these babies yours, the better for everyone." Most people I respected agreed. But my gut wouldn't accept it. I couldn't stop imagining how it would feel from Jayden's side of the crib.

Last October, on the way to a doctor's appointment, Callie and I had joked about the passing of the baton. I was calling the shots. Soon, it would be her. We laughed. Now, the baton was in her hands. It looked heavier than we'd laughed about. She was their mother. This was her turn. And I would honor that.

Still, I worried. About the noise. The holiday chaos. About Jayden's silence around new people. Her distress didn't come with tears or tantrums. It showed up in the numbers. Her glucometer readings told the story no one else could. She wasn't speaking yet. Just her eyes. Just the meter. Just the hope that someone would notice what she could not say.

---

GRIEF ARRIVED like an old visitor we recognized. Dudley claimed his place first, leaping into my lap the moment I sat in the rocker. He pressed himself close, insistent, as if declaring I wouldn't face this alone.

But first, the work. I boxed bottles and folded clothes in silence. Each onesie a goodbye. Baby things slid into the basement shadows. The Christmas lights went dark. I flipped the calendar.

Our house exhaled, quieter than I'd ever known it. The space that once held them was too clean, too still. The highchairs were gone, packed away. A vase of fresh flowers on the table. Candles on the counter. It looked like home again. Too much like it used to.

I set my iced tea on the end table and waited for the tiny Deedle hand that used to reach for it. She didn't. Of course she didn't. But my heart hadn't caught up. I took a shower and cried. The water turned cold. I stayed. Next shower. Same tears. Third shower. Still there.

At night, I went to bed before John, needing the privacy. Dudley curled along my spine, his breath warm, his chin on my shoulder. At 2:00 a.m., I cried again. My chest remembered her shape, her weight, her warmth, the rhythm of her breathing against my collarbone. That was her feeding time. But she wasn't there. Only air. And ache. I'd known this goodbye would hurt. I hadn't known it would hollow me out.

---

THE NEXT MORNING, John noticed my swollen eyes and pulled me close. He reminded me she had been born into a house that couldn't hold her, held safely in ours, then brought into one built around her. He was so amazed by it all he couldn't let sadness in. To him, sorrow felt like ingratitude.

I believed him. Every word. But my arms ached with the quiet devastation of skin that no longer held her. Jayden didn't understand custody, caseworkers, or court-rooms. She just knew someone was gone. I hoped she knew I hadn't left her on purpose.

The house felt empty. Our grown children had returned to their lives. Our babies were gone. And John's career was still on hold. He remained grounded since last June, unable to fly, pouring himself into home and hospital and hope. Now, when the babies left, there was still no sky waiting for him.

Even church felt out of reach. I couldn't imagine mustering the strength to answer the questions without breaking. So we stayed home, watching the service on the computer, holding hands in the glow of the screen, praying for patience.

I still laced up my running shoes each morning, muscle memory from the Michael months. But there was nowhere to run. I used to sit and give a bottle while choreographing the next move. "As soon as he's done drinking, I'll change his diaper, then lay him in the bouncy seat, then get her up, change her diaper, do her reading, give her an injection, feed her, empty the dishwasher."

The list never ended. I had never propped a bottle in my life. I believed babies needed cuddling as much as they needed calories. And I needed them too. Now there was no routine. No choreography. No 2:00 a.m. bottles. No notebooks of numbers. Just work that was no longer required. There was no cue for how to leave.

My calendar, once scribbled with 284 appointments for Jayden alone, now stood blank on the wall. I had tasks. But no will. Just the hush of a house that no longer needed me.

---

ON JANUARY 3, Callie texted me. Jayden had been singing. Sitting in the living room while her toy played *"Twinkle, Twinkle, Little Star."*

I pictured her, finger pointing up, a whole constellation in her mind. I replied, "Thank you. This text is a gift."

She still remembered music. She still reached for wonder. She hadn't let go. Neither had I. Her little voice, singing in her new home, reminded me I could still find light in this. I tucked the phone to my chest, a small light in the dark. A lullaby for my heart.

---

JOHN and I planned a trip to celebrate our 35th wedding anniversary at the end of the month. The first night in Chicago with theater tickets. We'd drive to Milwaukee for the weekend. An adventure. We hadn't had many of those. I tried to focus on the trip. The itinerary. A restaurant he'd found. A promise of something different.

On January 10, our actual anniversary, we went out to dinner. I put on makeup and earrings. John was the love of my life. My constant. I wanted to be present for him. I wanted to rise to the occasion. But I couldn't stop sinking.

I felt guilty that I wasn't enjoying the night. We hadn't

eaten in a restaurant for nearly two years. I owed him more than I had to give. I smiled with my lips. The rest of me stayed home.

The next evening, he ordered pizza. I curled beside him on the couch. We put a movie on, something light-hearted. A continuation of the tradition that helped us survive the hospital months. He tried to keep me there beside him, even as I unraveled.

---

TWO WEEKS AFTER THE MOVE, Callie emailed. Jayden wasn't eating. She stopped singing. She didn't play with her favorite toys. No sparkle. Just silence. Callie was worried. And she told me. I wept. She told me, and that mattered more than she knew.

I walked the living room as if it were a maze. I prayed. I tried to pull myself out of the center of the story. *Would seeing me help? Or make it worse? Would she think I'd left her? Would her blood sugar suffer because of the separation?* I sat at the computer and typed. One word at a time.

---

JAYDEN HAD likely seen us as a team. For months, Callie and I braided ourselves into her life. We went places together. Shared feedings, errands, meals. Then came Thanksgiving. And after that, handoffs. No play or visits. Just passing through doorways.

She might've thought we were still a team. And then we weren't. In one sweeping transition, she lost Papa John, Mama Judy, Dudley, and even Miss Pam. Mark and Callie lived in a different school district, which meant a different Early On program. The people, the rhythms, the scaffolding of her world all gone.

My heart ached with the enormity of that loss. I suggested I visit her house, sit with her mama, and play with her toys. Let Jayden see this wasn't a betrayal. Let her see me loosen my grip. We'd weaned her into Callie's care, slowly. Maybe now we needed to wean me out just as gently. Callie agreed.

I PACKED a small bag of toys from the basement bins. Familiar ones. My knees shook as I climbed the steps.

*Dear Lord,*
*Please give me the strength to help her accept this.*

Callie opened the door. Jayden ran. Arms flung wide. She wrapped herself around my neck, head buried in my shoulder. I froze. Afraid moving would break me. Holding her, the stillness felt like grace. Eventually, I eased off my coat. We played with lap toys. Callie offered tea. Jayden stayed.

Callie gave the insulin. I gave the enzymes. I fed her the bottle. No blanket available. Just my arms. I sang, patted her bottom. Callie told me about bedtime. How Jayden, half-asleep, reached behind and began to pat her own bottom. Familiar. Grounding.

We planned the goodbye. Michael on the floor. Callie holding Jayden. I'd wave and blow kisses. Walk to my car. Two beeps, then I'd pull away. We rehearsed the goodbye, but my heart missed its cue.

I crouched to eye level. "Mama Judy is going home now. But I'll be back Thursday. Yay for Thursday!"

She clapped.

I left a small gift. Callie held her at the window. I waved and blew kisses. Just like we planned. Just like we practiced.

I turned the corner, pulled over, and sobbed.

---

THAT NIGHT, I cried myself to sleep. At 2:00 a.m., I woke. *Was she awake too? Was someone patting her bottom?*

At 4:00, I broke. *I missed her. I missed her. I missed her.*

John stirred. He pulled me into him. No words. Just breath and arms. Just presence. We started this together. Now we were here. At the end.

# February, March, April 2011

I was asked the most devastating question of my life: *Would you please just hold her until she dies?* But the question that changed everything was, *what if she doesn't?*

---

THE NEXT MORNING, I woke up with something new to carry. Not to hold on. But to hold her up.

John and I were recovering from the exhaustion of the past year and a half. We returned to our routine, except for John's aviation career, which he longed for. His lungs had not healed enough for him to pass the first-class medical required to fly again.

I found comfort in cleaning, playing the piano, and reading again. With no word yet from the agency, I enjoyed staying in bed a little longer in the mornings, just because I could.

It was good for me to see Jayden in her new home. She ran from room to room, full of giggles and confidence.

She belonged there. Back home, I'd catch myself smiling, remembering her peeking around the corner of the kitchen, trying to catch the cat.

Jayden had always been extremely cautious. If there were toys in her path, she would turn sideways to step between them. At her new house, the slate floor in the kitchen was raised about an inch from the carpeted family room. Each time Jayden went from the carpet into the kitchen, she bent over, placed her hands on the slate, and carefully stepped up before standing again. I chuckled.

Our visits together were sweet and simple. Jayden's eyes sparkled the moment she saw the bag I carried. She knew there was something inside. I always brought a small project for us to try together, something she and Mommy (the name Callie chose for herself) could keep exploring after I left. Homemade playdough. Bubbles. Nothing fancy, just simple ways to share joy.

Sometimes, I brought meals for the family. I remembered what a difference that made when I had two babies. If Callie didn't have to worry about dinner, she might have extra time to play with her babies.

I would wait for Callie to email me about which days I could visit. Even last-minute visits were welcome. I'd do what I could to help. One day she asked if I could watch Michael while she took Jayden to the doctor. Of course, I said yes. But I suggested she back her minivan into the driveway, maybe Jayden wouldn't recognize where they were and wouldn't get upset. I even crated Dudley so he wouldn't give it away.

We thought we were clever, but Jayden wasn't about to be fooled. As Callie pulled onto our street, Jayden sat straight up at the bump in the road and began chattering. It had been six weeks, a long time in a baby's world, but Jayden recognized the road. When the car door opened,

Callie handed Michael to John and gave me a quick hug. I heard Jayden in the car crying. She knew.

Papa John was thrilled to get his hands on Buster, who at ten months wasn't so little anymore. Michael greeted him with a big smile, buzzing his lips while drool soaked Papa's shirt. Obviously, a new trick. John laughed and tickled Michael's belly, giving him raspberries in the soft fold on his neck.

Callie shared that Jayden needed her glasses full-time now, not just a few hours a day. She wasn't excited about keeping them on Jayden's face. And honestly, I was glad it was her and not me managing that challenge.

Callie had found a highly recommended pediatric dentist and made an appointment for March. Jayden's baby teeth were rotten.

Later, I offered to watch both babies if Callie ever needed to run errands or meet a friend. She said she might take me up on it. But a few weeks passed with no visits. I wondered: had I overstepped? Was Jayden's crying when she left our house making things harder for Callie? Was she waiting for me to ask to visit? My mind ran wild. Waiting was hard.

Finally, Callie emailed me to ask if we could watch the babies while she attended a church meeting. Yes, of course. We were excited to see them.

When she arrived, all three of us greeted her at the minivan. Dudley's tail started wagging double time when he smelled the babies. Once inside, Jayden squirmed to get down and ran straight to the family room with Dudley behind her. She found her toys and began chatting to them.

Callie shared the morning review and instructions. I placed Jayden's insulin in the fridge beside the bottles of breast milk. They'd nap here. Callie would be back soon after.

Jayden weighed twenty pounds three ounces at her last appointment. That was only a seven-ounce gain in nearly three months. I did the math again. She still wore size twelve-month clothes I bought in August. It was February.

Jayden waved and smiled when her mommy said goodbye. Callie seemed comforted knowing she could leave them with us. John and I enjoyed our time with the babies, but it reminded us why we chose not to adopt them ourselves. John tried to carry Michael around the house, but the tour was cut short. His lungs couldn't handle the exertion. So he settled into his rocker, held Buster, and played "*This Little Piggy.*"

Jayden snuggled in my lap with *Goodnight Moon*. Afterwards, she dragged a plush blanket from the couch across the floor to me, reached for her bottle, and curled into my arms. She remembered this room, this rhythm. I quickly swapped the oversized blanket for a smaller, fluffy baby one. We rocked, I patted, and she drank her bottle filled with donated breast milk.

When Callie came to pick them up, I mustered my happy voice. "Yay! Mommy's coming! You get to see your sister, Hope!" But Jayden ran the opposite way when she heard the door.

Callie carried Michael to the car. I packed the diaper bag. When she returned, I handed Jayden to her. Jayden looked up at me, then started to cry, arms outstretched.

"Thank you for coming to play with me," I called after her, waving. There was no next visit on the calendar. I did my well-rehearsed bye-bye dance. Then I closed the door and cried.

Every time Callie left the babies, Jayden struggled. We

tried everything. We walked her to the car, tried sending her home with something special. Nothing helped. I feared Callie might step back if she thought it was too painful for Jayden. I held my breath between visits.

I believed distance made things harder, not easier. Many insisted children in transition should be separated from their first parents so they would bond with the new ones. I never believed that was for the child's sake.

One day I asked Callie how she handled Jayden's tears when she left our house. She said it reminded her of leaving her grandma's house as a child. She knew her parents loved her, but still cried every single time she left her grandma. That comforted me. Callie understood Jayden's heart. She understood our connection.

We watched Michael on the day of Jayden's dental surgery. The dentist found exposed nerves and gum disease. He capped all twelve teeth. Jayden's gums were infected and would bleed with brushing, but healing would come. Callie needed to stay focused on her. I offered to keep Michael overnight, but she said Jayden might need time with Mama Judy later.

I knew better. Callie had to be the one to comfort her. Jayden needed to see that her new Mama could handle her pain. It could change their bond. We returned Michael late that night with meals for the coming days. Mark greeted us on the front porch. I offered to return tomorrow if help was needed.

Weeks passed quietly. We continued to "POP," leaving donated breast milk on the porch, and respected Callie's space. Then she emailed us a list of dates she needed help. We said yes.

The next visit, all four of them knocked on our door: Mark, Callie, Michael, and Jayden. Jayden grinned as she reached for me, showing her new teeth and tiny wire-framed glasses. Mark and Callie left for their meeting. I put the babies in the highchairs we retrieved from the basement. Jayden devoured half a hamburger before even glancing at the fruit and vegetables. In just two months, she gained over a pound. She was eating. She was growing. One bite, one breath, one step at a time.

John popped out from behind the kitchen door and tapped her cheeks. "Pickle, pickle, pickle juice!" Jayden's belly laughs filled the room.

After lunch, Jayden ran to me with her blanket and said, "Bottle." Then, "Book."

Jayden Wright. Rewriting the odds that once defined her.

Later, when Callie came to pick them up, Jayden stayed in the kitchen, calling out, "Hi!" as her two mamas sat and talked. Callie invited us to Jayden's upcoming second birthday. I hesitated. Not because I didn't want to go, but because I didn't want her to feel obligated. I told her so.

Callie looked at me, certain and kind. "You're the reason I have her," she said. "Jayden survived because of you. I want you in her life. Always."

Then she shook her finger at me and laughed. "I don't ever want to have this discussion again!"

I hugged her.

Jayden left our home that day without a fuss. She danced on her way to the front door singing "pickle, pickle, pickle juice" as Papa John chased after her.

I told her, "I'll see you on Sunday!" She waved and said, "Bye, bye, bye," blowing kisses as the car pulled away with two beeps.

In the end, I could see it clearly, not just her survival, but the timing of it all. Every piece had fallen into place. I had to believe my gut was right all along: if Jayden was okay, I would be okay.

It sounds simple. It wasn't. Jayden didn't come into our lives just to survive. She came to thrive. She taught us how to wait without knowing. How to trust without answers. That was enough. I didn't need to understand why she came to us. I was simply thankful.

———

JOHN and I carried helium balloons and gifts into Mark and Callie's home for brunch on April 17, 2011. Jayden ran to the front door doing a little dance of joy. "Hi! Hi! Hi!" she shouted, jumping into my arms. Papa John reached for his Buster. We carried both babies into the kitchen, arms full, memories rising. Deedle with her Mama Judy. Buster with his Papa John.

We gave each baby a balloon to carry into the party, then we set our packages on the sofa. In the kitchen, siblings buzzed around, parents prepared the brunch buffet. Cameras clicked. Stories flowed.

We had been asked to hold her until she died. Now, in a kitchen full of joy and frosting, she clapped her hands and sang her own name.

Jayden. Two years old.

The girl we were asked to hold was home.

Epilogue

In June of 2011, John and I drove my Aunt Ethel and Uncle Floyd to visit Amish Country in Lancaster, Pennsylvania, to celebrate their 60th anniversary. Their dream vacation. The roads wound through green fields and white farmhouses, laundry snapping on clotheslines and buggies clip-clopping along the shoulders. John told stories and sang along to the old songs on the radio, the scent of his vanilla coffee creamer drifting through the car.

After several hours of touring, buggy rides, and sitting on stiff-backed benches listening to lectures, we went to our separate hotel rooms completely spent.

I scrolled aimlessly through my Facebook page and saw a post from someone trying to mail breast milk to Jayden. The mother lived too far away for our regular transport teams. I replied that if the milk was anywhere along our route home from central Pennsylvania back to Michigan, we would be happy to transport it.

She lived in Maryland. Just over the state line from Lancaster. Forty minutes away. Amanda drove twenty minutes to meet us halfway in a store parking lot, where John bought three extra-large coolers. She had reached out to several other moms in her group and gathered their frozen breast milk, too.

Aunt Ethel rode with us just to be there. She stood beside the cars as we opened trunks and lifted bag after bag from one cooler to another, the life-saving milk passing from hand to hand in the warm summer air.

With the back of our SUV filled with coolers, my aunt and uncle rode home snuggled together in the back seat, making room for our luggage beside them. The car hummed through the patterned farmland while John sang softly with the radio. For years afterward, Aunt Ethel spoke about that day, but never with a dry eye.

JOHN and I continued to foster nine more babies after Jayden and Michael. Over twelve years of fostering, we cared for fifty-five babies. In October 2012, my husband was diagnosed with non-small cell lung cancer, linked to Agent Orange exposure during his time in Vietnam.

As John's hospital stays grew longer, Kelly came to help care for her dad, brewing coffee, rubbing his feet, cuffing his socks at the ankle, the way he liked them.

Then a letter came from the Michigan Supreme Court. We learned that we had been named Michigan's Foster Parents of the Year. The honor traced back to Jayden's story.

Kelly insisted I go. Andy drove from Milwaukee to accompany me to the event at the Capitol in Lansing, about two hours away. On our way home from the event, I called Kelly to check in.

"Dad began having an episode and couldn't breathe.

The doctors and nurses rushed in. They treated him, and eventually he began to breathe again." Kelly paused, her voice shaking.

"As soon as he could talk, while everyone was still around his bed, his first words were, 'Do you know where my wife is right now?' And then he began telling them about his Deedle and her story," she said.

"He is so proud of you, Mom."

I didn't speak. I just swallowed. And wept.

———

MARK AND CALLIE brought Jayden and Michael to the hospital or to our home for time with their Papa John. While the adults gathered around the kitchen table, we would often find them at the foot of his bed, rubbing his feet with quiet reverence.

My dear husband passed away on November 30, 2012, with all of our children by his bed. Mark led the funeral service after days of sitting vigil with us. Callie sang *In the Garden*, her voice holding even through the ache. Jayden sat on my lap during the service.

———

JAYDEN CONTINUES to defy her prognosis. She's seventeen. Smart. Funny. Sharp. Diagnosed with social anxiety, she still struggles around people she doesn't know well. But to us, she shines.

I am grateful that Jayden and Michael continue to be part of my life. They send me messages and FaceTime from their tablets. I often get tours of their bedrooms, their farm animals, or simply the chance to see their sweet faces.

We have seen each other often over the years, never letting too much time pass. We were always connected. There have been times when Jayden has talked about missing her Papa John.

Two years after my husband passed away, I had Jayden for a visit. I put her in the booster seat to go on an adventure. We sang nursery rhymes together as we traveled to our destination. I stopped the car and opened the back door to help her out. Before she jumped down, she hesitated. I began to worry that something was wrong. She looked up and held my gaze. "You can call me Pickle Juice if you want to."

Mark and Callie have made trips to North Carolina since my move here in 2022. Jayden has her own room here now. She hangs her hoodie on the same hook by the door every time, like she never left.

There has been no greater gift than watching Mark and Callie love our little ones and give them a place that was theirs. The children struggled in school, affected by the addictions they were born into, so Mark and Callie moved to a farm to help them learn practical life skills. There have been hard seasons, but Jayden and Michael have always known they have their family, and Mama Judy, behind them.

Now they know their story. How it began. I'm sharing this book with Jayden, chapter by chapter. This is her story. I'm just the one who got to tell it. The one who got the call. The one who got to hold her.

---

Soon after the adoption process was complete, Callie invited me to speak with her at church. To talk about fostering and what we had witnessed with Jayden and

Michael. To give thanks for the 350 Pumpin' Mamas, spread over ten states and Canada, who contributed to Jayden's life through the milk they shared. It showed up in foot rubs. In casseroles on the porch. In FaceTime pings. In coolers of donated breast milk.

The sermon that day was about the widow's oil from 2 Kings 4. She had almost nothing, just a small jar. No title. No training. No plan beyond survival. When the prophet told her to pour, she poured. And as long as she kept pouring, the oil did not run out. She didn't multiply the miracle. She simply made herself available.

I didn't have much either. No degree. No medical license. No background in special needs, trauma, or glucose monitoring. I had the spiral notebook. A quiet house. A pair of tired arms. A heart that said yes before it knew the cost.

But when I started to pour, there was always enough. Enough courage. Enough strength. Enough milk in the cooler. We showed up with what we had. Somehow, it was enough.

***

MY SWEET HUSBAND, John, used to say, "If you don't believe in miracles, come to our house. We see miracles every day."

*Afterword*

## The Other Side of the Hallway

*Mama Callie*

There are moments that look ordinary to anyone passing by. A church hallway. Fluorescent lights. Folding chairs stacked against the wall. I saw them before they saw me.

Judy was walking toward me with a baby against her chest. The baby wore the smallest pink glasses I had ever seen. They seemed too delicate for her face. She seemed too delicate for the world. But she was in it. Looking out from it. Taking her time. The two of them moved together, not just close but attuned. The baby's hand rested against Judy's collarbone. Every few steps her eyes lifted to Judy's face, checking. Judy did not grip her tightly. She did not need to. The security between them was already settled.

I did not know their story yet. I only knew I was looking at something that had been fought for.

When we stopped to talk, the baby studied me. I

learned her name was Jayden. I learned she had been very sick. I learned she had just become eligible for adoption. Adoption did not sound like a possibility in that moment. It felt heavy. I remember saying I would pray for the right parents.

That afternoon I carried their faces home with me. Mark sat at the kitchen table while I tried to explain it. The glasses. The way she rested into Judy. The sense of having brushed up against something already sacred. We did not speak in dramatic terms. We just kept circling the same quiet question.

*What if?*

By the time Jayden came into our home, she already knew how to trust. She already knew that when she reached, someone would be there. That had been built long before I arrived. In hospital rooms. In long nights. In steady hands.

I did not feel the need to replace it.

I felt thankful for it.

There were early evenings when the house would grow quiet and Jayden would drift toward the door at the sound of a car outside. She would stand there a moment, listening. When it was not Judy, she would turn back, climb into my lap, and press her head against me with the same certainty.

It took me time to understand that this was not divided loyalty. It was abundance.

Our family grew in directions I could never have mapped from that hallway. A bonus baby. Michael learned to follow his big sister's lead. Mark learned to give her insulin injections without making her flinch. Our dinner table settled into its own ordinary chaos. Homework papers. Mismatched cups. Laughter that arrived too loud and too sudden and did not apologize for it.

And Judy was never outside of it.

There were church programs where Jayden scanned the audience until she found both of us. Hard days when she needed the voice that first sang her to sleep. Easier days when she ran past me straight into Judy's arms, then circled back for mine.

Love did not divide her. It widened what she could carry.

One afternoon not long ago, Jayden was at the kitchen counter drawing, her glasses pushed up into her hair the way she does when she is thinking. Michael was showing his latest sock puppets to anyone who would pay attention, one on each hand. The house was loud in that familiar, settled way.

I was at the stove, hands full, apron on, half listening to whatever Michael's puppets were joking about, when I turned around and saw Jayden holding up the phone. Judy's face on the screen. Jayden had already called her. I hadn't even noticed.

"Oh! Hi, Judy."

Jayden propped the phone against the flour canister. She kept drawing while talking. Michael leaned in immediately, both puppets raised, eager for an introduction. I turned back to dinner.

No one stopped. No one stiffened. The room didn't change. It already knew her.

I used to think the hardest thing would be saying yes to her adoption.

I understand now that I said yes to entering a story that had already begun. To loving a child who had already learned what it meant to be held.

Jayden moves between our homes the way a child

moves between rooms. Certain the door will open. Certain someone will answer.

That certainty is not something I created. It was something I inherited.

And I will spend the rest of my life grateful to the woman who first said yes.

# *Acknowledgements*

This book exists because of the people who showed up.

To my husband, John, without whom none of this would have been possible. Not the fostering. Not the vigil. Not the life we built. You are on every page.

To the NICU nurses, who knew this baby before I did and trusted us anyway. You cared for her in the long weeks before we could. This story begins with you.

To Dr. Sonja Earles, for listening, for caring, and for asking the question no one else thought to ask. You gave Jayden a chance. You became a friend.

To Dr. Sinclair, for knowing how to see a person beyond their chart. For dancing.

To Dr. Nancy, for her patience and her willingness to try.

To Miss Pam. There are no words that fit what you gave us. Only gratitude, and the memory of your quilted blue bag coming through the front door.

To Nicole, our caseworker, for the tireless work no one saw. For the paperwork she almost didn't bother filing, and for understanding, from the very first visit, what we were carrying.

To Ms. Chase, who held Jayden in her arms and told me to make the call. Thank you for not letting me wait.

To Terri, Murielle, and Cressie. You were there in my darkest moments. You knew what I needed before I did. You fed me, held her, and kept me steady.

To Courtenay and the Pumpin' Mamas. What you

gave was ordinary to you and miraculous to us. Every ounce mattered.

To the medical staff at every hospital and clinic who cared for this little girl. The ones who learned her name. The ones who stayed an extra moment just to see. You are not forgotten.

To every friend, neighbor, and stranger at the edges — in the church hallways, the grocery store aisles, the parking lots. You listened. That was enough.

To Callie and Mark, for saying yes. You know what that word cost, and you know what it gave.

To Kelly, Casey, and Emily. My girls. My loves. You held me while I held her. And you taught me more than I ever expected to learn. You are my inspiration.

To my sister Doreen, for knowing when I needed help. For listening. For always believing I had a story to tell. You flew to North Carolina, then drove me to Pennsylvania and Michigan for this book. I didn't need to say anything. That said everything.

To my sisters Sonya and Donna, for reading every draft with a critical eye, catching the misspelled words. Sonya, especially, for saving my first draft, printing it on paper. You revived this story when I thought it was lost forever.

To my niece Stacie Doughtie and my daughter-in-law Stephanie Sun, for reading every word with care. For catching what others missed.

To Conor Gallogly, for the questions that opened the manuscript, and the thoughtfulness that carried it through.

To Gloria Nixon-John, PhD, for tea and sweets at her kitchen table, and for teaching me that the story I was carrying was worth learning how to tell.

And to my son, Andrew Wright. This book would

not exist without you. You helped me find the words when grief made language impossible. You shepherded every draft with love and clarity. You are your father's son.

---

"Jayden taught me so much. I am honored for you to use my name, as long as you point out that it took an awful lot of people to keep that kiddo alive. I believe without the Wrights, she would have perished."
— Dr. Sonja Earles | November 14, 2025

JUDY WRIGHT

Judy Wright is a foster mother, caregiver, and advocate whose life has been shaped by the demanding, ordinary work of staying.

She and her late husband, John, a Vietnam veteran and corporate pilot, shared a conviction that children matter not abstractly but concretely, in the daily decisions of a household. After raising four children of their own, they became foster parents through Michigan's foster care system. Over twelve years, their home became a place of readiness for fifty-five children, many of them medically fragile. Judy learned to advocate inside systems that often failed to see children clearly, showing up when others did not and loving without guarantees.

In 2012, Judy and John were named Michigan's Foster Parents of the Year by the Michigan Supreme Court. Their legacy also inspired the Judy Wright Volunteer of the Year Award at Muskego High School and the John and Judy Wright Scholarship for Foster Children, established with the Ennis Center for Children to support foster youth pursuing higher education.

Her debut memoir, *Just Hold Her*, is drawn from the spiral notebooks she kept during a 674-day vigil for a medically fragile infant. It is not a story about saving. It is a story about the labor of presence.

Judy lives with the conviction that while children may not remember every face that held them, they remember what it felt like to be held.

*Judy Wright*

In 2012, Judy and John Wright were named Michigan's Foster Parents of the Year. The recognition came after more than a decade of service and fifty-five children welcomed into their home.

The award was meaningful. But the work was never about recognition. It was about the child in the next room.

Many of those children grew up and aged out of the foster care system at eighteen. Not with a family behind them, but with a small check and a closing door. For too many, education or vocational training remained just out of reach.

A portion of the proceeds from *Just Hold Her* supports the John and Judy Wright Scholarship, established in the wake of John's death in 2012. Administered in partnership with Ennis Center for Children, the scholarship provides financial assistance for higher education and vocational training to foster youth who have aged out of the system.

The children in these pages were held. The scholarship is one way to keep holding.

To learn more or to contribute directly, visit www.jjwrightscholarship.com or contact the Ennis Center for Children at www.enniscenter.org.

www.ingramcontent.com/pod-product-compliance
Lightning Source LLC
Chambersburg PA
CBHW051258130726
47987CB00004B/1579